0
D22
591.03
VIS
Checked
Feb 2011
OP

VISUAL

ENCYCLOPEDIA OF

animals

RECEIVED

1 6 MAR 2005

D1331584

WITHDRAWN WARWICKSHIRE
COLLEGE
LIBRARY

WITHDRAWN

Warwickshire College

00526839

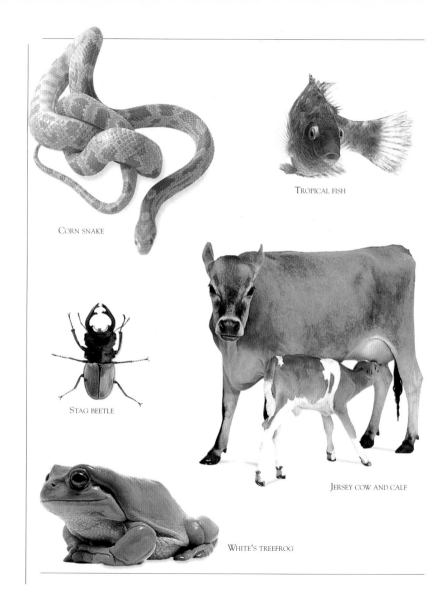

CORN SNAKE

TROPICAL FISH

STAG BEETLE

JERSEY COW AND CALF

WHITE'S TREEFROG

WARWICKSHIRE
COLLEGE
LIBRARY

VISUAL

E N C Y C L O P E D I A 1 OF
animals

AMMONITE

CRESTED WATER
DRAGON

LESSER
FLAMINGO

DK

Warwickshire College
Library
Moreton Morrell Centre

Class No: 591.03

Acc No: 00526839

LONDON, NEW YORK,
MUNICH, MELBOURNE, and DELHI

Writers and consultants:
David Alderton, Steve Brooks, Dr. Barry Clarke,
John Farndon, Mark Lambert, Laurence Mound,
Scarlett O'Hara, Barbara Taylor, Steve Parker,
Joyce Pope, David Taylor

Project Editor Lucy Hurst
Managing Editor Jayne Parsons
Managing Art Editor Jacquie Gulliver
Production Kate Oliver

First published in Great Britain in 1999
as *Pockets Animals of the World.*
Original edition produced for Dorling Kindersley by
PAGE*One*, Cairn House, Elgiva Lane, Chesham, Buckinghamshire, HP5 2JD

2 4 6 8 10 9 7 5 3 1

Copyright © 2001 Dorling Kindersley Ltd., London
This edition published in 2004

All rights reserved. No part of this publication may be reproduced, stored in a
retrieval system, or transmitted in any form or by
any means, electronic, mechanical, photocopying, recording,
or otherwise, without the prior written
permission of the copyright owner.

A CIP catalogue record for this book is available
from the British Library.

ISBN 1-4053-0675-0

Colour reproduction by Colourscan, Singapore
Printed and bound in Singapore by Star Standard

See our complete catalogue at
www.dk.com

Note to Parent
Every effort has been made to ensure that the information in this book is as up-to-date as possible at the time of going to
press. The internet, by its very nature, is liable to change. Homepages and website content is constantly being updated,
as well as website addresses. In addition, websites may contain material or links to material that may be unsuitable for
children. The publishers, therefore, cannot accept responsibility for any third party websites or any material contained in
or linked to the same or for any consequences arising from use of the internet, nor can the publishers guarantee that any
website or urls featured in this book will be as shown. Parents are strongly advised to ensure that access to the internet by
children is supervised by a responsible adult.

CONTENTS

BIRDWING
BUTTERFLY

GREEN MANTELLA

TAWNY OWL

MAMMALS 366

ARMADILLO

GREAT DANE

HOW TO USE THIS BOOK

These pages show you how to use the *Visual Encyclopedia of Animals*. The book is divided into seven sections about the animal kingdom. There is also an introductory section about the origins of animal life, and how animals are classified. At the back of the book, there is a comprehensive index.

HEADING AND INTRODUCTION
Every spread has a subject heading. This is followed by the introduction, which outlines the subject and gives a clear idea of what these pages are about.

Label

Heading

Introduction

Data box

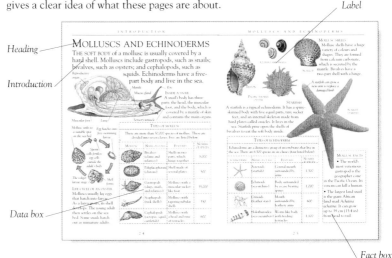

Fact box

DATA BOX
Some pages have data boxes, which contain detailed numerical information. This box gives data about types of mollusc.

FACT BOXES
Many pages have fact boxes. The information in these is related to the main topic on the page.

LABELS
For clarity, some pictures have labels. These give extra information about the picture, or provide clearer identification.

SECTION NAMES
Along the sides of the pages there are section names. The lefthand page gives the section, the righthand the subject.

SIZE INDICATORS
In some sections of this book, you will find clear symbols next to photography. These indicate the average size of an animal.

Size indicator

Annotation

Caption

ANNOTATION
Pictures often have extra information around them, which picks out features. This text appears in *italics*, and uses leader lines to point to details.

CAPTIONS
Each illustration in the book is accompanied by a detailed, explanatory caption.

INDEX
There is an index at the back of the book that alphabetically lists every subject. By referring to the index, information on particular topics can be found quickly.

11

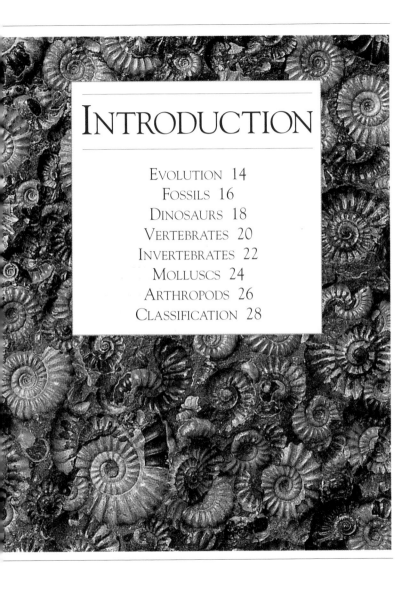

INTRODUCTION

EVOLUTION

SINCE LIFE appeared 3.8 billion years ago, millions of different creatures have come and gone. As habitats altered, some life forms survived by adapting to change, while others died out. This gradual change over time is known as evolution.

PORPOISE'S FRONT FLIPPER

"Finger" bones form a powerful flipper for swimming

Two sets of short "arm" bones

Two sets of long bones make up the arm

ADAPTATION
Evidence for evolution comes from the adaptation of the forearm in humans and porpoises – two related species that live in very different habitats, land and water.

Five sets of finger bones make up the hand

HUMAN ARM

LIFE FORMS
THROUGH THE AGES
By working out when certain rocks formed, and then studying the fossils found in them, paleontologists – who study the life forms of the past – have built up a remarkable picture of the way species have changed since the dawn of the Cambrian period 545 million years ago. Little is known of Precambrian life forms because very few fossils remain.

PRECAMBRIAN	PALEOZOIC	
	Cambrian	Ordovician

4,600–545 mya
Single-celled life forms, such as bacteria and algae, appear, then soft multi-celled life forms, such as worms and jellyfish.

545–495 mya
No life on land. Invertebrates flourish in the seas. First molluscs and trilobites.

495–443 mya
First crustaceans and early jawless fish appear. Coral reefs form. Sahara glaciated.

HOW EVOLUTION WORKS

According to Darwin's theory of evolution, only the best-adapted members of species survive to breed, leading to a gradual change in living organisms over millions of years. His theory challenged the accepted 19th-century view that life forms did not change after being created by a deity (god).

CHARLES DARWIN (1809–1882)

The theory of evolution was developed by English naturalist Charles Darwin after studying animals and plants during a world voyage. He published his findings in 1859 in his book *On the Origin of Species*.

EVOLUTION OF THE HORSE

Hyracotherium
This animal of 50 million years ago had four toes on its front feet.

Mesohippus
Mesohippus, which lived 30 million years ago, had three toes on its front feet.

Merychippus
One of Merychippus's three toes formed a large hoof. Merychippus existed 20 million years ago.

Equus (modern horse)
Modern horses, which have a single toe or hoof on each foot, evolved about 2 million years ago.

Silurian	Devonian	Carboniferous	Permian

443–417 mya
First jawed fish. Huge sea scorpions hunt in the sea. Small land plants colonize the shore.

417–354 mya
Age of sharks and fish. Insects and amphibians appear on land. Giant ferns form forests.

354–290 mya
Warm swampy forests leave remains that will turn to coal. First reptiles.

290–248 mya
Reptiles diversify, conifers replace tree ferns. Mass extinction as Earth turns cold.

FOSSILS

THE REMAINS of living things preserved naturally, often for many millions of years, are called fossils. Most fossils are formed in rocks; however, remains can also be preserved in ice, tar, peat, and amber. Fossils tell us nearly all we know about the history of life on Earth.

Spider trapped inside resin

SPIDER IN AMBER
Amber is fossilized tree resin that may also preserve trapped insects.

AMMONITES BECAME EXTINCT 65 MYA

KINDS OF FOSSIL

Many fossils form on the seabed, so shells and sea creatures are very common. Fossils of land animals and plants are more rare. Footprints, burrows, or droppings may also be preserved.

Fossilized shell

MESOZOIC			CENOZOIC	
Triassic	Jurassic	Cretaceous	Tertiary	
			Palaeocene	Eocene
248–206 mya Mammals and dinosaurs appear. The climate warms and seed-bearing plants dominate.	*206–142 mya The age of the dinosaurs. The first known bird, Archaeopteryx, appears.*	*142–65 mya First flowering plants. Period ends with a mass extinction that wipes out dinosaurs.*	*65–55 mya Warm, humid climate. Mammals, insects, and flowering plants flourish.*	*55–34 mya Mammals grow larger and diversify. Primates evolve.*

1 ANIMAL DIES
The body of a dead animal lies decaying on the surface of the land.

2 REMAINS SINK
Gradually, the body becomes covered with sand or mud.

FOSSILIZATION AT SEA
Dead organisms sink to the sea bed and are buried. As the sediment turns to rock, their remains are either chemically altered or dissolve to leave a cavity, which may fill with minerals to form a cast.

3 BONES ALTER
Over time, the bones are altered, and the sand and mud turn to rock.

4 FOSSIL IS EXPOSED
Eventually, weather and erosion expose the fossil at the surface.

			Quaternary	
Oligocene	Miocene	Pliocene	Pleistocene	Holocene

34–24 mya	*24–5 mya*	*5–2 mya*	*2 mya–10,000 ya*	*10,000 ya to present*
First human-like creatures appear. Hunting birds thrive. Some mammals die out.	*Climate cools, and forests shrink. Deer-like hoofed mammals flourish. First hominids.*	*Cold and dry. Mammals reach maximum diversity. Many modern mammals appear.*	*Ice Ages. Homo sapiens evolves. Mammoths and sabre-toothed tigers die out.*	*Humans develop agriculture and technology. Human activity threatens many species.*

17

DINOSAURS

FOR 150 MILLION YEARS the
Earth was dominated by giant
reptiles called dinosaurs, including
Seismosaurus, the largest creature
ever to walk on land. Then,
65 million years ago, all the
dinosaurs mysteriously died out.

Light bones
for flying

Wings
of skin

Furry
body

DINOSAUR GROUPS
Scientists divide dinosaurs into two orders according
to the arrangement of their hip bones. Saurischians
have lizard-like hips and include both plant and
meat-eaters. Ornithischians have
bird-like hips and are all plant
eaters. The two orders are
divided into five subgroups.

PTEROSAUR
While dinosaurs ruled the
land, giant reptiles, like
Pterosaur, flew
in the air.

Muscular
tail balanced
the front of
the body

Long neck
for browsing
in treetops

Ruff

SALTASAURUS

Sauropods (Saurischians) were huge,
long-necked four-legged plant eaters.

STYRACOSAURUS

Horn

Marginocephalians (Saurischians) had
a bony ruff and horns for self-defence.

STEGOSAURUS

TYRANNOSAURUS

CORYTHOSAURUS

Thyreophorans (Ornithischians)
were spiny-backed plant eaters.

Theropods (Saurischians) were
two-legged meat eaters.

Ornithopods (Ornithischians)
had a horny beak and bird-like feet

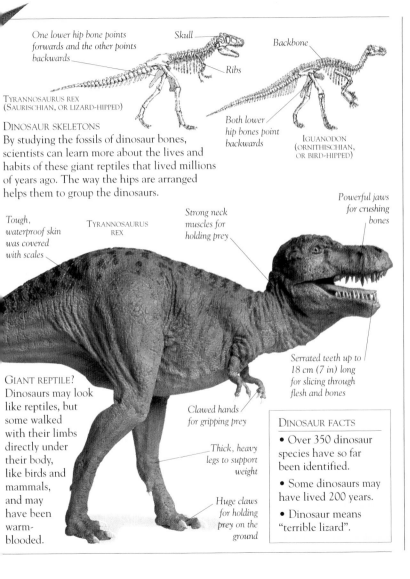

One lower hip bone points
forwards and the other points
backwards

Skull

Ribs

Backbone

TYRANNOSAURUS REX
(SAURISCHIAN, OR LIZARD-HIPPED)

DINOSAUR SKELETONS

By studying the fossils of dinosaur bones,
scientists can learn more about the lives and
habits of these giant reptiles that lived millions
of years ago. The way the hips are arranged
helps them to group the dinosaurs.

Both lower
hip bones point
backwards

IGUANODON
(ORNITHISCHIAN,
OR BIRD-HIPPED)

Powerful jaws
for crushing
bones

Tough,
waterproof skin
was covered
with scales

TYRANNOSAURUS
REX

Strong neck
muscles for
holding prey

Serrated teeth up to
18 cm (7 in) long
for slicing through
flesh and bones

GIANT REPTILE?

Dinosaurs may look
like reptiles, but
some walked
with their limbs
directly under
their body,
like birds and
mammals,
and may
have been
warm-
blooded.

Clawed hands
for gripping prey

Thick, heavy
legs to support
weight

Huge claws
for holding
prey on the
ground

DINOSAUR FACTS

• Over 350 dinosaur
species have so far
been identified.

• Some dinosaurs may
have lived 200 years.

• Dinosaur means
"terrible lizard".

VERTEBRATES

ONLY ABOUT five per cent of all animals have backbones, and these are called vertebrates. There are more than 50,000 different species of vertebrate, divided into classes of mammals, birds, fish, reptiles, and amphibians. Their sense organs and nervous systems are well developed, and they have adapted to almost every habitat.

GORILLA SKELETON

BACKBONE
Vertebrates have a skeleton of bone, with a backbone, two pairs of limbs, and a skull that protects the brain. Inside are the heart, lungs, and other organs.

REPTILES
Lizards, snakes, crocodiles, and geckos are reptiles. They all have a tough, scaly skin. Young reptiles hatch from eggs, and look like tiny versions of their parents. This chameleon is a type of lizard.

Spines along backbone give protection from attack

Scaly skin

Female frog lays eggs, called frogspawn

MADAGASCAN CHAMELEON

Male fertilizes spawn

ANIMAL REPRODUCTION
In vertebrates, offspring are created when males and females come together and the male's sperm join the female's eggs. This is called sexual reproduction, and usually involves mating. A few animals are neither male nor female, and they reproduce asexually.

Prehensile tail for holding on to branches

SENSES

Mammals and other vertebrate animals have senses to help them find their way, locate food, and avoid enemies. For land animals, such as this caracal, sight, hearing, and smell are the most important senses. Sea creatures rely more on smell and taste to escape danger and find food.

Sharp eyesight for hunting, even at night

Strong sense of smell

Sharp teeth

Long, sensitive ears pick up even the faintest sounds

CARACAL

FISH

TWINSPOT WRASSE

With streamlined bodies covered in slippery scales, these vertebrates are perfectly suited to life in the water.

Scales covered in slimy mucus

BIRDS

The only animals that have feathers are birds, and most of them are powerful fliers. Birds have a beak, or bill, instead of teeth, and all reproduce by laying eggs.

COUNT RAGGI'S BIRD OF PARADISE

RED-EYED TREE FROG

Large eyes spot prey

AMPHIBIANS

Frogs, toads, newts, and salamanders are amphibians. These vertebrates spend part of their lives in water and part on land. They all reproduce by laying eggs.

Long legs for jumping

PORCUPINE

Spiny quills protect body

Fur helps keep body warm

MAMMAL

A mammal is usually covered in fur or hair. It gives birth to live young, which it feeds with milk.

INVERTEBRATES

NINETY-FIVE PER CENT of all animals are invertebrates, which means they have no backbone. They include jellyfish, sponges, starfish, coral, worms, crabs, spiders, and insects.

Intestine

Body shape maintained by fluid

Dorsal blood vessel

Gizzard (part of stomach)

Ovary

Spermatheca (reproductive organ)

Ventral nerve cord

Mouth

EARTHWORM CROSS-SECTION

Hard shell to protect soft body

Soft body

Eyes on stalks

MOLLUSCS
These soft-bodied invertebrates are often protected by a hard shell. Most molluscs, such as squid and octopuses, clams, mussels, and scallops, live in water, but some, like snails and slugs, live on land.

WORMS
A worm is an animal with a long soft body and no legs. There are many different kinds, including flatworms, tapeworms, earthworms, roundworms, and leeches.

Echinoderms have a five-part body plan.

Arm

Ossicles are hard plates just under the skin that keep the body rigid

STARFISH AND URCHINS
Starfish, sea urchins, and sea cucumbers are all echinoderms. All are predators, and most have sucker-tipped "tube feet" through which they pump water to move along and feed. The five broad arms of a starfish can wrench open a shellfish to suck out the contents.

Arm

Underside of arm is covered with fluid-filled tube feet for moving and feeding

LIFE CYCLE
Each invertebrate has its own life cycle, but most species lay eggs. Some go through several larval stages, while others hatch as miniature adults.

Buds break away as free-swimming adults

Jellyfish

Fertilized larva

Polyp divides into eight-part buds

Larva grows into a polyp

SPIDER

ARTHROPODS
Insects, spiders, and lobsters are all arthropods. They have jointed limbs and a tough external skeleton.

CROSS-SECTION OF A JELLYFISH

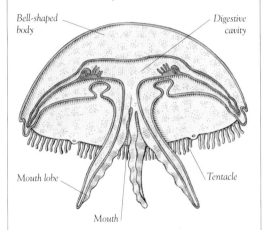

Bell-shaped body

Digestive cavity

Mouth lobe

Tentacle

Mouth

Jellyfish, anemones, and coral are all kinds of cnidarians – sea creatures with a mouth surrounded by tentacles. These tentacles usually carry a sting to stun or kill prey. Some cnidarians, called polyps, always attach to solid objects, such as a rock; others, called medusas, move by contracting their bell-shaped bodies.

SPONGES
These primitive sea creatures feed by drawing water into the holes in their soft bodies and filtering out any food.

INVERTEBRATE FACTS
• Up to 500 million hookworms may be found in a single human.

• Roundworms are probably the most numerous animals on Earth.

MOLLUSCS AND ECHINODERMS

THE SOFT BODY of a mollusc is usually covered by a hard shell. Molluscs include gastropods, such as snails; bivalves, such as oysters; and cephalopods, such as squids. Echinoderms have a five-part body and live in the sea.

Reproductive organ

Mantle

Mucus gland

Eye

Muscular foot

Lung

Sensory tentacle

INSIDE A SNAIL
A snail's body has three parts: the head, the muscular foot, and the body, which is covered by a mantle of skin and contains the main organs.

Mollusc sinks to a suitable spot on the sea bed

Egg hatches into free-swimming larvae

Sperm cells fertilize egg cells outside the adult's body

The veliger larvae stage

Shell forms

LIFE CYCLE OF AN OYSTER
Molluscs usually lay eggs that hatch into larvae. As a larva grows, its shell develops. The young adult then settles on the sea bed. Some snails hatch out as miniature adults.

TYPES OF MOLLUSC			
There are more than 50,000 species of mollusc. These are divided into seven classes. Five are listed below.			
MOLLUSC	NAME OF CLASS	FEATURES	NUMBER OF SPECIES
	Bivalves (clams and relatives)	Shells in two parts, which hinge together	8,000
	Polyplacophorans (chitons)	Shell made of several plates	600
	Gastropods (slugs, snails, and relatives)	Molluscs with a muscular sucker-like foot	40,000
	Scaphopods (tusk shells)	Molluscs with tapering tubular shells	350
	Cephalopods (octopus, squid, cuttlefish)	Molluscs with a head and ring of tentacles	650

24

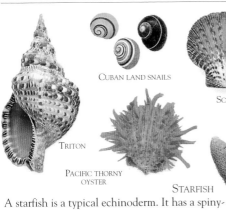

CUBAN LAND SNAILS

SCALLOP

TRITON

PACIFIC THORNY OYSTER

MOLLUSC SHELLS
Mollusc shells have a huge variety of colours and shapes. They are formed from calcium carbonate, which is secreted by the mantle. Bivalves have a two-part shell with a hinge.

A starfish can grow a new arm to replace a damaged limb

SCARLET STARFISH

STARFISH
A starfish is a typical echinoderm. It has a spiny-skinned body with five equal parts, tiny sucker feet, and an internal skeleton made from hard plates called ossicles. It lives in the sea. Starfish prise open the shells of bivalves to eat the soft body inside.

TYPES OF ECHINODERM

Echinoderms are a distinctive group of invertebrates that live in the sea. There are 7,000 species in six classes (four listed below).

ECHINODERM	NAME OF CLASS	FEATURES	NUMBER OF SPECIES
	Asteroids (starfish)	Central mouth surrounded by arms	1,500
	Echinoids (sea urchins)	Body surrounded by a case bearing spines	1,000
	Crinoids (feather stars)	Mouth surrounded by feathery arms	625
	Holothuroidea (sea cucumbers)	Worm-like body with feeding tentacles	1,150

MOLLUSC FACTS
• The world's most venomous gastropod is the geographer cone in the Pacific Ocean. Its venom can kill a human.

• The largest land snail is the giant African land snail *Achatina achatina*. It can grow up to 39 cm (15.4 in) from head to tail.

ARTHROPODS

ARACHNIDS, CRUSTACEANS, and
insects are part of the arthropod
group of invertebrates. Insects are by
far the largest of these three groups.
All arthropods have a jointed body
with a tough body case. The case is
shed as the animal grows.

The egg is laid
in a silk sac
to protect it

Spiderlings
resemble the
adult spider

Spiderling
moults

LIFE CYCLE OF A SPIDER
Arachnids such as spiders
lay eggs that hatch into
tiny versions of adults.
They moult several times
before they are mature.

IMPERIAL SCORPION

Poison
gland

Sting

Heart

Cephalothorax

Pedipalps – a pair of
pincers for feeding

Intestine

Abdomen

Spiracle –
air hole

INSIDE AN ARACHNID
The body of an
arachnid is divided into a front and
middle part (cephalothorax)
and a rear part (abdomen).
Arachnids have four
pairs of walking legs.

TYPES OF ARACHNID

The class Arachnida includes spiders, mites, and scorpions. It contains 73,000 species,
which are grouped into 12 orders. Six orders are listed below.

ARACHNID	NAME OF ORDER	NUMBER OF SPECIES	ARACHNID	NAME OF ORDER	NUMBER OF SPECIES
	Scorpiones (scorpions)	1,200		Uropygi (whip scorpions)	100
	Solifugae (camel spiders)	900		Opiliones (harvestmen)	5,000
	Acari (mites and ticks)	30,000		Araneae (spiders)	35,000

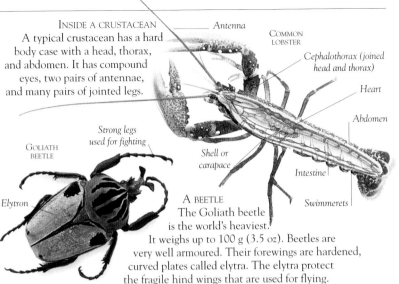

INSIDE A CRUSTACEAN

A typical crustacean has a hard body case with a head, thorax, and abdomen. It has compound eyes, two pairs of antennae, and many pairs of jointed legs.

Antenna

COMMON LOBSTER

Cephalothorax (joined head and thorax)

Heart

Abdomen

GOLIATH BEETLE

Strong legs used for fighting

Shell or carapace

Intestine

Elytron

Swimmerets

A BEETLE

The Goliath beetle is the world's heaviest. It weighs up to 100 g (3.5 oz). Beetles are very well armoured. Their forewings are hardened, curved plates called elytra. The elytra protect the fragile hind wings that are used for flying.

TYPES OF CRUSTACEAN

There are more than 50,000 species of crustaceans divided into eight classes. These include the four classes below.

CRUSTACEAN	NAME OF CLASS	FEATURES	NUMBER OF SPECIES
	Branchiopods (fairy shrimps, water fleas)	Small animals of freshwater and salty lakes	1, 000
	Cirripedia (barnacles)	Immobile animals with a box-like case	1,000
	Copepods (cyclopoids and relatives)	Small animals often found in plankton	9,000
	Malacostracans (shrimps, crabs, lobsters)	Many-legged animals, often with pincers	≥ 20, 000

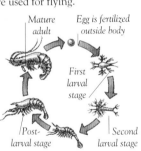

Mature adult

Egg is fertilized outside body

First larval stage

Post-larval stage

Second larval stage

LIFE CYCLE OF A SHRIMP

Crustaceans usually lay their eggs in water. Once hatched, the egg begins its first larval stage. After two more larval stages, there is a final post-larval stage before adulthood.

CLASSIFICATION

BIOLOGISTS HAVE identified and classified most species of vertebrates (animals with backbones), although it is likely that new species of fish await discovery. Invertebrate animals have not been so well documented, and there are many species to be identified.

Springtails	Lice
Bristletails	Thrips
Diplurans	Booklice
Silverfish	Zorapterans
Mayflies	Bugs
Stoneflies	Beetles
Webspinners	Ants, bees, wasps
Dragonflies	Lacewings and
Grasshoppers and	antlions
crickets	Scorpionflies
Stick and leaf insects	Stylopids
Grylloblattids	Caddisflies
Earwigs	Butterflies and moths
Cockroaches	Flies
Praying mantids	Fleas
Termites	

INSECTS
(Insecta)
1,000,000 species

ANIMALS (Animalia)

ROTIFERS
(Rotifera)
2,000 species

MOLLUSCS
(Mollusca)

ECHINODERMS
(Echinodermata)
7,000 species in 6 classes, including:

MOSS ANIMALS
(Bryozoa)
4,000 species

OCTOPUSES, SQUIDS
(Cephalopoda)
650 species

SNAILS
(Gastropoda)
40,000 species

SEA URCHINS
(Echinoidea)
1,000 species

BRITTLE STARS
(Ophiuroidea)
2,000 species

C.13 OTHER SMALL
PHYLA
c. 2,000 species

SOLENOGASTERS
(Aplacophora)
250 species

CHITONS
(Polyplacophora)
600 species

STARFISH
(Asteroidea)
1,500 species

SEA CUCUMBERS
(Holothuroidea)
1,150 species

VELVETWORMS
(Onychophora)
80 species

MUSSELS, CLAMS
(Bivalvia)
8,000 species

TUSK SHELLS
(Scaphopoda)
350 species

ROUNDWORMS
(Nematoda)
20,000 species

SPONGES
(Porifera)
9,000 species

DEEP-SEA LIMPETS
(Monoplacophora)
11 species

SPINY
STARFISH

HORSEHAIR WORMS
(Nematomorpha)
250 species

COMB JELLIES
(Ctenophora)
90 species

WATERBEARS
(Tardigrada)
400 species

FLATWORMS,
FLUKES,
TAPEWORMS
(Platyhelminthes)
20,000 species

SEA ANEMONES,
HYDRAS, CORALS,
JELLYFISH
(Cnidaria)
9,500 species

SPINY-HEADED
WORMS
(Acanthocephala)
700 species

LAMPSHELLS
(Brachiopoda)
300 species

WORMS, LEECHES
(Annelida)
15,000 species

HORSESHOE CRABS
(Merostomata)
4 species

SAND SHRIMPS
(Cephalocarida)
9 species

MYSTACOCARIDEANS
(Mystacocarida)
10 species

PARROT

Scorpions
Tick spiders
Micro-whip
scorpions
Tail-less whip
scorpions
Whip scorpions
Camel spiders
Pseudoscorpions
Harvestmen
Mites and ticks
Spiders

SEA SPIDERS
(Pycnogonida)
1,000 species

SPINY SAND
SHRIMPS
(Branchiura)
125 species

CRABS, LOBSTERS,
AND SHRIMPS
(Malacostraca)
20,000 species

Ostriches
Rheas
Cassowaries, emus
Kiwis
Albatrosses, petrels,
shearwaters, fulmars
Pelicans, gannets,
cormorants,
frigatebirds, darters
Penguins
Grebes
Divers or loons
Tinamous
Herons, storks,
ibises, flamingos
Ducks, geese, swans
Eagles, hawks,
vultures, falcons,
kites, buzzards
Pheasants,
partridges, grouse,
turkeys
Cranes, rails, coots,
bustards
Wading birds, gulls,
terns, auks
Sandgrouse
Pigeons, doves
Parrots
Cuckoos,
roadrunners, turacos
Owls
Nightjars,
frogmouths
Swifts,
hummingbirds
Trogons
Mousebirds
Kingfishers,
bee-eaters, rollers,
hoopoes
Woodpeckers,
toucans, barbets,
honeyguides,
puffbirds, jacamars
Passerines

CENTIPEDES
(Chilopoda)
2,500 species

BARNACLES
(Cirripedia)
1,000 species

MUSSEL SHRIMPS
(Ostracoda)
2,000 species

MILLIPEDES
(Diplopoda)
10,000 species

BRANCHIOPODS
(Branchiopoda)
1,000 species

COPEPODS
(Copepoda)
9,000 species

ARACHNIDS
(Arachnida)
73,000 species

ARTHROPODS
(Arthropoda)

CRUSTACEANS
(Crustacea)
50,000 species

BIRDS
(Aves)
9,600 species

CHORDATES
(Chordata)

MAMMALS
(Mammalia)
4,600 species

AMPHIBIANS
(Amphibia)
4,000 species

Frogs and toads
Newts and salamanders
Caecilians

Monotremes (egg-laying mammals)
Marsupials (pouched mammals)
Insectivores
Elephant shrews
Flying lemurs
Bats
Tree shrews
Primates
Edentates (anteaters, sloths,
armadillos)
Pangolins
Aardvarks
Hares, rabbits, pikas
Rodents
Whales and dolphins
Carnivores
Seals, sea lions, walrus
Elephants
Hyraxes
Sea cows
Odd-toed hoofed mammals
Even-toed hoofed mammals

REPTILES
(Reptilia)
6,500 species

Lizards and snakes
Turtles, tortoises, and terrapins
Crocodilians
Tuataras

JAWLESS FISH
(Agnatha)
75 species

SHARKS AND RAYS
(Chondrichthyes)
800 species

Sharks, dogfish
Skates, rays

BONY FISH
(Osteichthyes)
24,000 species

More than 20 orders including:
Eels
Herrings, anchovies
Salmon, trout
Carp
Catfish
Perch, marlin, swordfish, tunas
Flying fish

SEA SQUIRTS
(Urochordata)
2,500 species

29

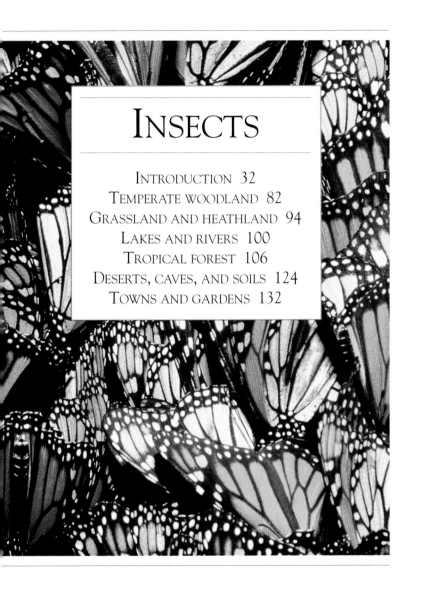

INSECTS

INSECTS

WHAT IS AN INSECT?

THERE ARE AT LEAST five million insect species – they are the most abundant animals on earth. All insects have six legs, and their skeleton is on the outside of their body. This outer skeleton forms a hard, protective armour around the soft internal organs.

SHEDDING SKIN

A young insect is called a larva. As each larva feeds and grows, it must shed its hard outer skin, which is also called an exoskeleton. When the larva grows too big for its skin, the skin splits, revealing a new, larger skin underneath.

The antennae of insects can sense smells and vibrations in the air.

DISSECTED BEETLE

Eye

First part of thorax bears the front legs

Jointed front leg

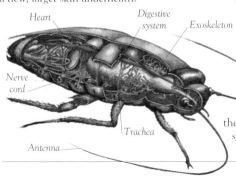

Heart

Digestive system

Exoskeleton

Nerve cord

Trachea

Antenna

INTERNAL ANATOMY

A typical insect breathes through holes in its sides and distributes air around the body in tubes called tracheae. It has a nerve cord which runs beneath the digestive system. The heart, a slender tube with several holes, pumps blood around the body.

32

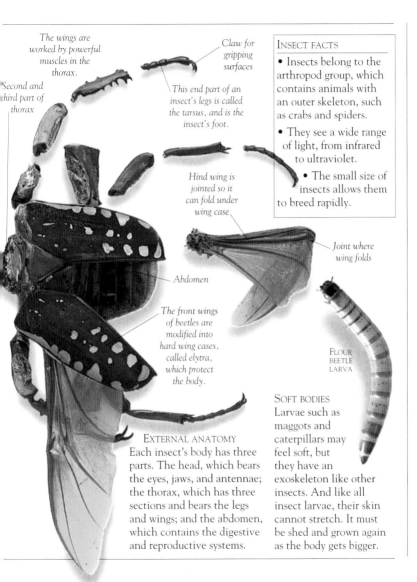

The wings are worked by powerful muscles in the thorax.

Second and third part of thorax

Claw for gripping surfaces

This end part of an insect's legs is called the tarsus, and is the insect's foot.

Hind wing is jointed so it can fold under wing case

Abdomen

The front wings of beetles are modified into hard wing cases, called elytra, which protect the body.

Joint where wing folds

FLOUR BEETLE LARVA

INSECT FACTS

• Insects belong to the arthropod group, which contains animals with an outer skeleton, such as crabs and spiders.

• They see a wide range of light, from infrared to ultraviolet.

• The small size of insects allows them to breed rapidly.

EXTERNAL ANATOMY
Each insect's body has three parts. The head, which bears the eyes, jaws, and antennae; the thorax, which has three sections and bears the legs and wings; and the abdomen, which contains the digestive and reproductive systems.

SOFT BODIES
Larvae such as maggots and caterpillars may feel soft, but they have an exoskeleton like other insects. And like all insect larvae, their skin cannot stretch. It must be shed and grown again as the body gets bigger.

33

THE FIRST INSECTS

INSECTS WERE the first animals to appear on land, and also the first to fly. They evolved at least 400 million years ago – long before humans, and even before dinosaurs. Fossils show that some ancient species were similar to modern dragonflies and cockroaches.

FLOWER FOOD
When flowering plants evolved 100 million years ago, insects gained two important new foods – pollen and nectar. Insects thrived on these foods. They pollinated the flowers, and many new species of plants and insects evolved together.

INSECT IN AMBER
Amber is fossilized tree resin from pine trees that grew over 40 million years ago. Well-preserved ancient insects are sometimes found in amber. This sweat bee is in fossilized copal, a resin from certain tropical trees.

MODERN EARWIG

Fossil earwig

FIRST INSECT FACTS

• The ancestors of insects – and all other animals alive on Earth today – were worm-like marine creatures.

• Some early insects had three pairs of wings.

• The oldest known butterfly or moth is known from England 190 million years ago.

ROCK REMAINS
This fossil of an earwig was found in 35-million-year-old lake sediment in Colorado, U.S.A. The fossil shows how similar in shape ancient earwigs are to modern ones.

FOSSIL DRAGONFLY

Dragonflies were one of the first types of insect. Fossils show that they have not changed very much in appearance over millions of years. Some ancient dragonflies were very large and may have had wingspans of up to 1 m (3 ft). This dragonfly fossil found in southern England is of a small species. The intricate wing veins can clearly be seen.

Wing laced with veins

End of abdomen

Large eye

Wing veins

MODERN DRAGONFLY

One of the largest present-day dragonflies is this species from Borneo, with a wingspan of 16 cm (6¼ in). Although the nymphs (young) of modern dragonflies live in water, we cannot be sure that this was true of prehistoric dragonflies.

AGILE FLIERS

Modern dragonflies are fast, agile fliers, and ancient dragonflies were probably the same. A prehistoric flying reptile would have had greater trouble catching a dragonfly than this fanciful engraving suggests.

TYPES OF INSECT

SCIENTISTS ARE CONSTANTLY DISCOVERING new insects. They currently know of about one million species, but it is likely that there may be at least five million in total. Each belongs to one of about 30 groups, or orders, which are defined according to body structure and larval development.

Beetles, wasps, bees, and ants

About 400,000 species of beetles are described – they are the largest order of insects. Wasps, bees, and ants form the second largest order of insects, made up of about 200,000 species. The common feature in this order is a narrow "waist".

Jaws

A STAG
BEETLE

*Hard wing
cases meet i
— mid-line.*

*Fringed legs
make swimming
easier.*

GREAT
DIVING
BEETLE

BEETLES

WINGS AND JAWS

The front pair of wings in beetles is hardened and forms a strong shield ove the folded hind wings. Some beetles, such as stag beetles, have greatly enlarged jaws which look like horns.

DIFFERENT FOODS

Plants, fungi, insects, and dead animals are among the wide variety of beetle foods. The great diving beetle lives in ponds. It is a fierce predator which hunts tadpoles and small fish.

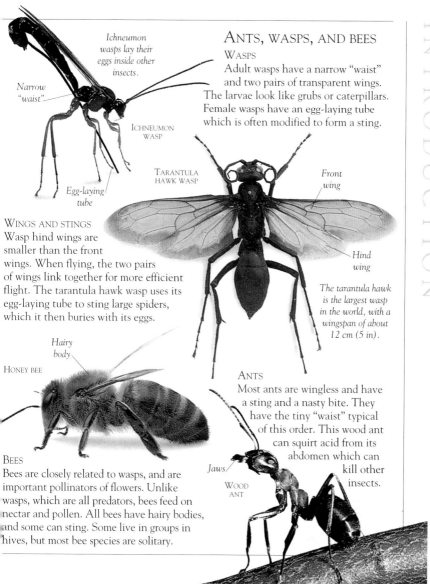

Ichneumon wasps lay their eggs inside other insects.

Narrow "waist"

ICHNEUMON WASP

ANTS, WASPS, AND BEES

WASPS

Adult wasps have a narrow "waist" and two pairs of transparent wings. The larvae look like grubs or caterpillars. Female wasps have an egg-laying tube which is often modified to form a sting.

Egg-laying tube

TARANTULA HAWK WASP

Front wing

WINGS AND STINGS

Wasp hind wings are smaller than the front wings. When flying, the two pairs of wings link together for more efficient flight. The tarantula hawk wasp uses its egg-laying tube to sting large spiders, which it then buries with its eggs.

Hind wing

The tarantula hawk is the largest wasp in the world, with a wingspan of about 12 cm (5 in).

Hairy body

HONEY BEE

ANTS

Most ants are wingless and have a sting and a nasty bite. They have the tiny "waist" typical of this order. This wood ant can squirt acid from its abdomen which can kill other insects.

BEES

Bees are closely related to wasps, and are important pollinators of flowers. Unlike wasps, which are all predators, bees feed on nectar and pollen. All bees have hairy bodies, and some can sting. Some live in groups in hives, but most bee species are solitary.

Jaws

WOOD ANT

Butterflies, moths, and flies

Two common insect orders are the two-winged flies and the butterflies and moths. Flies are distinctive because their second pair of wings is converted into balancing organs which look like drumsticks. Their young stages are maggots. Butterflies and moths have a coiled feeding tube, and their wings are covered in minute, flattened scales. Butterfly and moth larvae are called caterpillars.

BUTTERFLIES AND MOTHS

CATERPILLARS

Although caterpillars' bodies are soft, they have an exoskeleton like other insects. Caterpillars grow at a very fast rate. They feed on leaves and have sharp jaws for slicing vegetation.

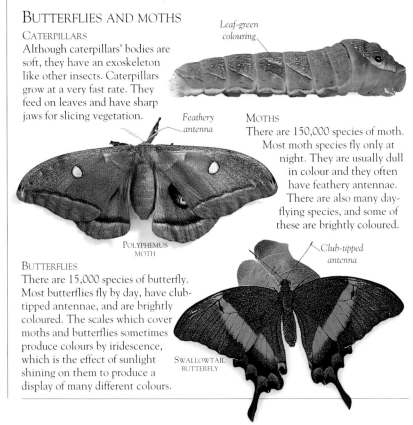

Leaf-green colouring

Feathery antenna

POLYPHEMUS
MOTH

MOTHS

There are 150,000 species of moth. Most moth species fly only at night. They are usually dull in colour and they often have feathery antennae. There are also many day-flying species, and some of these are brightly coloured.

Club-tipped antenna

BUTTERFLIES

There are 15,000 species of butterfly. Most butterflies fly by day, have club-tipped antennae, and are brightly coloured. The scales which cover moths and butterflies sometimes produce colours by iridescence, which is the effect of sunlight shining on them to produce a display of many different colours.

SWALLOWTAIL
BUTTERFLY

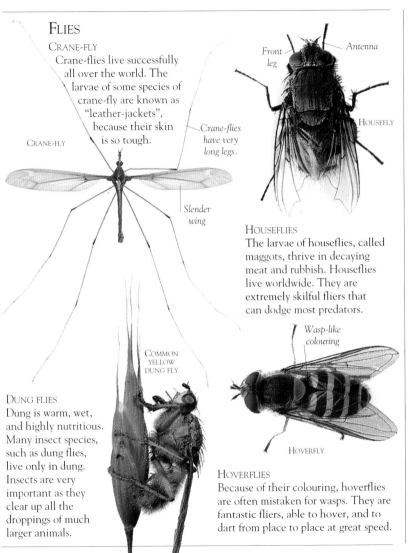

FLIES

CRANE-FLY

Crane-flies live successfully all over the world. The larvae of some species of crane-fly are known as "leather-jackets", because their skin is so tough.

CRANE-FLY

Crane-flies have very long legs.

Front leg

Antenna

HOUSEFLY

Slender wing

HOUSEFLIES

The larvae of houseflies, called maggots, thrive in decaying meat and rubbish. Houseflies live worldwide. They are extremely skilful fliers that can dodge most predators.

Wasp-like colouring

COMMON YELLOW DUNG FLY

DUNG FLIES

Dung is warm, wet, and highly nutritious. Many insect species, such as dung flies, live only in dung. Insects are very important as they clear up all the droppings of much larger animals.

HOVERFLY

HOVERFLIES

Because of their colouring, hoverflies are often mistaken for wasps. They are fantastic fliers, able to hover, and to dart from place to place at great speed.

39

Bugs and other types

There are about 67,500 species of bug – they are the fifth largest order of insects. Bugs have a feeding tube folded back between the legs, and most of them eat plant food. The many other orders of insects contain fewer species. Some of these orders are well known, such as fleas, cockroaches, dragonflies, and locusts.

BUGS

FEEDING TUBES
The mandibles (jaws) found in most insects are modified into needle-like tubes in bugs. The bug pierces food with the feeding tube and then sucks up juices.

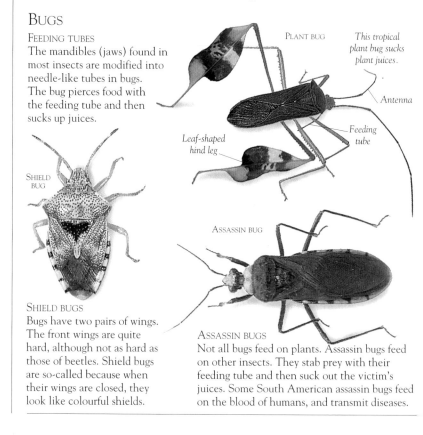

PLANT BUG

This tropical plant bug sucks plant juices.

Antenna

Feeding tube

Leaf-shaped hind leg

SHIELD BUG

ASSASSIN BUG

SHIELD BUGS
Bugs have two pairs of wings. The front wings are quite hard, although not as hard as those of beetles. Shield bugs are so-called because when their wings are closed, they look like colourful shields.

ASSASSIN BUGS
Not all bugs feed on plants. Assassin bugs feed on other insects. They stab prey with their feeding tube and then suck out the victim's juices. Some South American assassin bugs feed on the blood of humans, and transmit diseases.

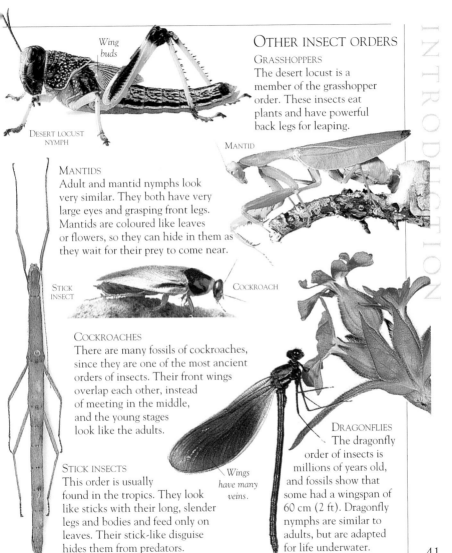

Wing buds

DESERT LOCUST NYMPH

OTHER INSECT ORDERS

GRASSHOPPERS
The desert locust is a member of the grasshopper order. These insects eat plants and have powerful back legs for leaping.

MANTID

MANTIDS
Adult and mantid nymphs look very similar. They both have very large eyes and grasping front legs. Mantids are coloured like leaves or flowers, so they can hide in them as they wait for their prey to come near.

STICK INSECT

COCKROACH

COCKROACHES
There are many fossils of cockroaches, since they are one of the most ancient orders of insects. Their front wings overlap each other, instead of meeting in the middle, and the young stages look like the adults.

DRAGONFLIES
The dragonfly order of insects is millions of years old, and fossils show that some had a wingspan of 60 cm (2 ft). Dragonfly nymphs are similar to adults, but are adapted for life underwater.

STICK INSECTS
This order is usually found in the tropics. They look like sticks with their long, slender legs and bodies and feed only on leaves. Their stick-like disguise hides them from predators.

Wings have many veins.

41

METAMORPHOSIS

INSECTS GO THROUGH several stages of growth before they become adults. This growing process is called metamorphosis. There are two types of metamorphosis: complete and incomplete. Complete metamorphosis has four main growth stages – egg, larva, pupa, and adult. Incomplete metamorphosis involves three main stages – egg, nymph, and adult.

Incomplete metamorphosis

This growing process is a gradual transformation. The insects hatch from their eggs looking like miniature adults. These young insects are called nymphs. As they grow, they shed their skin several times before they reach the adult stage.

Clawed feet hook onto stem

Wing buds

Adult head

Adult head and thorax emerge

1 DAMSELFLY NYMPH
A damselfly nymph lives underwater. Paddle-like plates on its tail help it swim and breathe. It sheds its skin several times as it grows towards adulthood.

2 HOLDING ON
When the nymph is ready to change into an adult it crawls out of the water up a plant stem.

3 BREAKING OUT
The skin along the back splits open and the adult head and thorax start to emerge.

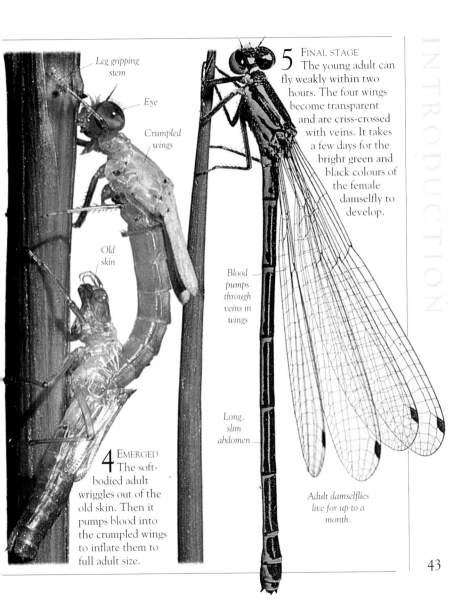

Leg gripping stem

Eye

Crumpled wings

Old skin

5 FINAL STAGE
The young adult can fly weakly within two hours. The four wings become transparent and are criss-crossed with veins. It takes a few days for the bright green and black colours of the female damselfly to develop.

Blood pumps through veins in wings

Long, slim abdomen

4 EMERGED
The soft-bodied adult wriggles out of the old skin. Then it pumps blood into the crumpled wings to inflate them to full adult size.

Adult damselflies live for up to a month.

Complete metamorphosis

The four main growth stages in a complete metamorphosis are egg, larva, pupa, and adult. The larva bears no resemblance to the adult it will become. The pupal stage is when the larva makes the amazing transformation into an adult. Insects such as wasps, butterflies, beetles, and flies undergo complete metamorphosis.

1 LAYING EGGS
Butterflies lay eggs near leaves which caterpillars can eat when they hatch. Newly hatched cater-pillars are too small to walk far to feed.

Eggshell

Egg

2 THE FIRST MEAL
When a caterpillar emerges, the first meal it eats is usually its own eggshell. The eggshell provides the caterpillar with valuable nutrients before it begins its diet of leaves.

Strong jaws slice food.

A caterpillar can increase its body weight by about 100 times in a few weeks.

3 GROWING
The caterpillar chews up hundreds of leaves and grows much bigger, shedding its skin several times. This growth prepares the caterpillar for the pupal stage of its life.

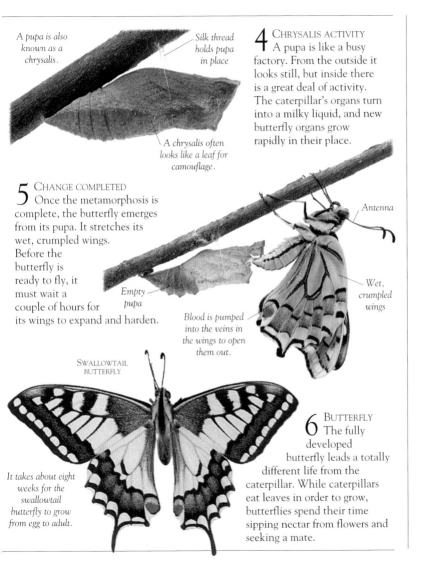

A pupa is also known as a chrysalis.

Silk thread holds pupa in place

A chrysalis often looks like a leaf for camouflage.

4 CHRYSALIS ACTIVITY
A pupa is like a busy factory. From the outside it looks still, but inside there is a great deal of activity. The caterpillar's organs turn into a milky liquid, and new butterfly organs grow rapidly in their place.

5 CHANGE COMPLETED
Once the metamorphosis is complete, the butterfly emerges from its pupa. It stretches its wet, crumpled wings. Before the butterfly is ready to fly, it must wait a couple of hours for its wings to expand and harden.

Empty pupa

Antenna

Wet, crumpled wings

Blood is pumped into the veins in the wings to open them out.

SWALLOWTAIL BUTTERFLY

It takes about eight weeks for the swallowtail butterfly to grow from egg to adult.

6 BUTTERFLY
The fully developed butterfly leads a totally different life from the caterpillar. While caterpillars eat leaves in order to grow, butterflies spend their time sipping nectar from flowers and seeking a mate.

HOW INSECTS MOVE

INSECTS MOVE using muscles which are attached
to the inner surfaces of their hard outer skeleton.
Many insects walk, but some larvae have no legs
so they crawl or wriggle along. Some insects swim,
others jump, but most adult insects can fly and in
this way they may travel long distances.

Legs

Insects use their legs for walking,
running, jumping, and swimming.
Many insects have legs modified
for a number of other purposes.
These include catching prey,
holding a female when mating,
producing songs, digging, fighting,
and camouflage.

LEGS FOR SWIMMING
The backswimmer has long, oar-
shaped back legs, allowing the insect
to "row" rapidly through water. The
legs have flattened ends and a fringe
of thick hairs. The front legs are short
to grasp prey on the water's surface.

MOVEMENT FACTS

• Fairyflies use
their wings to "fly"
underwater.

• Many butterflies walk
on four legs; the front
pair are used for tasting.

• The legless larvae of
some parasitic wasps
hitch a ride on a
passing ant in order to
enter an ant's nest.

1 PREPARING TO JUMP
The back legs of locusts are swollen and packed
with strong muscles for jumping. Before leaping, a
locust holds its back legs tightly under its body, near its
centre of gravity. This is the best position for the legs
to propel the insect
high into the air.

Long back
legs

Wing

Shorter
front legs

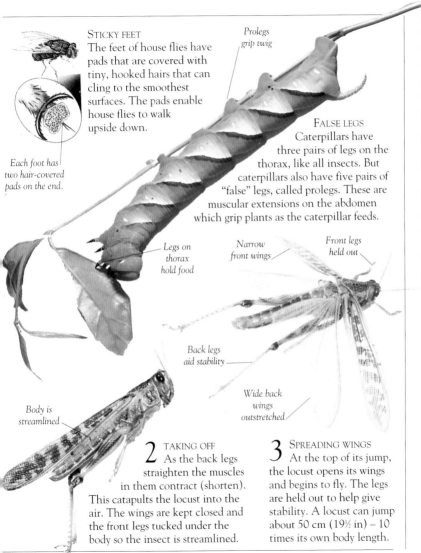

STICKY FEET
The feet of house flies have pads that are covered with tiny, hooked hairs that can cling to the smoothest surfaces. The pads enable house flies to walk upside down.

Each foot has two hair-covered pads on the end.

Prolegs grip twig

FALSE LEGS
Caterpillars have three pairs of legs on the thorax, like all insects. But caterpillars also have five pairs of "false" legs, called prolegs. These are muscular extensions on the abdomen which grip plants as the caterpillar feeds.

Legs on thorax hold food

Narrow front wings

Front legs held out

Back legs aid stability

Wide back wings outstretched

Body is streamlined

2 TAKING OFF
As the back legs straighten the muscles in them contract (shorten). This catapults the locust into the air. The wings are kept closed and the front legs tucked under the body so the insect is streamlined.

3 SPREADING WINGS
At the top of its jump, the locust opens its wings and begins to fly. The legs are held out to help give stability. A locust can jump about 50 cm (19½ in) – 10 times its own body length.

47

Wings and scales

Insect wings are a wide variety of shapes and sizes. They are not used just for flying, but also for attracting a mate or hiding from predators. Most insects have two pairs of wings, each with a network of veins to give strength. Flies have only one pair of wings – the second pair is modified into small balancing organs called halteres. Small insects have few wing veins since their wings are so tiny.

EXPERT FLIERS
Dragonflies are among the most accomplished fliers in the insect world. They can hover, fly fast or slow, change direction rapidly, and even fly backwards. As they manoeuvre, their two pairs of wings beat independently of each other.

WING FACTS

• The scales of butterflies and moths contain waste products from the pupal stage.

• There is a hearing organ in one of the wing veins of green lacewings for hearing the shrieks of bats.

• Many species of island insects are wingless because of the risk of being blown out to sea.

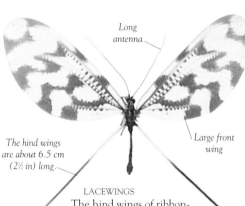

Long antenna

Large front wing

The hind wings are about 6.5 cm (2½ in) long.

LACEWINGS
The hind wings of ribbon-tail lacewings are modified into long graceful streamers. Scientists are not sure what these are for, but they may act as stabilizers in flight, or even divert predators from attacking the lacewing's body. The lacewing's mottled patterns probably help to conceal it in the dry sandy places where it lives.

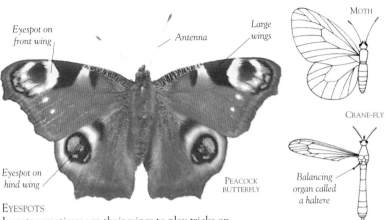

Eyespot on front wing

Antenna

Large wings

Eyespot on hind wing

PEACOCK BUTTERFLY

MOTH

CRANE-FLY

Balancing organ called a haltere

WASP

Hind wings are slightly smaller than front wings

EYESPOTS

Insects sometimes use their wings to play tricks on their enemies. Many butterflies and moths have eyespots on their wings. These are probably used to startle predators when flashed suddenly. This gives the butterfly or moth a little more time to escape.

SCALES

The wings of moths and butterflies are covered in overlapping scales. The scales are formed from specially flattened and ridged hairs.

FRINGED WINGS

Tiny insects have difficulty in flying as air is very dense for them. To increase the size of their wings and so help improve lift, they often have fringes of hairs around the edges of the wings.

Fringes along edge

Wing case

Large hind wing

BEETLE

DIFFERENT WINGS

Most moths have two pairs of large wings. True flies have only one pair of wings. The wings of wasps are transparent. A beetle's second pair of large wings is folded under the hardened first pair, or wing cases.

Flight

The ability to fly is one of the main reasons insects have survived for millions of years, and continue to flourish. Flight helps insects escape from danger. It also makes it easier to find food and new places to live. Sometimes insects fly thousands of kilometres to reach fresh food or warmer weather.

FLYING GROUPS
This African grasshopper has broad hind wings which allow it to glide for long distances. Locusts are a type of grasshopper which fly in huge groups when they need new food. Sometimes as many as 100 million locusts fly together for hundreds of kilometres.

WARMING UP
An insect's flight muscles must be warm before the wings can be moved fast enough for flight. On cool mornings, insects like this shield bug shiver, vibrating their wings to warm themselves up.

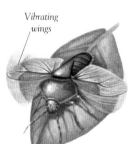

Vibrating wings

1 PREPARING TO FLY
This cockchafer beetle prepares for flight by climbing to the top of a plant and facing into the wind. It may open and shut its elytra (wing cases) several times while warming up.

Elytra protect body

2 OPENING THE WINGS
The hardened elytra, which protect the fragile hind wings, begin to open. The antennae are spread so the beetle can monitor the wind direction.

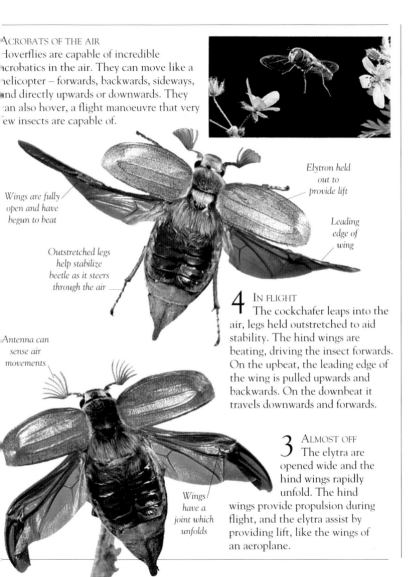

ACROBATS OF THE AIR
Hoverflies are capable of incredible
acrobatics in the air. They can move like a
helicopter – forwards, backwards, sideways,
and directly upwards or downwards. They
can also hover, a flight manoeuvre that very
few insects are capable of.

*Wings are fully
open and have
begun to beat*

*Outstretched legs
help stabilize
beetle as it steers
through the air*

*Antenna can
sense air
movements*

*Elytron held
out to
provide lift*

*Leading
edge of
wing*

4 IN FLIGHT
The cockchafer leaps into the
air, legs held outstretched to aid
stability. The hind wings are
beating, driving the insect forwards.
On the upbeat, the leading edge of
the wing is pulled upwards and
backwards. On the downbeat it
travels downwards and forwards.

3 ALMOST OFF
The elytra are
opened wide and the
hind wings rapidly
unfold. The hind
wings provide propulsion during
flight, and the elytra assist by
providing lift, like the wings of
an aeroplane.

*Wings
have a
joint which
unfolds*

51

INSECT SENSES

INSECTS NEED to be fully aware of the world around them in order to survive. Although insects are tiny, they have keener senses than most larger animals. They can see colours and hear sounds that are undetectable to humans, as well as being able to detect smells from many kilometres away.

Sight

There are two types of insect eyes – simple and compound. Simple eyes can probably detect only light and shade. Compound eyes have hundreds of lenses, giving their owner excellent vision.

HEAD OF COMMON DARTER DRAGONFLY

SIMPLE EYES
Caterpillars never need to look far for their plant food – they are constantly surrounded by it. Because of this, they do not need sharp eyesight. They can manage perfectly well with a group of simple eyes.

GOOD VISION
The eyes of dragonflies take up most of their head. This allows them to see what is in front, above, below, and behind them all at the same time. Dragonflies use their sight more than any other of their senses to catch prey.

COMMON DARTER DRAGONFLY

Simple eyes

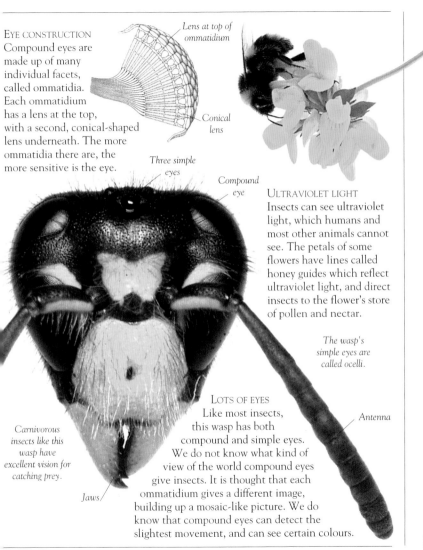

EYE CONSTRUCTION
Compound eyes are made up of many individual facets, called ommatidia. Each ommatidium has a lens at the top, with a second, conical-shaped lens underneath. The more ommatidia there are, the more sensitive is the eye.

Lens at top of ommatidium

Conical lens

Three simple eyes

Compound eye

ULTRAVIOLET LIGHT
Insects can see ultraviolet light, which humans and most other animals cannot see. The petals of some flowers have lines called honey guides which reflect ultraviolet light, and direct insects to the flower's store of pollen and nectar.

The wasp's simple eyes are called ocelli.

LOTS OF EYES
Like most insects, this wasp has both compound and simple eyes. We do not know what kind of view of the world compound eyes give insects. It is thought that each ommatidium gives a different image, building up a mosaic-like picture. We do know that compound eyes can detect the slightest movement, and can see certain colours.

Antenna

Carnivorous insects like this wasp have excellent vision for catching prey.

Jaws

53

Smelling, hearing, and touching

The bodies of insects are covered in short hairs which are connected to the nervous system. These hairs can feel, or "hear", vibrations in the air due to sound or movement. Some hairs are modified to detect smells and flavours. Sensory hairs are often found on the antennae, but also occur on the feet and mouthparts.

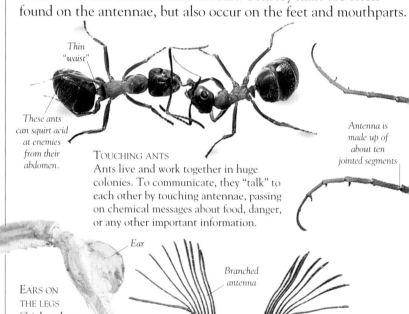

Thin "waist"

These ants can squirt acid at enemies from their abdomen.

Antenna is made up of about ten jointed segments

TOUCHING ANTS
Ants live and work together in huge colonies. To communicate, they "talk" to each other by touching antennae, passing on chemical messages about food, danger, or any other important information.

Ear

Branched antenna

EARS ON THE LEGS
Crickets have a swelling just below the knee on each front leg. They are the cricket's ears, which are formed like drums and pick up the mating songs of other crickets.

BEETLE ANTENNAE
The fringes on the antennae of this Indian beetle greatly enlarge their surface area. This increases their sensitivity to scents carried in the wind.

54

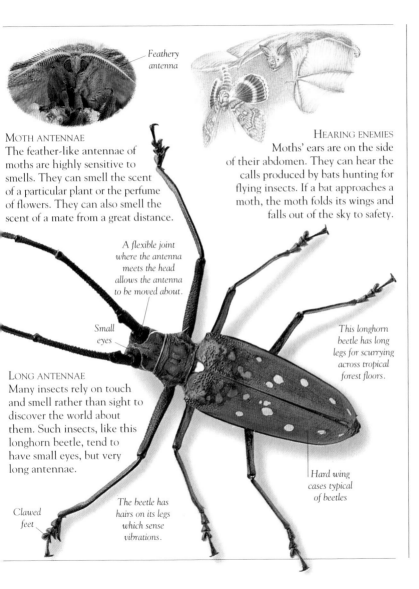

Feathery
antenna

MOTH ANTENNAE
The feather-like antennae of
moths are highly sensitive to
smells. They can smell the scent
of a particular plant or the perfume
of flowers. They can also smell the
scent of a mate from a great distance.

HEARING ENEMIES
Moths' ears are on the side
of their abdomen. They can hear the
calls produced by bats hunting for
flying insects. If a bat approaches a
moth, the moth folds its wings and
falls out of the sky to safety.

A flexible joint
where the antenna
meets the head
allows the antenna
to be moved about.

Small
eyes

This longhorn
beetle has long
legs for scurrying
across tropical
forest floors.

LONG ANTENNAE
Many insects rely on touch
and smell rather than sight to
discover the world about
them. Such insects, like this
longhorn beetle, tend to
have small eyes, but very
long antennae.

Hard wing
cases typical
of beetles

Clawed
feet

The beetle has
hairs on its legs
which sense
vibrations.

55

Jaws chew leaf

Caterpillar holds leaf with its legs

HOW INSECTS FEED

INSECTS HAVE complex mouthparts. The insects that chew their food have a pair of strong jaws for chopping, a smaller pair of jaws for holding food, and two pairs of sensory organs, called palps, for tasting. Some insects drink only liquid food and have special tubular mouthparts like a straw.

Chewing

Predatory, chewing insects need sharp, pointed jaws for stabbing, holding, and chopping up their struggling prey. Insects that chew plants have blunter jaws for grinding their food.

PLANT CHEWER
A caterpillar needs powerful jaws to bite into plant material. Their jaws are armed with teeth that overlap when they close. Some caterpillars' jaws are modified into grinding plates for mashing up the toughest leaves.

THRUSTING JAWS
Dragonfly larvae have pincers at the end of a hinged plate folded under the head. When catching prey, the plate unfolds, shoots forwards, and the pincers grab the prey. Toothed jaws in the head reduce the victim to mincemeat.

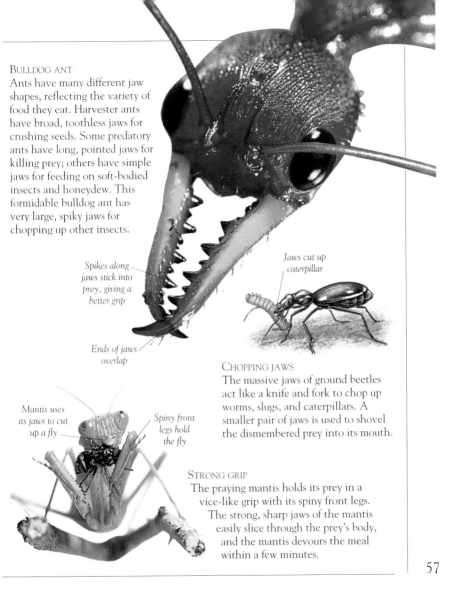

BULLDOG ANT
Ants have many different jaw shapes, reflecting the variety of food they eat. Harvester ants have broad, toothless jaws for crushing seeds. Some predatory ants have long, pointed jaws for killing prey; others have simple jaws for feeding on soft-bodied insects and honeydew. This formidable bulldog ant has very large, spiky jaws for chopping up other insects.

Spikes along jaws stick into prey, giving a better grip

Ends of jaws overlap

Jaws cut up caterpillar

CHOPPING JAWS
The massive jaws of ground beetles act like a knife and fork to chop up worms, slugs, and caterpillars. A smaller pair of jaws is used to shovel the dismembered prey into its mouth.

Mantis uses its jaws to cut up a fly

Spiny front legs hold the fly

STRONG GRIP
The praying mantis holds its prey in a vice-like grip with its spiny front legs. The strong, sharp jaws of the mantis easily slice through the prey's body, and the mantis devours the meal within a few minutes.

57

Drinking

For many insects, the main way of feeding is by drinking. The most nutritious foods to drink are nectar and blood. Nectar is rich in sugar, and blood is packed with proteins. Some insects drink by sucking through straw-like mouthparts. Others have sponge-like mouthparts with which they mop up liquids.

HAWK-MOTH
Butterflies and moths have a long, tongue-like tube called a proboscis through which they drink. Darwin's hawk-moth has an extremely long proboscis for reaching the nectar in an extra-long flower.

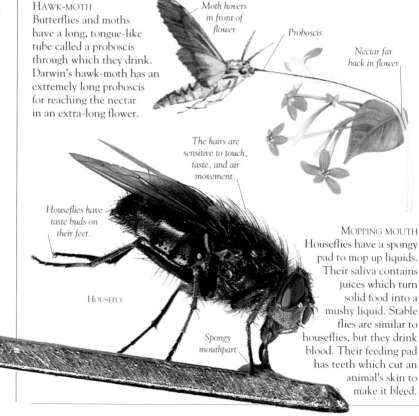

Moth hovers in front of flower

Proboscis

Nectar far back in flower

The hairs are sensitive to touch, taste, and air movement.

Houseflies have taste buds on their feet.

HOUSEFLY

MOPPING MOUTH
Houseflies have a spongy pad to mop up liquids. Their saliva contains juices which turn solid food into a mushy liquid. Stable flies are similar to houseflies, but they drink blood. Their feeding pad has teeth which cut an animal's skin to make it bleed.

Spongy mouthpart

ROSTRUM

The saliva kills the prey and dissolves its insides which the bug drinks.

Assassin bug

ROSTRUM

Assassin bugs pierce prey with needle-like stylets enclosed in a sheath called a rostrum. The stylets form a double tube so that saliva goes down one side while food comes up the other.

Antenna

COILED PROBOSCIS

When the proboscis of butterflies and moths is not in use it is coiled beneath the head. Different species have different lengths of proboscis. The longest known proboscis belongs to a Madagascan moth, and is about 33 cm (13 in) long.

Long proboscis

Coiled proboscis

HORSEFLIES

Most horseflies have knife-like jaws to make animals bleed. But this curious oriental horsefly has short, stout mouthparts to feed on blood, and a long slender proboscis to collect nectar from flowers.

COURTSHIP, BIRTH, AND GROWTH

REPRODUCTION is hazardous for insects. A female must first find and mate with a male of her own species, and lay eggs where the newly hatched young can feed. The larvae must shed their skin several times as they grow. All this time the insects must avoid being eaten.

Courtship and mating

Males and females use special signals to ensure that their chosen mate is the right species. Courtship usually involves using scents, but may include colour displays, dancing, caressing, and even gifts.

The light is produced by a chemical reaction.

GUIDING LIGHT
Glowworms are the wingless females of certain beetle species. They attract males by producing a light near the tip of their abdomen. Some species flash a distinctive code to attract the correct males.

COURTSHIP FLIGHTS
Butterflies may recognize their own species by sight, but scent is more reliable. Butterfly courtship involves dancing flights with an exchange of scented chemical signals specific to each species.

Butterflies find the scented chemicals, called pheromones, very attractive.

MATING DANGER
Mating between some insect species may last for several hours, with the male gripping the female's abdomen with claspers. This keeps other males away, but the pair are vulnerable to predators at this time.

Male

Female receives male's sperm

Tip of male's abdomen grips female

Female

DAMSELFLIES

When mating, a male damselfly grips a female's neck with the tip of his abdomen. She receives a packet of sperm from a pouch near his legs, and he continues to hold her neck while she lays eggs. This prevents other males mating with her.

Female

PREDATORS MATING

Males of some predatory species, such as empid flies, give the female a meal of a dead insect when mating so they are not eaten themselves. Some males trick the female. They give an empty parcel, and mate while the female opens it.

MATING ASIAN SWALLOWTAIL BUTTERFLIES

UNNATURAL BEHAVIOUR

It is often said that a female mantis will eat a male while he is mating with her. But this probably only happens when the mantises are in captivity and their behaviour is not natural.

Male

61

Eggs and egg-laying

Insects use up a lot of energy producing eggs. To make sure this energy is not wasted, insects have many ways of protecting their eggs from predators. A few species of insect stay with their eggs to protect them until the larvae hatch. Some insects lay their eggs underground with a supply of food waiting for the newly hatched larvae. Most insects lay their eggs either in food, or near food, so the young larvae do not have to travel far to eat.

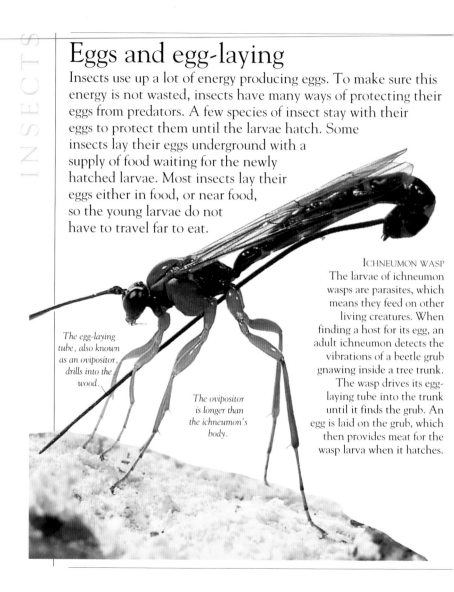

The egg-laying tube, also known as an ovipositor, drills into the wood.

The ovipositor is longer than the ichneumon's body.

ICHNEUMON WASP
The larvae of ichneumon wasps are parasites, which means they feed on other living creatures. When finding a host for its egg, an adult ichneumon detects the vibrations of a beetle grub gnawing inside a tree trunk.

The wasp drives its egg-laying tube into the trunk until it finds the grub. An egg is laid on the grub, which then provides meat for the wasp larva when it hatches.

SUITABLE FOOD

Butterflies desert their eggs once they are laid. Different butterflies lay their eggs on different plants, depending on what the larvae eat. The Malay lacewing butterfly lays its eggs on vine tendrils.

Wasp carrying beetle to nest

Beetles are stored in underground nest

CARING EARWIGS

female earwig looks
r her eggs, licking
hem regularly to
eep them clean.
en the nymphs
atch, she feeds
hem until they
big enough to
leave the nest.

Earwig eggs

rticle
nain
nnel

Beetles mould dung into balls

Beetle filling tunnel with dung as food for newly hatched grubs

JNG BEETLES

e males and females of some dung
etle species work together to dig an underground
nel with smaller tunnels branching off it. A female
s an egg in each of the smaller tunnels and fills them
h animal dung, which the beetle grubs will feed on.

HUNTING WASPS

Most species of hunting wasp collect soft-bodied prey, such as caterpillars or spiders, for their grubs. But the weevil-hunting wasp collects adult beetles which it stings in the throat, and then stores in a tunnel as food for its larvae.

INSECT EGG FACTS

• Whitefly eggs have stalks that extract water from leaves.

• Tsetse flies develop their eggs internally and lay mature larvae.

• Green lacewing eggs have long stalks, making them difficult for predators to eat.

Birth and growth

As an insect grows from egg to adult it sheds its skin several times to produce a larger exoskeleton. Whilst this new skin hardens the insect is soft and vulnerable. Insects show many life-cycle adaptations to protect their soft young stages.

EGGS LARVA PUPA ADULT LADYBIRD

LADYBIRD GROWTH
Ladybirds and all other beetles go through a complete metamorphosis. An adult ladybird lays its eggs on a plant where small insects called aphids feed. Ladybird larvae eat aphids and shed their skin three times as they grow. The colourful adult emerges from the dull resting stage, or pupa.

APHIDS
Female aphids can reproduce without mating. They give birth to live young rather than lay eggs and each female may have about 100 offspring. The newborn aphids can give birth after only a few days.

FROTHY PROTECTION
Froghoppers are soft-bodied bugs like aphids. A froghopper nymph produces a frothy liquid from its anus. The froth protects the nymph from drying out, and also hides it from predators.

Frothy hideaway

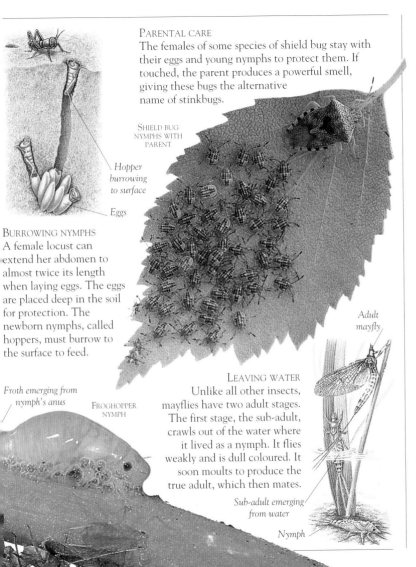

PARENTAL CARE

The females of some species of shield bug stay with their eggs and young nymphs to protect them. If touched, the parent produces a powerful smell, giving these bugs the alternative name of stinkbugs.

SHIELD BUG NYMPHS WITH PARENT

Hopper burrowing to surface

Eggs

BURROWING NYMPHS

A female locust can extend her abdomen to almost twice its length when laying eggs. The eggs are placed deep in the soil for protection. The newborn nymphs, called hoppers, must burrow to the surface to feed.

Froth emerging from nymph's anus

FROGHOPPER NYMPH

Adult mayfly

LEAVING WATER

Unlike all other insects, mayflies have two adult stages. The first stage, the sub-adult, crawls out of the water where it lived as a nymph. It flies weakly and is dull coloured. It soon moults to produce the true adult, which then mates.

Sub-adult emerging from water

Nymph

65

Survival of the young

Predators eagerly hunt insect larvae since many are slow-moving, soft, and nutritious. To ensure survival, most insect species produc large numbers of young which grow rapidly. Most insect larvae are defenceless and have developed special ways of hiding from predators. But many insect larvae are fierce predators themselves, consuming other creatures for nourishment as they grow.

Grub in pupal cell

WELL HIDDEN
The larvae of chafer beetles live underground, safely hidden from most predators. The larvae, or grubs, may take many weeks to develop. They then produce a cell of hardened earth in which they will change into an adult.

Caterpillar rears up when threatened

Fearsome "face"

Sharp spines

True legs

Proleg

SPINY LARVA
Mexican bean beetle larvae eat leaves and develop rapidly. They are covered with long, branched spines which may deter birds and other predators from attacking them.

SCARY DISPLAY
Caterpillars are a favourite food of birds. Some caterpillars try to hide to stay safe. But if the puss moth caterpillar is threatened, it puts on a startling display which can frighten off birds.

NIGHT FEEDER

The mormon butterfly caterpillar feeds in the dark of night to avoid being seen by predators. In less than eight hours it will chew away a leaf which is more than twice its own length. During the day it rests as inconspicuously as possible.

For a more frightening, display, the caterpillar waves these "tails" as if they were stings.

WATER LARVA

Stone-fly larvae live in cold water and grow slowly, spending about three years as a larva. They are slow-moving and hide from predators under rocks and amongst plants.

SOFT BODIES

Young mantids are fierce predators. The body of some species resembles a flower. This disguise helps them to go unnoticed by prey, and also by predators such as birds.

Eye

Leg

Pink, flower-like body

Legs are striped pink and green

67

INSECTS

NESTS AND SOCIETIES

MOST INSECTS lead solitary lives, but some, particularly wasps, ants, bees, and termites, live in societies which are sometimes very ordered. There are queens, kings, workers, and soldiers. Each of these has particular jobs to do. Social insects live in nests which are often elaborate, where they protect each other and rear their young.

TROPICAL WASP NEST MADE OF CHEWED-UP PLANT FIBRES

The nest is cemented together with wasp saliva.

Wasps, ants, and bees

These insects produce a wide range of nests. Some are small with only a few dozen members, while larger nests may contain thousands of insects. Most have a single queen, and all the nest members are her offspring.

ANTS

A species of African tree ant builds its nest from fragments of plants and soil to produce a substance like dark cement. The ants live on a diet of honeydew which they get from aphids. The aphids feed on the sap of leaves in the tree tops and discharge the honeydew from their rear ends.

BEES

A bumblebee queen starts her nest alone in spring in a hole in the ground. She makes cells for her eggs out of wax. She also makes a wax pot which she fills with honey for food.

The queen uses her antennae to measure the cells as she builds them.

1 A NEW START

European wasp colonies die out each winter. In spring a queen begins a new nest of "paper" made with chewed-up wood. She makes a few cells for her eggs, building walls around the cells to shield them.

Entrance hole

2 PROTECTIVE LAYERS

The queen builds more and more paper layers around the cells. The layers will protect the larvae from cold winds as well as from predators. The queen leaves an entrance hole at the bottom.

Finished nest

3 HARD-WORKING FAMILY

The first brood the queen rears become workers, gathering food for more larvae and expanding the nest. By summer, a nest may have 500 wasps, all collecting caterpillars for the larvae. A large nest may be as much as 45 cm (18 in) in diameter.

INSIDE THE NEST

The queen lays a single egg in each cell. When the larvae hatch they stay in their cell and the queen feeds them with pieces of caterpillar.

Termite nests

Termites have the most complex insect societies. Their elaborate nests, which may be in wood or underground, last for several years. Each nest has a single large queen and king, which are served by specialized small workers and large soldiers. Termites feed and protect each other, and one generation will help to raise the next generation of offspring.

QUEEN TERMITE
In a termite society, the queen lays all the eggs. She is too fat to move, so the workers bring food to her. The queen lays 30,000 eggs each day and, as she lays them, the workers carry them off to special chambers for rearing.

Layers of "umbrellas"

NEST DEFENDERS
Termite soldiers fight enemies that attack the nest. Most termite species have soldiers with enlarged heads and powerful jaws. In some species, each soldier's head has a snout that squirts poison at invaders.

STRANGE NEST
The function of the "umbrellas" on this African nest is a mystery to scientists. The termite species which builds this type of nest lives underground. If an "umbrella" is damaged, it does not get repaired, but a new one may be built.

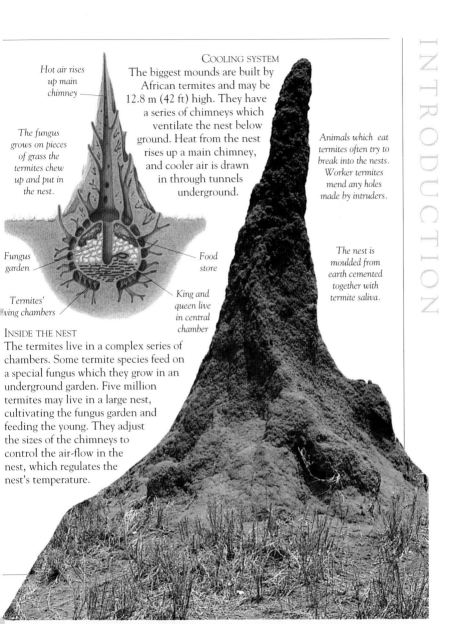

Hot air rises up main chimney

The fungus grows on pieces of grass the termites chew up and put in the nest.

COOLING SYSTEM

The biggest mounds are built by African termites and may be 12.8 m (42 ft) high. They have a series of chimneys which ventilate the nest below ground. Heat from the nest rises up a main chimney, and cooler air is drawn in through tunnels underground.

Animals which eat termites often try to break into the nests. Worker termites mend any holes made by intruders.

Fungus garden

Food store

Termites' living chambers

King and queen live in central chamber

The nest is moulded from earth cemented together with termite saliva.

INSIDE THE NEST

The termites live in a complex series of chambers. Some termite species feed on a special fungus which they grow in an underground garden. Five million termites may live in a large nest, cultivating the fungus garden and feeding the young. They adjust the sizes of the chimneys to control the air-flow in the nest, which regulates the nest's temperature.

HUNTING AND HIDING

SOME INSECT SPECIES are deadly hunters, killing prey with poisonous stings and sharp jaws. Insects are also hunted by a huge number of animals. To hide from predators, many insects have developed special disguises and patterns of behaviour.

Hunting insects

About one third of insect species are carnivorous (they eat meat). Some species eat decaying meat and dung, but most carnivorous insects hunt for their food.

KILLER BEETLE
Some insects are easily recognized as predators. The large jaws of this African ground beetle indicate that it is a hunter, and its long legs show that it can run fast after its insect prey.

KILLER WASPS
There are many types of hunting wasp. Most adult hunting wasps are vegetarians – they hunt prey only as food for their larvae. Each hunting wasp species hunts a particular type of prey. The weevil-hunting wasp hunts only a type of beetle called a weevil.

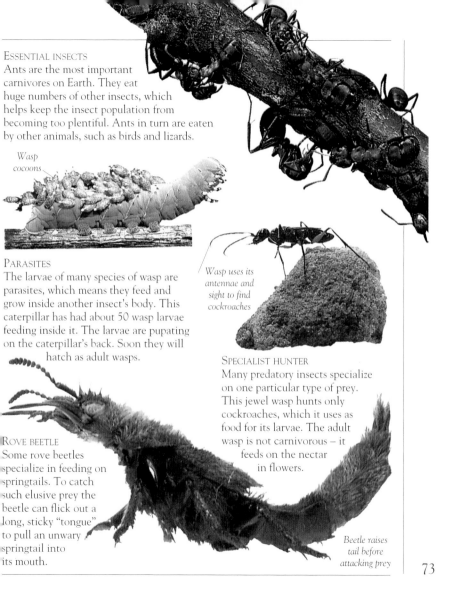

ESSENTIAL INSECTS

Ants are the most important carnivores on Earth. They eat huge numbers of other insects, which helps keep the insect population from becoming too plentiful. Ants in turn are eaten by other animals, such as birds and lizards.

Wasp cocoons

PARASITES

The larvae of many species of wasp are parasites, which means they feed and grow inside another insect's body. This caterpillar has had about 50 wasp larvae feeding inside it. The larvae are pupating on the caterpillar's back. Soon they will hatch as adult wasps.

Wasp uses its antennae and sight to find cockroaches

SPECIALIST HUNTER

Many predatory insects specialize on one particular type of prey. This jewel wasp hunts only cockroaches, which it uses as food for its larvae. The adult wasp is not carnivorous – it feeds on the nectar in flowers.

ROVE BEETLE

Some rove beetles specialize in feeding on springtails. To catch such elusive prey the beetle can flick out a long, sticky "tongue" to pull an unwary springtail into its mouth.

Beetle raises tail before attacking prey

73

Camouflage

Insects whose body colouring matches their background are almost impossible to see. This method of hiding is known as camouflage. One of the first rules of successful camouflage is to keep still, as any movement can betray an insect to a sharp-eyed predator. Some insects use another type of camouflage called disruptive coloration. They disguise their body by breaking up its shape with stripes and blocks of colour.

GRASSY DISGUISE
The stripe-winged grasshopper can be heard singing in meadow grasses, but its camouflaged body is very hard to spot.

Grasshopper kicks any attackers with its back legs

DISRUPTIVE COLORATION
This tropical moth has disruptive coloration. The patterns on the wings break up their shape. A predator might notice the patterns, but not the whole moth.

LOOKING DISTASTEFUL
This treehopper has twig-like extensions on its thorax and abdomen. It looks like an inedible piece of wood, so hunters are likely to overlook it.

Extension on thorax

Eye

Wing

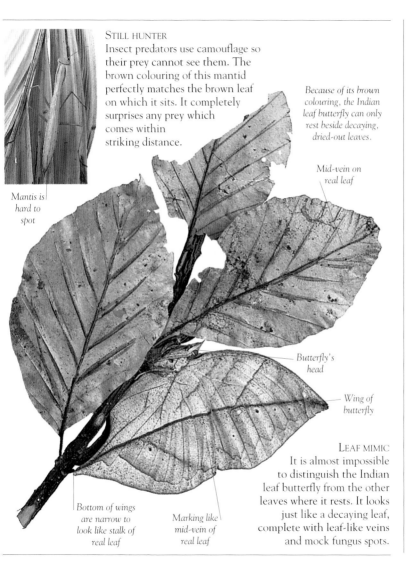

STILL HUNTER

Insect predators use camouflage so their prey cannot see them. The brown colouring of this mantid perfectly matches the brown leaf on which it sits. It completely surprises any prey which comes within striking distance.

Mantis is hard to spot

Because of its brown colouring, the Indian leaf butterfly can only rest beside decaying, dried-out leaves.

Mid-vein on real leaf

Butterfly's head

Wing of butterfly

LEAF MIMIC

It is almost impossible to distinguish the Indian leaf butterfly from the other leaves where it rests. It looks just like a decaying leaf, complete with leaf-like veins and mock fungus spots.

Bottom of wings are narrow to look like stalk of real leaf

Marking like mid-vein of real leaf

75

Warning coloration

Birds, mammals, and other intelligent
predators learn through experience that
some insects are poisonous or harmful.
Such insects do not camouflage themselves.
Instead they have brightly coloured bodies
which warn predators that they have an
unpleasant taste or a nasty sting. The
most common warning colours are red,
yellow, and black. Any insect with those
colours is probably poisonous.

BASKER MOTH
Moths that fly by day are
often brightly coloured,
particularly when they
taste unpleasant. The
red, yellow, and black
colouring of this basker
moth tells birds that it is
not a tasty meal.

PAINFUL REMINDER
The saddle-back caterpillar is
eye-catching with its vivid
colouring and grotesque
appearance. No young bird
would ever forget the
caterpillar if it tried a
mouthful of the poisonous,
stinging spines.

*Poisonous
spines*

*Vivid green
colouring
across back*

*Bright
spot*

WARNING SPOTS
This assassin bug is easily seen
because of the two bright spots on
its back. These bold markings warn
predators that there is a reason for
them to stay away. The bug's
weapon is a needle-sharp beak
which can give a very painful bite.

EYESPOTS
This silk moth is camouflaged when its wings are closed. But when attacked by a predator, the moth flashes the eyespots on its hind wings. This startles the attacker briefly, and may give the moth time to escape.

Camouflaged front wings

Eyespot

POISONOUS BODY
This grasshopper tastes horrible. It gets its terrible flavour from eating poisonous plants and storing the poisons in its body. The yellow and black stripes advertise its unpleasantness to birds and other predators.

Grasshopper uses the spines on its legs for defence

Eyes are black to blend with rest of colouring

Mimicry

Predators usually avoid preying on dangerous animals. Many harmless insects take advantage of this by mimicking harmful creatures. Mimicking insects copy a dangerous animal's body shape and colouring. They also behave like the animal they are copying to make the disguise more convincing. Inedible objects, such as twigs and thorns, are also mimicked by insects.

The treehoppers only move when they need a fresh source of food.

Markings make head resemble alligator's head

Real eye of bug

ALLIGATOR MIMIC
Scientists can often only guess at the reasons for the strange look and behaviour of some animals. It is not known why this tree-living bug looks like a tiny alligator. Perhaps its appearance briefly startles monkey predators, giving the bug time to fly off to safety.

HORNET MIMIC
The hornet moth looks very like a large wasp called a hornet. When flying, the moth even behaves like a hornet. Many insects find protection by mimicking wasps – birds avoid them because they might sting.

THORN MIMICS
These treehoppers mimic green thorns, a disguise which seems to fool most predators. The treehoppers have piercing mouthparts and sit motionless for hours feeding on the sap of a plant.

Legs are held close to body

Head

TWIG MIMIC
Inchworms, the larvae of geometrid moths, often mimic dead twigs. They feed at night and are almost unrecognizable as an insect by day, sticking out motionless at the end of a twig.

Legs of moth

Moth has same colouring as flower

Hanging flower

Real twig

FLOWER MIMIC
Insects which are active by night need to rest by day. But resting insects are vulnerable, and the daylight makes it easier for predators to see them. To go unnoticed, this moth from Trinidad mimics the hanging flowers on a bush where it rests during the day.

Prolegs at end of caterpillar clutch twig

79

WHERE INSECTS LIVE

INSECTS LIVE everywhere there is warmth and
moisture. Many of the five million or more species
have specialized habitat requirements. They can
live only in particular places, and easily
become extinct when humans change
or destroy their surroundings.
Other species are able to
adapt to changing
conditions; these
adaptable insects
often become pests.

NORTH
AMERICA

SOUTH
AMERICA

TEMPERATE WOODLAND
The varied plant life and
complex structure of
temperate woodland provides
insects with many different
habitats. Trees, shrubs, and
herbs all have flowers, fruits,
and buds for insects to feed
on, as well as stems and roots
for insects to bore into.

GRASSLAND AND HEATHLAND
These habitats offer little shelter
from bad weather. But they warm
up quickly in the sun, and have a
rich variety of flowering plants.

TOWNS AND GARDENS
Hundreds of insect species take advantage of human habitats. Insects find food and shelter in our roofs, cellars, food stores, kitchens, rubbish bins, farms, and in our flower-filled gardens.

DESERTS, CAVES, AND SOILS
These are inhospitable habitats. Food and water are scarce in deserts. Caves are dark and cold. And it is hard for insects to move and communicate in dense soil.

TROPICAL FOREST
This is the richest habitat for insect species. Thousands of species of plants provide countless niches for insects to live in, from treetop fruits, to dead leaves and twigs on the ground.

LAKES AND RIVERS
Freshwater insects are highly specialized. They have had to modify their bodies to be able to swim and breathe underwater.

TEMPERATURE WOODLAND

FIELD SCABIOUS
FLOWER

TEMPERATE WOODLANDS are often dominated by one tree species, such as oak, which is deciduous (the trees lose their leaves in winter). The types of insect found, and their numbers, will vary with the seasons, and also with the types of tree species in the woodlands.

DRAINING
Forests in wetlands have many different plant species. But people often drain this habitat because it is good for farming. Draining kills plants such as milk-parsley, the only plant the English swallowtail butterfly will breed on. This beautiful insect is now rarely seen.

+1.75

Although the English swallowtail will only lay eggs on milk-parsley, adults feed on a variety of flowers.

WOODLAND FACTS

• The woodland edge supports the greatest number of insect species.

• Each pair of blue tit birds needs about 5,000 caterpillars to feed to its chicks.

• In Britain, over 280 species of insect live on native oak trees.

• Temperate rainforests in the northwestern United States are disappearing faster than tropical rainforests.

Bumblebees are very common in woodlands.

+2.5

FLOWERS

Woodlands contain many types of flower. These attract various species of insect, such as bumblebees, which nest in the ground in animal burrows and pollinate many woodland flowers.

Vapourer moth caterpillar is covered with tufts of hair

VAPOURER MOTH CATERPILLAR

This attractive caterpillar eats the leaves of many different trees in Europe and North America. It will also attack rosebushes and heather plants.

Processionary caterpillars are covered in poisonous hairs.

PROCESSIONS

Conifer forests have fewer types of plant and animal than deciduous forests, although some, such as processionary moth caterpillars, can be common. These are named for their habit of following each other head to tail.

83

OAK TREE

IN EUROPE AND North America, oak trees support a rich variety of insects. There are insects living on every part of the oak tree – the leaves, buds, flowers, fruits, wood, bark, and on decaying leaves and branches. All these insects provide food for the many birds and other animals found in oak woodland.

OAK TREE

GREEN OAK TORTRIX MOTH ON LEAF

GREEN OAK TORTRIX CATERPILLAR

GREEN OAK TORTRIX MOTH

The green wings of the green oak tortrix moth camouflage it on leaves. Green oak tortrix caterpillars are extremely common on oak trees. The caterpillars hide from predators by rolling themselves up in a leaf.

+1.5

+2.5

Leaf rolled around green oak tortrix caterpillar

Mine

MAKING A TUNNEL

The caterpillars of some small moths tunnel between the upper and lower surfaces of a leaf. They eat the green tissues between these surfaces as they tunnel, and leave a see-through trail called a mine.

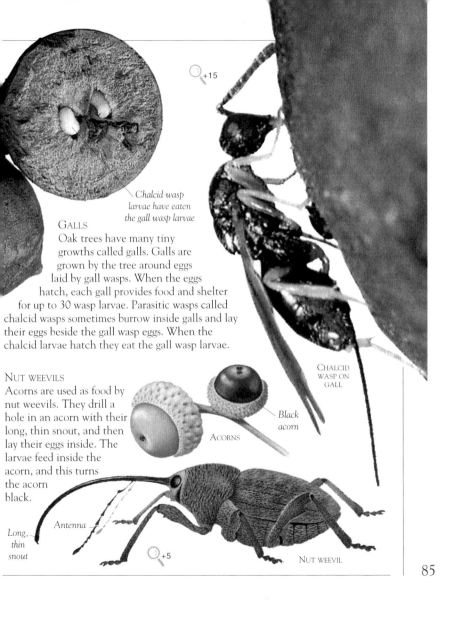

+15

*Chalcid wasp
larvae have eaten
the gall wasp larvae*

GALLS

Oak trees have many tiny
growths called galls. Galls are
grown by the tree around eggs
laid by gall wasps. When the eggs
hatch, each gall provides food and shelter
for up to 30 wasp larvae. Parasitic wasps called
chalcid wasps sometimes burrow inside galls and lay
their eggs beside the gall wasp eggs. When the
chalcid larvae hatch they eat the gall wasp larvae.

CHALCID
WASP ON
GALL

NUT WEEVILS

Acorns are used as food by
nut weevils. They drill a
hole in an acorn with their
long, thin snout, and then
lay their eggs inside. The
larvae feed inside the
acorn, and this turns
the acorn
black.

*Black
acorn*

ACORNS

*Long,
thin
snout*

Antenna

+5

NUT WEEVIL

TREE CANOPY

THE UPPER BRANCHES and leaves
of a tree are called the canopy.
Like a living green umbrella, the
canopy forms a protective
covering over the lower plants.
Countless insects find their food
in the canopy and they, in turn,
are food for many different birds.

*Inchworm
on leaf*

*Silken thread
suspends
inchworm*

INCHWORMS
Some young birds like
to feed on inchworms,
the caterpillars of
geometrid moths.
When in danger, inchworms
can drop from a leaf and hang
below by a silken thread.

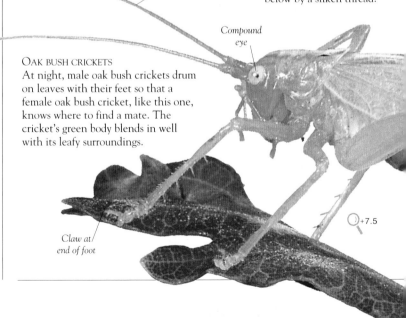

*Very long antennae help
cricket find its way in the
dark and alert it to the
approach of enemies*

*Compound
eye*

OAK BUSH CRICKETS
At night, male oak bush crickets drum
on leaves with their feet so that a
female oak bush cricket, like this one,
knows where to find a mate. The
cricket's green body blends in well
with its leafy surroundings.

*Claw at
end of foot*

⊙+7.5

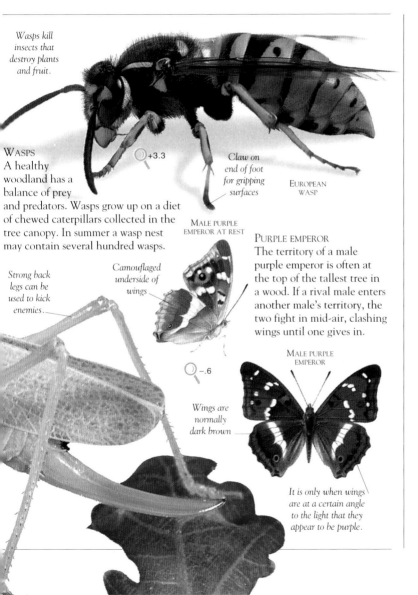

Wasps kill insects that destroy plants and fruit.

WASPS
A healthy woodland has a balance of prey and predators. Wasps grow up on a diet of chewed caterpillars collected in the tree canopy. In summer a wasp nest may contain several hundred wasps.

+3.3

Claw on end of foot for gripping surfaces

EUROPEAN WASP

MALE PURPLE EMPEROR AT REST

Strong back legs can be used to kick enemies.

Camouflaged underside of wings

PURPLE EMPEROR
The territory of a male purple emperor is often at the top of the tallest tree in a wood. If a rival male enters another male's territory, the two fight in mid-air, clashing wings until one gives in.

MALE PURPLE EMPEROR

−.6

Wings are normally dark brown

It is only when wings are at a certain angle to the light that they appear to be purple.

WOODLAND BUTTERFLIES

THE RICH VARIETY of habitats in woodland supports many butterfly species. Some live in the canopy, others feed on low shrubs. But most butterflies need sunshine and can be found on flowers in sunny clearings.

Q −.6

SILVER-WASHED FRITILLARY
This butterfly lays its eggs in cracks in the bark of mossy tree trunks, close to where violets are growing. The caterpillars feed on the leaves of these plants.

Brown upperside

Q −.8

Green underside

GREEN HAIRSTREAK
Whether it is sitting on a branch or resting on a leaf, the green hairstreak butterfly is well camouflaged. Its upperside is a woody brown while its underside is a leafy green.

PURPLE HAIRSTREAK BUTTERFLY

Female

Male

Eyespots on underwings

PURPLE HAIRSTREAK
High in the canopy of oak trees the caterpillars of the purple hairstreak butterfly feed on flowers and young leaves. Adult purple hairstreaks spend most of their lives in the treetops, feeding and sunbathing with their wings open.

Q –1

SPECKLED WOOD
When a speckled wood male finds a sunny spot in a shady woodland, he claims it as his territory. If a rival male challenges him, the two will fight in the air, clashing their wings as they spiral upwards into the treetops.

Eye

Comma butterflies live for about 10 months, hibernating during the winter.

Mottled brown and green colouring

This butterfly gets its name from the comma-shaped mark on each hind wing.

Oak-leaf-shaped edge of wing

COMMA BUTTERFLY
This woodland butterfly has a remarkable camouflage. When it closes its ragged-edged wings it looks just like a dead oak leaf. This helps to hide the butterfly from birds when it settles among the leaf litter on the woodland floor.

Q +3.75

TREE TRUNKS AND BRANCHES

CRACKS IN THE bark of trees provide a hiding place for many species of insect. Some burrow into the wood and live completely concealed from predators. Many insects also live and feed among the different plant life that grows on tree trunks and branches.

BARK INSECTS
Insects which live on bark are usually camouflaged, such as barklice which feed on tiny fungi and algae. Another bark insect, the snakefly, is a predator. When it hunts, it looks like a tiny snake about to strike, holding its head high looking for prey.

○+5

BARKLOUSE
Mesopsocus

SNAKEFLY

○+3.3

○+1.8

BARKLOUSE
Loensia fasciata

Giant wood wasp larvae feed on wood

Head

WOOD WASP
This female giant wood wasp has a long, stout egg-laying tube, or ovipositor, which looks like a fearsome sting. It lays eggs deep inside the soft wood of dead or dying trees.

Antenna

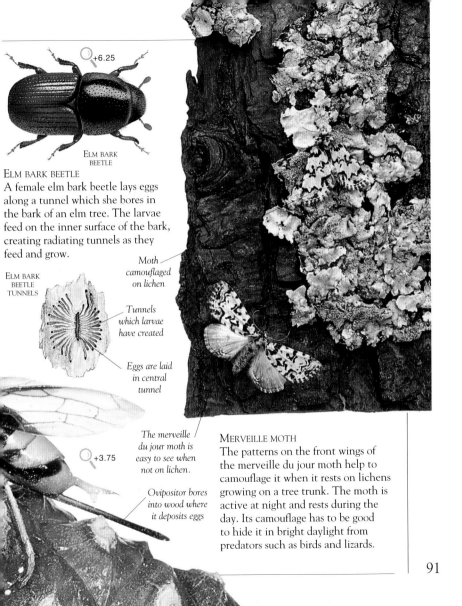

+6.25

ELM BARK
BEETLE

ELM BARK BEETLE
A female elm bark beetle lays eggs
along a tunnel which she bores in
the bark of an elm tree. The larvae
feed on the inner surface of the bark,
creating radiating tunnels as they
feed and grow.

ELM BARK
BEETLE
TUNNELS

*Moth
camouflaged
on lichen*

*Tunnels
which larvae
have created*

*Eggs are laid
in central
tunnel*

*The merveille
du jour moth is
easy to see when
not on lichen.*

+3.75

*Ovipositor bores
into wood where
it deposits eggs*

MERVEILLE MOTH
The patterns on the front wings of
the merveille du jour moth help to
camouflage it when it rests on lichens
growing on a tree trunk. The moth is
active at night and rests during the
day. Its camouflage has to be good
to hide it in bright daylight from
predators such as birds and lizards.

GROUND LEVEL

THE WOODLAND floor does not get much sunlight, so few plants grow there. Most insects at ground level feed on plant and animal debris falling from the canopy, or, if they are carnivorous, eat other insects.

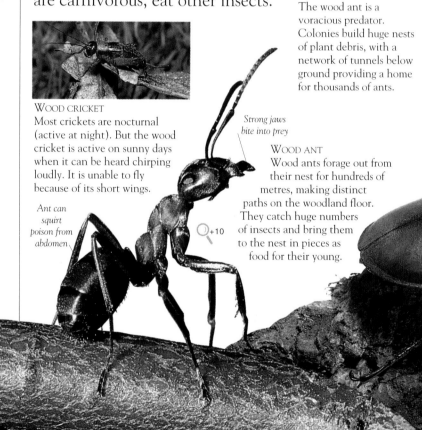

ANT NEST
The wood ant is a voracious predator. Colonies build huge nests of plant debris, with a network of tunnels below ground providing a home for thousands of ants.

WOOD CRICKET
Most crickets are nocturnal (active at night). But the wood cricket is active on sunny days when it can be heard chirping loudly. It is unable to fly because of its short wings.

Ant can squirt poison from abdomen

Strong jaws bite into prey

WOOD ANT
Wood ants forage out from their nest for hundreds of metres, making distinct paths on the woodland floor. They catch huge numbers of insects and bring them to the nest in pieces as food for their young.

+10

VIOLET GROUND BEETLE
This beetle can run fast on its long legs, catching other insects among the leaf litter. It grips its prey with powerful jaws, and hunts mainly at night.

–1.25

WHITE ADMIRALS
On sunny days, white admiral butterflies can be spotted near the ground feeding on the nectar of bramble flowers. They can often be seen in the morning sipping water from puddles. They spend much of their time in the tree canopy, basking in the sunshine.

+3

UPPERSIDE OF
WHITE ADMIRAL

UNDERSIDE OF
WHITE ADMIRAL

STAG BEETLE
The larvae of stag beetles spend about three years feeding on rotting wood inside a dead tree. These handsome beetles are now becoming rare because dead wood is often cleared away and burnt.

Antenna

Only male stag beetles have enlarged jaws.

+3.75

This grass is called cocks-foot.

FIELD CHAFER

+1.5

GRASSLAND AND HEATHLAND

HERE, THE LACK OF PROTECTIVE tree canopy results in quick changes in the weather – from hot and dry, to windy, cold, or wet. Grassland and heathland habitats provide fewer dwelling places for insects than forest or woodland, as there is little wood for them to burrow into, and hardly any leaf litter to live underneath.

FOOD SOURCE
Plant roots are an important food for insects in these habitats. Field chafer larvae eat roots, while the adults fly from plant to plant seeking a mate.

SPRINGTAILS
Cultivated grass fields, such as sports pitches, support few insect species. Bu they do contain vast numbers of tiny insects called springtails. An area the size of a tennis court might be home to up to three hundred million springtail

OXFORD RAGWORT

A weed called the Oxford ragwort is a common invader of neglected pasture in Europe. The cinnabar moth lays its eggs on this weed, and its caterpillars eat the leaves.

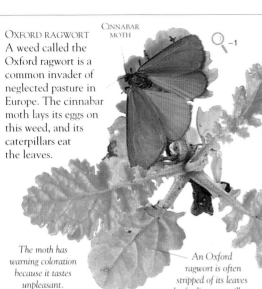

CINNABAR MOTH

The moth has warning coloration because it tastes unpleasant.

An Oxford ragwort is often stripped of its leaves by feeding caterpillars

GRASSLAND AND HEATHLAND FACTS

• The grassland of Argentina are called Pampas, or "plains" in the language of the native people.

• Prairies of the U.S.A. have long grasses.

• Steppes (prairie-like land) of Siberia have short grasses.

RICH IN PLANT LIFE

Natural grassland and heathland have a huge variety of grasses and flowering plants. These rich habitats buzz with insect life in the summer months.

CRANESBILL

RARE BUTTERFLY

The English large copper butterfly was once common in fenland but is now extinct. This is a result of intensive land development for agriculture, which destroyed the butterfly's special food plant.

GRASSLAND INSECTS

MOST INSECT species cannot survive in cultivated grass
land, such as garden lawns, since they usually contain
only one type of grass. Also, fertilizers and other
chemicals harm many insects. But natural grassland,
with their variety of plants, support thousands of insect
species which have adapted to this open, windy habitat

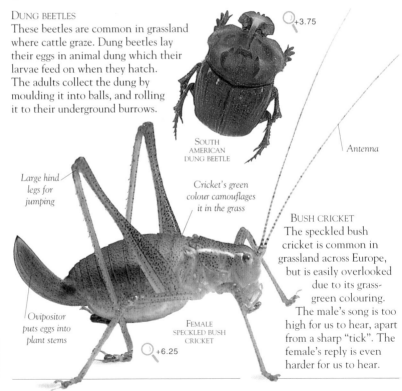

DUNG BEETLES
These beetles are common in grassland
where cattle graze. Dung beetles lay
their eggs in animal dung which their
larvae feed on when they hatch.
The adults collect the dung by
moulding it into balls, and rolling
it to their underground burrows.

+3.75

SOUTH
AMERICAN
DUNG BEETLE

Antenna

*Large hind
legs for
jumping*

*Cricket's green
colour camouflages
it in the grass*

BUSH CRICKET
The speckled bush
cricket is common in
grassland across Europe,
but is easily overlooked
due to its grass-
green colouring.
The male's song is too
high for us to hear, apart
from a sharp "tick". The
female's reply is even
harder for us to hear.

*Ovipositor
puts eggs into
plant stems*

FEMALE
SPECKLED BUSH
CRICKET

+6.25

ANTEATER

There are so many ants in the grassland of South America and Africa that specialized ant-eating mammals have evolved. They have powerful claws to break open ant nests, and long sticky tongues to collect the ants.

ANTEATER

LARGE BLUE BUTTERFLY

This butterfly lays its eggs on the wild thyme plant, and the newly hatched caterpillars feed on thyme flowers. The caterpillars attract red ants with a special milk. The ants are deceived into carrying the caterpillars into their nest, where the caterpillars eat the ant eggs and larva.

Ragwort plant

MARBLED WHITE BUTTERFLY

This butterfly can be found in a variety of grassland habitats, including grassy areas inside a wood. Marbled whites often gather in groups to bask in the early morning and early evening sunshine.

Mating soldier beetles

SOLDIER BEETLES

Some insects feed on one particular flower, while others, such as soldier beetles, eat pollen from various flowers. These feeding sites are also good places for insects to find a mate.

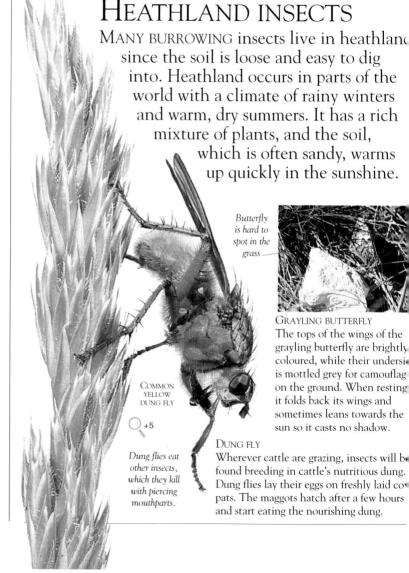

HEATHLAND INSECTS

MANY BURROWING insects live in heathland
since the soil is loose and easy to dig
into. Heathland occurs in parts of the
world with a climate of rainy winters
and warm, dry summers. It has a rich
mixture of plants, and the soil,
which is often sandy, warms
up quickly in the sunshine.

*Butterfly
is hard to
spot in the
grass*

COMMON
YELLOW
DUNG FLY

+5

*Dung flies eat
other insects,
which they kill
with piercing
mouthparts.*

GRAYLING BUTTERFLY
The tops of the wings of the
grayling butterfly are brightly
coloured, while their underside
is mottled grey for camouflage
on the ground. When resting
it folds back its wings and
sometimes leans towards the
sun so it casts no shadow.

DUNG FLY
Wherever cattle are grazing, insects will be
found breeding in cattle's nutritious dung.
Dung flies lay their eggs on freshly laid cow
pats. The maggots hatch after a few hours
and start eating the nourishing dung.

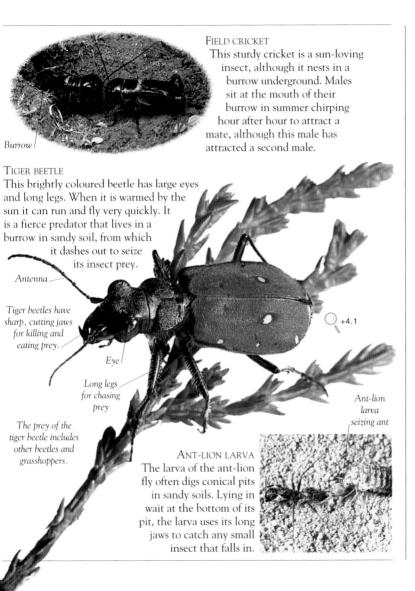

FIELD CRICKET

This sturdy cricket is a sun-loving insect, although it nests in a burrow underground. Males sit at the mouth of their burrow in summer chirping hour after hour to attract a mate, although this male has attracted a second male.

Burrow

TIGER BEETLE

This brightly coloured beetle has large eyes and long legs. When it is warmed by the sun it can run and fly very quickly. It is a fierce predator that lives in a burrow in sandy soil, from which it dashes out to seize its insect prey.

Antenna

Tiger beetles have sharp, cutting jaws for killing and eating prey.

Eye

Long legs for chasing prey

The prey of the tiger beetle includes other beetles and grasshoppers.

+4.1

Ant-lion larva seizing ant

ANT-LION LARVA

The larva of the ant-lion fly often digs conical pits in sandy soils. Lying in wait at the bottom of its pit, the larva uses its long jaws to catch any small insect that falls in.

99

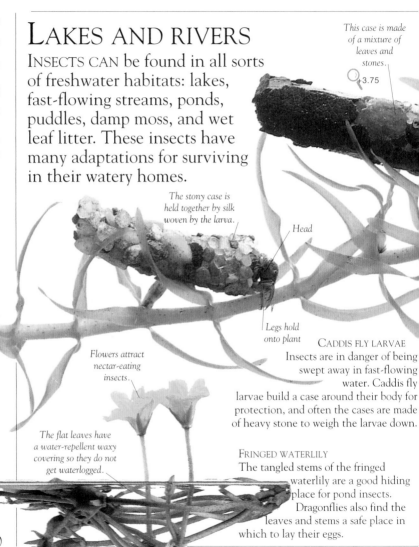

LAKES AND RIVERS

INSECTS CAN be found in all sorts
of freshwater habitats: lakes,
fast-flowing streams, ponds,
puddles, damp moss, and wet
leaf litter. These insects have
many adaptations for surviving
in their watery homes.

*This case is made
of a mixture of
leaves and
stones.*

+3.75

*The stony case is
held together by silk
woven by the larva.*

Head

Legs hold
onto plant

*Flowers attract
nectar-eating
insects.*

*The flat leaves have
a water-repellent waxy
covering so they do not
get waterlogged.*

CADDIS FLY LARVAE
Insects are in danger of being
swept away in fast-flowing
water. Caddis fly
larvae build a case around their body for
protection, and often the cases are made
of heavy stone to weigh the larvae down.

FRINGED WATERLILY
The tangled stems of the fringed
waterlily are a good hiding
place for pond insects.
Dragonflies also find the
leaves and stems a safe place in
which to lay their eggs.

100

Head of caddis fly larva

Leg

Breathing tube

Case made of leaves

+2.5

A caddis fly larva has gills for taking oxygen from the water. The larva undulates its body to create a flow of oxygen-rich water over its gills inside the case.

SPRINGTAILS

In corners of ponds sheltered from the wind, swarms of springtails sometimes gather on the surface of the water. They feed on organic debris that has blown into the pond.

FAST STREAMS

Insects that live in fast-flowing streams have streamlined bodies and strong claws to help them cling to stones. The water that passes over their gills is always rich in oxygen, but cool temperatures mean that larvae develop more slowly than they would in a shallow, sun-warmed pond.

WATER SCORPION

The water scorpion has a breathing tube on its rear end so it can breathe the outside air while it is underwater. Insects with breathing tubes can survive in warm ponds or polluted waters which are low in oxygen.

LAKE AND RIVER FACTS

• Fish populations depend on plenty of insects as food.

• Dragonfly larvae are considered a delicacy in New Guinea.

• Swarms of non-biting midges are sometimes so dense in African lakes that fishermen have been suffocated.

WATER SURFACE INSECTS

A WATER SURFACE behaves like a skin due to a force called surface tension. This force enables certain insects to walk on the "skin" and others to hang beneath it. Many of these insects are predators, and much of their food comes from the constant supply of flying insects which have fallen into the water.

⊕+7.5

WHIRLIGIG
The whirligig beetle swims round and round very fast on the water surface. It hunts insects trapped on the surface tension. The whirligig's eyes are divided into two halves, allowing it to see both above and below the water surface at the same time.

BACKSWIMMER
Using its oar-shaped back legs, this water bug swims along upside down as it patrols in search of insects trapped on the water's surface. The backswimmer is a hungry hunter and will even attack fish and young frogs.

Piercing mouthparts inject poison into prey and suck out the prey's body fluids.

Large, compound eyes for spotting prey

⊕+6.25

POND SKATER

With feet scarcely denting the surface, the pond skater walks on the water. This bug detects ripples caused by any insect struggling on the pond surface, and runs across the water to capture and kill the trapped insect.

WATER MEASURER

This insect walks slowly on a pond surface, supported by water-repellent feet. It feeds on water fleas, sucking its victims' body fluids through piercing mouthparts.

+3.75

+3

A backswimmer may leave the water to fly to other ponds or rivers for fresh food, or to find a mate.

Breathing tube has water-repellent hairs which break through surface tension.

Hairs widen the back legs, giving them their oar-like shape.

MOSQUITO LARVAE

The larvae of mosquitoes have a breathing tube which they poke through the water surface. The larvae are legless and swim by wriggling, rising to the surface now and again to take air.

+5.6

Thorax

Eye

UNDERWATER INSECTS

MANY OF THE insects that live underwater are carnivorous, either hunting their prey or scavenging. Some of these insects are fierce, sometimes killing prey larger than themselves.

DIVING BEETLE
The great diving beetle collects air from the water surface and stores it under its wings to breathe as it swims underwater.

+1.8

As well as insects, this mighty beetle can catch small fish and tadpoles.

Antenna

Larva waits for prey to swim past

+1.8

The great diving beetle sometimes flies from one pond to another.

Water plants provide food and shelter for water insects.

DAMSELFLY LARVA

LARVAL CASES
Caddis fly larvae sometimes use pieces of plant to make their protective cases. This body armour also acts as camouflage.

Pieces of plant

MAYFLY NYMPH
A mayfly spends one year as a larva living underwater before it leaves the water to become an adult. The larva breathes through gills along the side of its abdomen.

+0

ADULT DRAGONFLY
Male darter dragonflies perch
on plants that emerge from the
water. They fiercely attack and
drive away any rival males of
the same species, but attempt
to mate with any female darter
dragonfly that flies past.

–.8

DRAGONFLY EGGS
Darter dragonflies scatter their
eggs in the water. The eggs are
surrounded by a sticky, jelly-
like substance, and hatch
after a few days.

*Jelly holds
eggs in place*

–.8

BEETLE LARVA
The larva of the great diving beetle
injects juices into prey with its jaws.
The juices turn the prey's insides
into liquid for the larva to suck out.

DRAGONFLY NYMPH
Dragonfly larvae breathe by
pumping water in and out of their
rear end, where they have
complex gills.

+1.8

ORCHID

TROPICAL FOREST

INSECTS THRIVE in the humid heat and flourishing plant life of tropical forests. These forests have a complex structure which provides many habitats for insects. Trees vary in shape and size; vines and dead branches are everywhere, and thick leaf litter covers the ground.

ORCHIDS
Tropical forests contain a spectacular variety of plants – there are about 25,000 species of orchid alone. It is quite dark near the forest floor, and orchids are strongly scented to help insects find them.

EPIPHYTES
Many plants grow on the trunks and branches of trees where birds have wiped seeds from their beaks. These tree-dwelling plants, called epiphytes, provide extra habitats for insects.

INSECT PREDATORS
A tropical forest is a rich habitat for birds as well as insects. Tropical birds feed on countless insects each day. This high rate of predation is a major reason for the evolution of camouflage and mimicry in tropical insects.

FRUITY NOURISHMENT
Some tropical butterflies live for several months. An important source of fuel for their continued activity is rotting fruit and dung on the forest floor. This gives them not only sugars for energy, but also amino acids and vitamins to stay healthy.

Blue face

Red eye

Bright green abdomen

Q +2.5

The cricket's colours fade when it dies.

TROPICAL FORESTS
Bright colours are typical of tropical forests, and they can be seen in both the plant and animal life. This Central American cricket looks as if it would be easy to spot with its multi-coloured body, but it is camouflaged among the shining leaves of the forest trees.

The bright colours of this cricket surprised even entomologists.

TROPICAL FOREST FACTS

• Tropical forests cover about five per cent of the Earth's land surface.

• They contain over half of all living species.

• Around 1,200 species of butterfly have been recorded in one forest in southern Peru.

• Over half the world's rainforest has been destroyed since 1945.

107

IN THE CANOPY

THERE IS WARMTH, light, and plenty of food to eat in the canopy of tropical trees. The canopy provides living space for thousands of insect species. In one day 3,000 different species were collected from a single tree in a forest in Borneo.

BRIGHT BEETLES
Many beetle species living on the leaves of tropical trees are brightly coloured. These gaily coloured beetles are difficult to see when they are sitting on shiny tree leaves in bright sunshine.

THREE LEAF BEETLES

–2.5

CICADAS
A male cicada produces a very loud mating song with drum-like organs called tymbals on the sides of its abdomen. A cavity beside each tymbal amplifies the sound. In the mating season, cicada males sing in the canopy, filling tropical forests with their shrill song.

Spines are spiked and poisonous

FROG BEETLE
This vividly coloured
jewelled frog beetle is
probably less noticeable
in the bright sunshine
of its leafy habitat.
Despite its name,
the frog-like hind
legs are not used for
jumping, but for
holding on to a
female while mating.

*Frog-like
hind leg*

+0

−3.1

VIOLIN BEETLE
Little is known about the curious
violin beetle, which got its name
because of its violin-like shape.
It is very flat, and has been seen
living between layers of bracket
fungi on tree-trunks in
Indonesian forests.

*Six simple eyes on either
side of the head can sense
whether it is light or dark.*

+5

PASSIONFLOWER

POISON SPINES
The body of the
postman butterfly
caterpillar contains
poisons. It gets the
poisons from chemicals
in the leaves of the
passionflower vines
which it eats. The
prickly spines remind
birds to avoid it.

NESTS IN THE CANOPY

WITH SO MANY insects feeding in the forest canopy, it is not surprising that the insect-eating ants and wasps build their nests there. But these ants and wasps are in turn hunted by mammals and lizards, so their nests must give protection.

Nest is made of paper-like material

GREEN WEAVER ANTS

Each green weaver ant colony has several nests made of leaves. To make a nest, the ants join forces to pull leaves together and sew the edges. They sew using silk which the larvae produce when they are squeezed by the adult ants. These carnivorous ants hunt through the tree canopy, catching other insects and carrying the prey in pieces back to the ants' nests.

WASP NESTS

Each wasp species makes a different type of nest. This nest from South America has been cut in half to reveal the "floors" which house the larvae. There is one small opening at the bottom where the wasps defend the nest from invading ants.

Ants pulling leaves together

This nest hangs from a branch of a tree.

There may be half a million ants in one weaver ant colony.

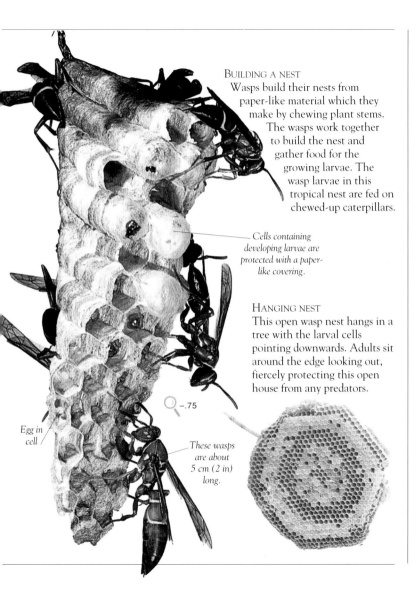

BUILDING A NEST
Wasps build their nests from paper-like material which they make by chewing plant stems. The wasps work together to build the nest and gather food for the growing larvae. The wasp larvae in this tropical nest are fed on chewed-up caterpillars.

Cells containing developing larvae are protected with a paper-like covering.

HANGING NEST
This open wasp nest hangs in a tree with the larval cells pointing downwards. Adults sit around the edge looking out, fiercely protecting this open house from any predators.

−.75

Egg in cell

These wasps are about 5 cm (2 in) long.

111

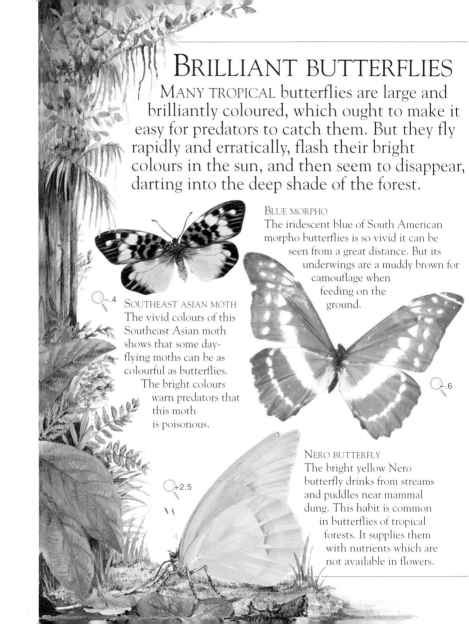

BRILLIANT BUTTERFLIES

MANY TROPICAL butterflies are large and brilliantly coloured, which ought to make it easy for predators to catch them. But they fly rapidly and erratically, flash their bright colours in the sun, and then seem to disappear, darting into the deep shade of the forest.

BLUE MORPHO
The iridescent blue of South American morpho butterflies is so vivid it can be seen from a great distance. But its underwings are a muddy brown for camouflage when feeding on the ground.

−.4

SOUTHEAST ASIAN MOTH
The vivid colours of this Southeast Asian moth shows that some day-flying moths can be as colourful as butterflies. The bright colours warn predators that this moth is poisonous.

−.6

+2.5

NERO BUTTERFLY
The bright yellow Nero butterfly drinks from streams and puddles near mammal dung. This habit is common in butterflies of tropical forests. It supplies them with nutrients which are not available in flowers.

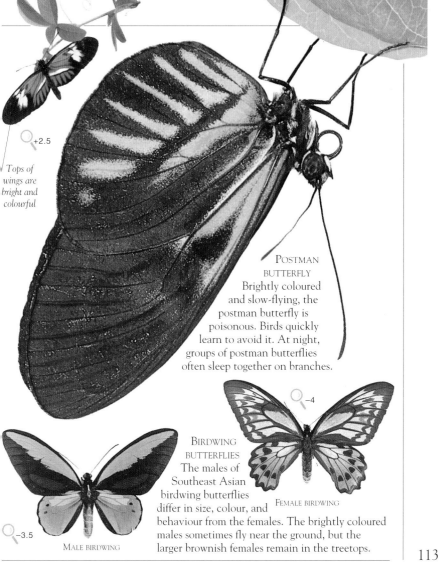

+2.5

Tops of wings are bright and colourful

POSTMAN
BUTTERFLY
Brightly coloured
and slow-flying, the
postman butterfly is
poisonous. Birds quickly
learn to avoid it. At night,
groups of postman butterflies
often sleep together on branches.

−4

BIRDWING
BUTTERFLIES
The males of
Southeast Asian
birdwing butterflies
differ in size, colour, and
behaviour from the females. The brightly coloured
males sometimes fly near the ground, but the
larger brownish females remain in the treetops.

FEMALE BIRDWING

−3.5

MALE BIRDWING

INSECTS

TROPICAL BUTTERFLIES

THOUSANDS OF butterfly species live in tropical forests. Each butterfly has to recognize members of its own species among all the others in order to mate. They find each other by sight – butterflies can see more colours than any other animal – and by smell.

-.75

Tail brush

USING SCENTS
Striped blue crow butterfly males have a yellow brush at the end of their abdomen. When a male has found a female, he uses his brush to dust scented scales on her. The arousing scent encourages the female to mate with him.

SCENT DETECTORS
Butterflies and moths detect smells with their antennae. Each antenna has thousands of microscopic sensory organs. These respond to airborne scent molecules, triggering nerve cells in the antennae to send signals to the insect's brain.

MOTH ANTENNA

Scent chemicals stimulate nerves in the moth's antennae.

-3

SITTING TOGETHER
At sunny spots in the forest, butterflies gather at muddy puddles to drink water and salts. Butterflies of the same species usually sit together, so that white-coloured species form one group, blue another, and so on.

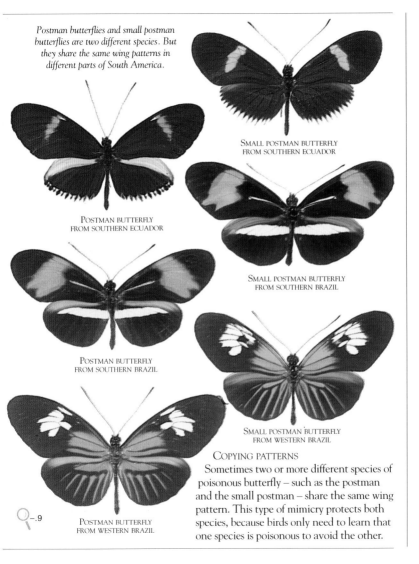

Postman butterflies and small postman butterflies are two different species. But they share the same wing patterns in different parts of South America.

SMALL POSTMAN BUTTERFLY
FROM SOUTHERN ECUADOR

POSTMAN BUTTERFLY
FROM SOUTHERN ECUADOR

SMALL POSTMAN BUTTERFLY
FROM SOUTHERN BRAZIL

POSTMAN BUTTERFLY
FROM SOUTHERN BRAZIL

SMALL POSTMAN BUTTERFLY
FROM WESTERN BRAZIL

POSTMAN BUTTERFLY
FROM WESTERN BRAZIL

COPYING PATTERNS

Sometimes two or more different species of poisonous butterfly – such as the postman and the small postman – share the same wing pattern. This type of mimicry protects both species, because birds only need to learn that one species is poisonous to avoid the other.

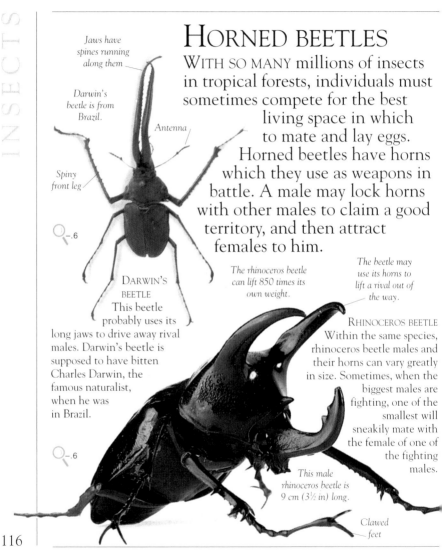

HORNED BEETLES

WITH SO MANY millions of insects in tropical forests, individuals must sometimes compete for the best living space in which to mate and lay eggs. Horned beetles have horns which they use as weapons in battle. A male may lock horns with other males to claim a good territory, and then attract females to him.

Jaws have spines running along them

Darwin's beetle is from Brazil.

Antenna

Spiny front leg

-.6

DARWIN'S BEETLE
This beetle probably uses its long jaws to drive away rival males. Darwin's beetle is supposed to have bitten Charles Darwin, the famous naturalist, when he was in Brazil.

-.6

The rhinoceros beetle can lift 850 times its own weight.

The beetle may use its horns to lift a rival out of the way.

RHINOCEROS BEETLE
Within the same species, rhinoceros beetle males and their horns can vary greatly in size. Sometimes, when the biggest males are fighting, one of the smallest will sneakily mate with the female of one of the fighting males.

This male rhinoceros beetle is 9 cm (3½ in) long.

Clawed feet

116

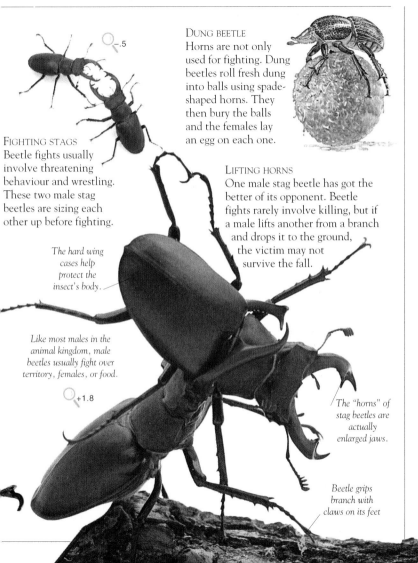

DUNG BEETLE
Horns are not only used for fighting. Dung beetles roll fresh dung into balls using spade-shaped horns. They then bury the balls and the females lay an egg on each one.

FIGHTING STAGS
Beetle fights usually involve threatening behaviour and wrestling. These two male stag beetles are sizing each other up before fighting.

LIFTING HORNS
One male stag beetle has got the better of its opponent. Beetle fights rarely involve killing, but if a male lifts another from a branch and drops it to the ground, the victim may not survive the fall.

–.5

The hard wing cases help protect the insect's body.

Like most males in the animal kingdom, male beetles usually fight over territory, females, or food.

+1.8

The "horns" of stag beetles are actually enlarged jaws.

Beetle grips branch with claws on its feet

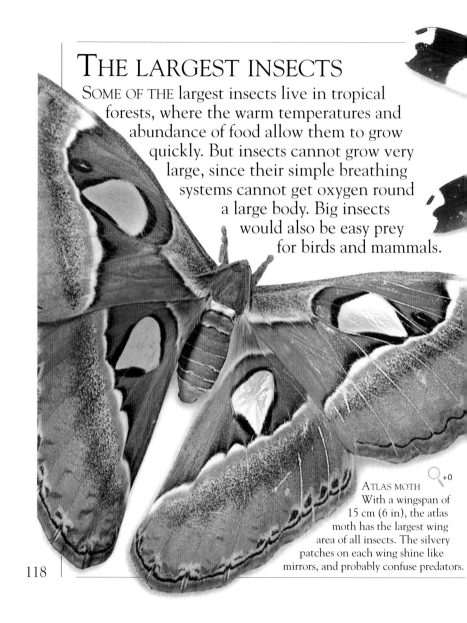

THE LARGEST INSECTS

SOME OF THE largest insects live in tropical forests, where the warm temperatures and abundance of food allow them to grow quickly. But insects cannot grow very large, since their simple breathing systems cannot get oxygen round a large body. Big insects would also be easy prey for birds and mammals.

ATLAS MOTH
With a wingspan of 15 cm (6 in), the atlas moth has the largest wing area of all insects. The silvery patches on each wing shine like mirrors, and probably confuse predators.

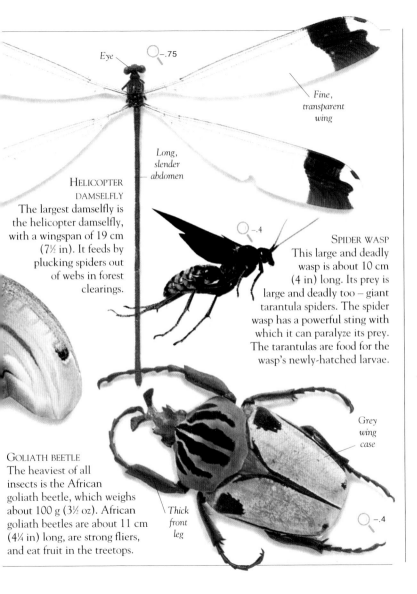

Eye

○−.75

Fine,
transparent
wing

Long,
slender
abdomen

HELICOPTER
DAMSELFLY
The largest damselfly is
the helicopter damselfly,
with a wingspan of 19 cm
(7½ in). It feeds by
plucking spiders out
of webs in forest
clearings.

○−.4

SPIDER WASP
This large and deadly
wasp is about 10 cm
(4 in) long. Its prey is
large and deadly too – giant
tarantula spiders. The spider
wasp has a powerful sting with
which it can paralyze its prey.
The tarantulas are food for the
wasp's newly-hatched larvae.

Grey
wing
case

GOLIATH BEETLE
The heaviest of all
insects is the African
goliath beetle, which weighs
about 100 g (3½ oz). African
goliath beetles are about 11 cm
(4¼ in) long, are strong fliers,
and eat fruit in the treetops.

Thick
front
leg

○−.4

119

STICK AND LEAF INSECTS

A TROPICAL FOREST is alive with animals, most of which eat insects. To survive, insects adopt many strategies. Stick and leaf insects hide from predators by keeping still and resembling their background of leaves and sticks.

STICK INSECTS
Some stick insects are slender, brown, or green, just like the twigs and leaf stalks they sit on. Other species are shorter and fatter, with spines and other projections. These often look like curled dead leaves.

Winged male of Macleay's spectre

Wingless female of Macleay's spectre

Indian stick insect

Spiny green nymph

LEAF MIMICS

Javanese leaf insects are leaf mimics. They have body markings which look like the midrib and veins of a leaf. Brown marks like those on a dying leaf add to the disguise.

Leg

When resting on a branch, a Javanese stick insect curls its body to look like the leaves it sits beside.

Head

Body is almost as slim as a real leaf

Real leaf

−.6

Imitation hole in "dying leaf"

Imitation midrib

−.4

Undeveloped wings indicate that this insect is immature

Green and brown colouring like a fading leaf

SPINY STICK INSECT

Good disguise is not just about appearance: it involves using the right behaviour in the right place. This spiny stick insect is easily seen on the white background of this page. But if it were sitting in a bush and swaying gently like a dead leaf, even a sharp-eyed bird may miss it.

121

ARMIES ON THE GROUND

ANTS ARE THE dominant creatures of tropical forests. They live in colonies made up of any number from 20 individuals to many thousands. Ants are mostly carnivorous. Some species make slaves of other ant species by invading their nest and killing their queen.

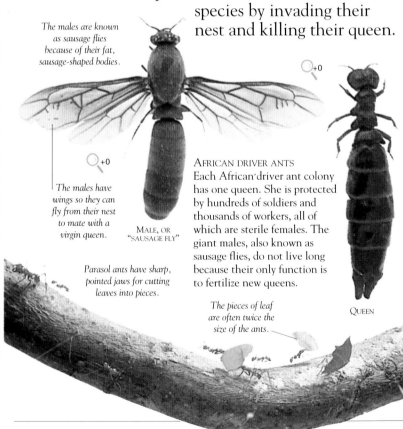

The males are known as sausage flies because of their fat, sausage-shaped bodies.

Q+0

Q+0

The males have wings so they can fly from their nest to mate with a virgin queen.

MALE, OR "SAUSAGE FLY"

Parasol ants have sharp, pointed jaws for cutting leaves into pieces.

AFRICAN DRIVER ANTS
Each African driver ant colony has one queen. She is protected by hundreds of soldiers and thousands of workers, all of which are sterile females. The giant males, also known as sausage flies, do not live long because their only function is to fertilize new queens.

The pieces of leaf are often twice the size of the ants.

QUEEN

DRIVER ANTS MARCHING

These ants get their name from the way a colony sweeps through an area catching all the insects it can find. They move their nests from place to place regularly, unlike most ants which have a permanent nest and territory.

+3.75

Beetle pupae are among the prey of driver ants.

CARRYING PREY

Ants in a column collaborate to cut large insects they have caught into smaller pieces. This is so they can carry their food back to the nest. Smaller prey can be carried whole.

ATTENTIVE SOLDIER

Driver ant soldiers have very large jaws. Often they can be seen standing beside a marching column of ants with their jaws wide open, waiting to attack intruders, such as parasitic flies.

Ant returning for more leaves

PARASOL ANTS

These South American ants are not carnivorous. They feed on fungus which they cultivate in huge underground nests. The fungus is grown on pieces of leaf which the ants bring to the nest.

123

DESERTS, CAVES, AND SOIL

SOME INSECTS flourish in habitats where it is difficult for living things to survive. Desert habitats, for example, lack water and have very high temperatures. Caves are dark and lack plant life for food. Life in soil makes communication, both by scent and sight, difficult for insects.

+5

A spike on the larva's back anchors it to the wall of the burrow.

HIDING IN SOIL

Life in the soil is only a passing phase for some insect species. This tiger beetle larva hides underground by day. At night it waits in its vertical tunnel with its jaws projecting at the ground surface, and snatches passing insects to devour in its burrow.

CAVE DWELLER

This cockroach lives all its life in the dark. Like other cave creatures, it feeds on debris from the outside world. Bat dung, dead animals, and pieces of plants washed into the cave provide the cockroach with its nourishment.

DESERT BEETLE

The lack of water in deserts means that insects have to find devious ways to obtain moisture. This darkling beetle lives in the Namib Desert where sea winds bring mists each night. The beetle holds its abdomen high to catch the moisture, which then runs down into its mouth.

DESERT HEAT

The hot and dry days in deserts can lead to rapid water loss and death for animals. Most living creatures hide under stones or in the sand to avoid drying out. These animals are active at night when it is much cooler.

DESERT FACTS

• The Sahara Desert is spreading at a rate of 5 km (3 miles) per year.

• In deserts the temperature may range from 30°C (90°F) in the day to below 0°C (32°F) at night.

• Caves are a nearly constant temperature throughout the year.

• 20% of the Earth's land surface is desert.

CACTUS FLOWER

DESERT PLANTS

Rain may not fall in a desert for months, or even years. Most desert plants store water so they can survive, and some desert animals rely on these plants for food. But many animals, including some insects, migrate in search of rain and the plant growth it produces.

125

DESERT INSECTS

HOT, DRY DESERTS are dangerous places in which to
live. Animals often die from sunstroke and dehydration
(drying out). To prevent this, insects avoid the sun by
staying in the shade or burrowing in the sand. Some
insects have special methods of collecting water. Many
feed only at night because the surface of the sand is too
hot for them to walk on during the day.

−.9

NAMIB DESERT BEETLE
Long legs keep the body of the Namib desert
beetle off the hot sand. The larvae live in the
sand, scavenging on detritus (organic debris),
and complete development in about six
months. The adults live for several years.

Antenna

DESERT LOCUSTS
Adult desert locusts fly in swarms
to find fresh food. When there
is enough food they breed
rapidly, and huge groups of
wingless nymphs hop
across the desert sand.

*Grasses and
other plants form
the diet of desert
locusts.*

*Desert locusts
get water from
plant food.*

TWO DESERT
LOCUST NYMPHS

+2.5

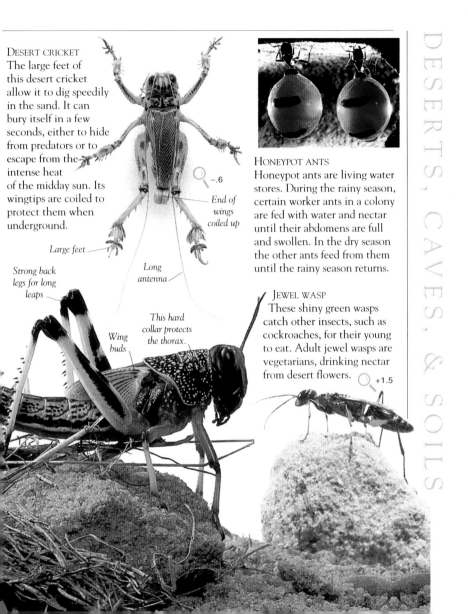

DESERT CRICKET
The large feet of this desert cricket allow it to dig speedily in the sand. It can bury itself in a few seconds, either to hide from predators or to escape from the intense heat of the midday sun. Its wingtips are coiled to protect them when underground.

−.6

End of wings coiled up

Large feet

Long antenna

Strong back legs for long leaps

Wing buds

This hard collar protects the thorax.

HONEYPOT ANTS
Honeypot ants are living water stores. During the rainy season, certain worker ants in a colony are fed with water and nectar until their abdomens are full and swollen. In the dry season the other ants feed from them until the rainy season returns.

JEWEL WASP
These shiny green wasps catch other insects, such as cockroaches, for their young to eat. Adult jewel wasps are vegetarians, drinking nectar from desert flowers.

+1.5

Long antenna

–4.4

AFRICAN CRICKET
Some insects have developed very long antennae to make up for lack of vision in the dark of caves. This African cricket has the longest antennae for its body size of any insect.

CAVE INSECTS

No plants can grow in the dark, inhospitable depths of caves, where the Sun's rays cannot reach. Despite this, cave-dwelling insects still manage to find enough food. Bat droppings, material washed in by floods, and the fungi that often grow on this decaying material all provide nourishment.

Long back legs for jumping out of danger

FEMALE AFRICAN CAVE CRICKET

Two sensitive spines, called cerci, can detect enemies approaching from behind.

Cricket uses its ovipositor (egg-laying tube) to lay eggs in soil.

+3

PEACOCK BUTTERFLY

For some insects, caves provide shelter from the uncomfortable weather conditions. During cold northern winters a cave is an ideal place for peacock butterflies to hibernate.

Dark underside of wings camouflages the peacock butterfly as it hibernates.

Top of wings are brightly coloured.

−1

PEACOCK BUTTERFLY

CAVE CRICKET

Crickets living in caves have smaller eyes and paler bodies than crickets living in sunlight. Cave crickets breed all year round because the temperature and the amount of food in the cave stay constant.

Very long, sensitive antennae

COCKROACH

Cave-dwelling cockroaches eat bat droppings and bat carcasses, as well as mites and fungi. Cockroaches often eat each other, too. Caves make an ideal home for cockroaches since they love dark, damp places.

+3.75

SURINAM COCKROACH

SOIL INSECTS

WHEN PLANTS and animals die, their remains usually get absorbed into the soil. Insects which live in soil are among the most important creatures on Earth because they help to recycle these remains, releasing their nutrients and so helping new crops and forests to grow. Soil insects are also an important food for many mammals and birds.

Q+0

BEETLE LARVA
Roots and decaying tree trunks provide food for many types of insect larva, such as this beetle grub. The grub breathes through holes called spiracles, which are along the side of its body. Although there is not very much air underground, there is enough for insects.

Spiracle

Pupa

GOOD HABITAT
Living in soil has advantages. Insects are unlikely to dehydrate, and there is plenty of food in plant roots and decaying plants. This spurge hawk-moth pupa has sharp plates on its abdomen which help it climb to the surface just before the adult emerges.

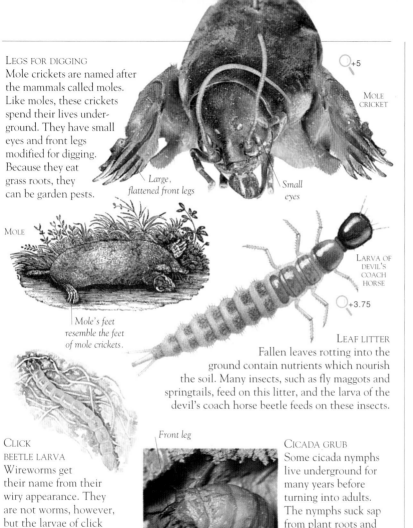

LEGS FOR DIGGING
Mole crickets are named after
the mammals called moles.
Like moles, these crickets
spend their lives under-
ground. They have small
eyes and front legs
modified for digging.
Because they eat
grass roots, they
can be garden pests.

*Large,
flattened front legs*

MOLE CRICKET

◯+5

*Small
eyes*

MOLE

*Mole's feet
resemble the feet
of mole crickets.*

LARVA OF
DEVIL'S
COACH
HORSE

◯+3.75

LEAF LITTER
Fallen leaves rotting into the
ground contain nutrients which nourish
the soil. Many insects, such as fly maggots and
springtails, feed on this litter, and the larva of the
devil's coach horse beetle feeds on these insects.

CLICK
BEETLE LARVA
Wireworms get
their name from their
wiry appearance. They
are not worms, however,
but the larvae of click
beetles. They crawl
through the soil, feeding
on the roots of plants.

Front leg

CICADA GRUB
Some cicada nymphs
live underground for
many years before
turning into adults.
The nymphs suck sap
from plant roots and
have enlarged front
legs for tunnelling
through the soil.

INSECTS

TOWNS AND GARDENS

SINCE INSECTS HAVE managed to make homes for themselves in practically every natural habitat, it is not surprising that they have turned human habitats into their homes, too. Insects live in our houses, feeding on our furniture, clothes, food-stores, and rubbish dumps. Our gardens and farms are also teeming with insect life, nourished by the abundance of flowers and vegetables.

Colorado beetle

−1.75

POTATO PESTS
When potatoes were brought to Europe from South America, the Colorado beetle came with them. This insect eats potato plant leaves, and can cause great damage to crops.

CABBAGE EATERS
Cabbage white butterflies lay eggs on cabbage plants so the larvae can eat the leaves. Farms provide acres of cabbages, and the butterflies become pests since they breed at an unnaturally high rate because of the abundance of food.

Leaves of potato plant

Potato

132

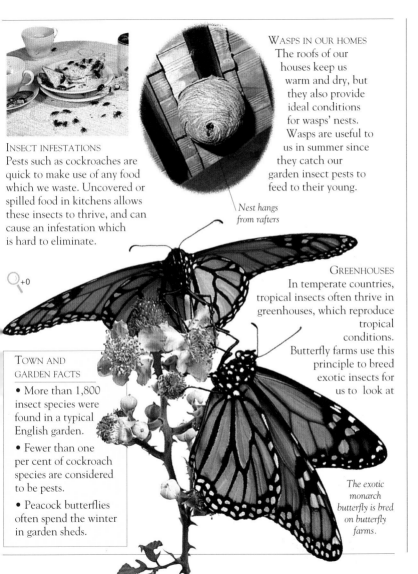

INSECT INFESTATIONS
Pests such as cockroaches are quick to make use of any food which we waste. Uncovered or spilled food in kitchens allows these insects to thrive, and can cause an infestation which is hard to eliminate.

WASPS IN OUR HOMES
The roofs of our houses keep us warm and dry, but they also provide ideal conditions for wasps' nests. Wasps are useful to us in summer since they catch our garden insect pests to feed to their young.

Nest hangs from rafters

Q_{+0}

GREENHOUSES
In temperate countries, tropical insects often thrive in greenhouses, which reproduce tropical conditions. Butterfly farms use this principle to breed exotic insects for us to look at

TOWN AND GARDEN FACTS
• More than 1,800 insect species were found in a typical English garden.

• Fewer than one per cent of cockroach species are considered to be pests.

• Peacock butterflies often spend the winter in garden sheds.

The exotic monarch butterfly is bred on butterfly farms.

133

HOUSEHOLD INSECTS

SINCE PREHISTORIC times, insects have lived in human homes, attracted by warmth, shelter, and food. These insects eat our food, our furniture, and some even eat our carpets. Parasitic insects also live in our homes, feeding on the human inhabitants.

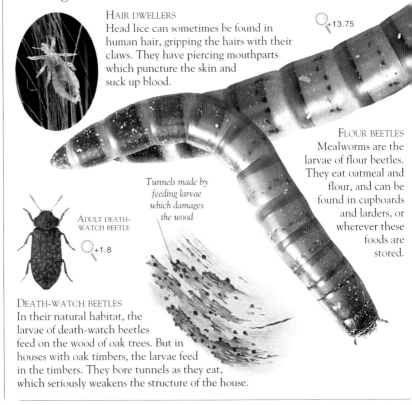

HAIR DWELLERS
Head lice can sometimes be found in human hair, gripping the hairs with their claws. They have piercing mouthparts which puncture the skin and suck up blood.

Q +13.75

FLOUR BEETLES
Mealworms are the larvae of flour beetles. They eat oatmeal and flour, and can be found in cupboards and larders, or wherever these foods are stored.

Tunnels made by feeding larvae which damages the wood

ADULT DEATH-WATCH BEETLE
Q +1.8

DEATH-WATCH BEETLES
In their natural habitat, the larvae of death-watch beetles feed on the wood of oak trees. But in houses with oak timbers, the larvae feed in the timbers. They bore tunnels as they eat, which seriously weakens the structure of the house.

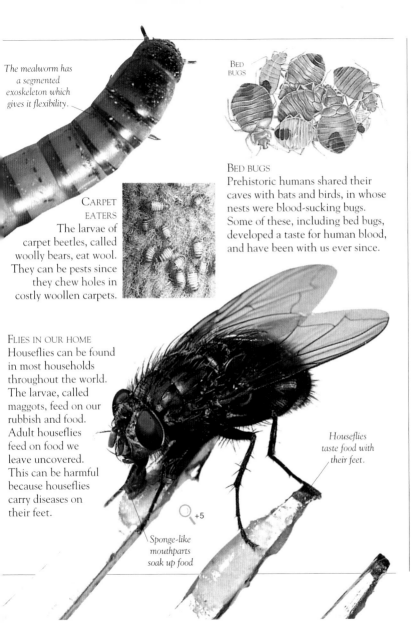

The mealworm has a segmented exoskeleton which gives it flexibility.

BED BUGS

BED BUGS
Prehistoric humans shared their caves with bats and birds, in whose nests were blood-sucking bugs. Some of these, including bed bugs, developed a taste for human blood, and have been with us ever since.

CARPET EATERS
The larvae of carpet beetles, called woolly bears, eat wool. They can be pests since they chew holes in costly woollen carpets.

FLIES IN OUR HOME
Houseflies can be found in most households throughout the world. The larvae, called maggots, feed on our rubbish and food. Adult houseflies feed on food we leave uncovered. This can be harmful because houseflies carry diseases on their feet.

Houseflies taste food with their feet.

+5

Sponge-like mouthparts soak up food

135

GARDEN INSECTS

A GARDEN IS a good place to watch and study insects. Many different insects are attracted into gardens to feed on the flowers, vegetables, and other plants. Some predatory insects come to eat the plant-eating insects. But most garden insects are just tourists, feeding on flower nectar as they pass through.

DEVIL BEETLES
Devil's coach horse beetles hunt at night, scouring the garden for insects to eat. These large beetles are common in compost heaps, scurrying away from the daylight when the compost is turned.

GARDENER'S FRIENDS
Hoverflies hover in front of flowers on hot, sunny days as they feed on nectar. They are particularly attracted to thistle flowers. Hoverfly larvae are the gardener's friends, feeding voraciously on plant-damaging aphids.

+3.1

+3.75

Eye

Antenna

HAWK-MOTH

The caterpillars of hawk-moths can be recognized by their short, erect "tail". Most adult hawk-moths fly at night, hovering in front of flowers to gather nectar with their long tongues.

SILVER-STRIPED HAWK-MOTH CATERPILLAR

"Tail"

+0

Caterpillar has eyespots to frighten off predators

Eyespot

Fuchsia flower

GARDEN GRASSHOPPER

The common field grasshopper is widespread in Europe on short grass in sunny places, and often finds a home in gardens. Like tropical locusts, common field grasshoppers sometimes develop swarms, but on a much smaller scale.

RED ADMIRAL

–.4

FOOD FOR BUTTERFLIES

The flower border of a garden is like a filling station for passing butterflies. They feed on nectar to give them energy as they search for suitable plants on which to lay eggs.

Butterflies often stop to sunbathe for a while.

PEACOCK

SILVER-SPOTTED SKIPPER

–.75

–.4

FRIENDS AND FOES

THE RELATIONSHIP between insects and humans is not always a good one. Many insects are useful to us, although others are pests. We enjoy seeing wild animals, but we destroy their habitats. This kills insects that other animals need as food. Ecology is about understanding the balance between our needs and the needs of other animals and plants.

Aphids drink the rose's sap. This eventually kills the rose, because the sap is like the plant's blood.

APHIDS
Aphids are major pests on our food plants and flowers. Some aphid species are common on roses, while others carry diseases which ruin potatoes and strawberries, as well as many other food crops.

Intricate pattern of veins in wings

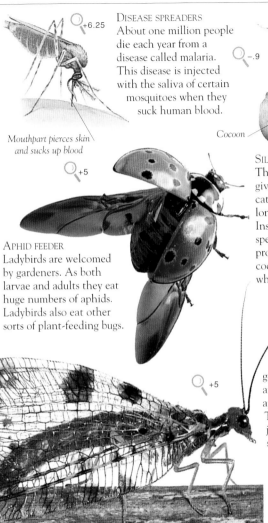

$Q_{+6.25}$

DISEASE SPREADERS

About one million people die each year from a disease called malaria. This disease is injected with the saliva of certain mosquitoes when they suck human blood.

Mouthpart pierces skin and sucks up blood

$Q_{-.9}$

Moth

Cocoon

SILK PROVIDERS

The silk we use in clothes is given to us by silk moth caterpillars. Silk moths no longer occur in the wild. Instead, they are bred in special farms. The caterpillars produce the silk to form cocoons which protect them when they pupate.

Q_{+5}

APHID FEEDER

Ladybirds are welcomed by gardeners. As both larvae and adults they eat huge numbers of aphids. Ladybirds also eat other sorts of plant-feeding bugs.

Q_{+5}

PEST EATERS

Lacewings are delicate insects, often with shining golden eyes. Their larvae are voracious predators of aphids and other plant lice. They have long, tubular jaws through which they suck the body contents of their prey. Lacewing larvae hide themselves from predators by sticking the remains of their prey onto small hairs on their back.

139

BEES AND POLLINATION

BEES AND PLANTS depend on each other.
Plants need bees to carry pollen
between flowers to produce seeds.
Bees collect pollen and nectar
from flowers to feed their larvae.
Nectar in a hive is made into
honey for winter food.

BEE-KEEPING

For thousands of years people have
kept bees for their honey. Modern hives
have racks of frames, each with a ready-made
comb of cells. Individual frames can be
removed and the honey drained.

POLLINATION

Other insects, such as butterflies, also
pollinate flowers. Many flowers are a
special colour or shape to attract
particular insects. These insects
receive pollen and nectar in
exchange for their work in
carrying pollen to
another flower.

+2.5

+7.5

140

POLLEN BASKETS
Bees carry pollen back to their hive in special pollen baskets on their back legs. The baskets are made from curved bristles. A bee uses its front legs to comb pollen dust from its furry body and put it in the baskets.

Shape of dance shows bees direction of flowers

BEE COMMUNICATION
When a bee finds flowers with nectar it tells other bees in the hive by dancing. The bee conveys the distance of the flowers by how fast it shakes its abdomen, and the direction by the angle of its dance.

Pollen basket

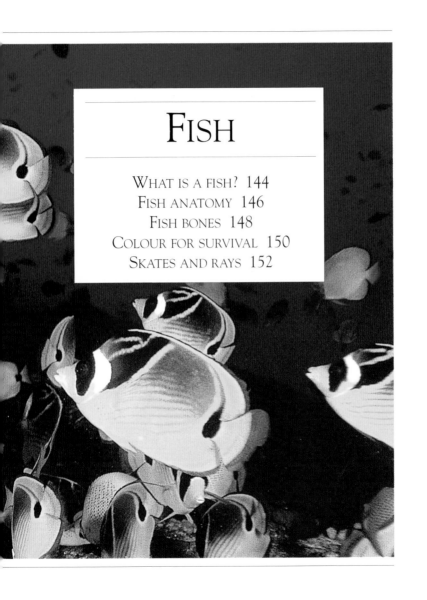

FISH

WHAT IS A FISH?

THE FIRST FISH appeared in the seas 500 million years ago. Today, there are about 25,000 known species. Fish live in water, breathe through gills, have a scaly body, and manoeuvre themselves using fins. All fish are vertebrates, which means that they have a backbone or similar structure, and an internal skeleton. The three main fish groups are bony fish, cartilaginous fish, and jawless fish.

Caudal fin or tail moves fish through water

Lateral line helps fish feel vibrations

BONY FISH FINS
Most bony fish have a dorsal fin, paired pectoral and pelvic fins, and a tail for movement. In some fish, fins have become specialized as lifting foils, walking legs, suckers for holding on, or poisoned spines for protection.

Anal fin

Pelvic fin for manoeuvring

WHALE SHARK

CARTILAGINOUS FISH
Sharks are cartilaginous fish, which means that they have skeletons made of strong, flexible cartilage, rather than bone. The world's biggest fish is the whale shark, which grows to 15 m (49 ft) in length.

WHAT IS NOT A FISH?
Some animals are confused with
"fish" just because they live
in water. Fish-shaped dolphins
and seals are mammals, and
come to the surface to breathe.
Shellfish like mussels and
cuttlefish are in fact molluscs.

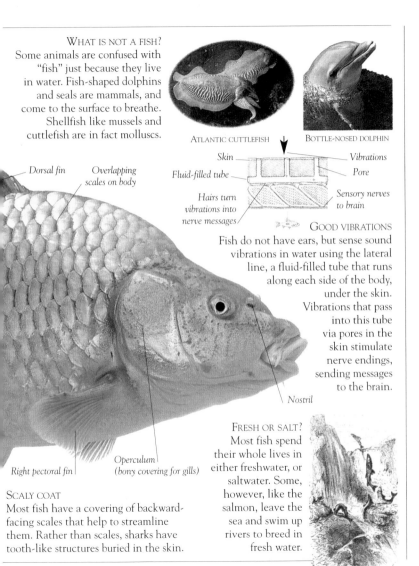

ATLANTIC CUTTLEFISH

BOTTLE-NOSED DOLPHIN

Skin

Fluid-filled tube

Hairs turn
vibrations into
nerve messages

Vibrations

Pore

Sensory nerves
to brain

GOOD VIBRATIONS
Fish do not have ears, but sense sound
vibrations in water using the lateral
line, a fluid-filled tube that runs
along each side of the body,
under the skin.
Vibrations that pass
into this tube
via pores in the
skin stimulate
nerve endings,
sending messages
to the brain.

Dorsal fin

Overlapping
scales on body

Nostril

Right pectoral fin

Operculum
(bony covering for gills)

SCALY COAT
Most fish have a covering of backward-
facing scales that help to streamline
them. Rather than scales, sharks have
tooth-like structures buried in the skin.

FRESH OR SALT?
Most fish spend
their whole lives in
either freshwater, or
saltwater. Some,
however, like the
salmon, leave the
sea and swim up
rivers to breed in
fresh water.

145

FISH ANATOMY

FISH HAVE MANY of the same internal organs found in reptiles, birds, and mammals, such as a heart, brain, lungs, and liver. However, in order to live and "breathe" underwater, a fish also needs some unique body parts.

BREATHING AND GILLS
Fish "breathe" in water using their gills. Oxygen passes from the water through the thin gill membranes into the fish's blood, and is then distributed around the body, to power the muscles.

Spinal cord inside backbone

Swim bladder

Kidney

BONY FISH

Tail fin

Roe

Liver

Heart

Gill arch

FLOATING ORGAN
Most bony fish have a balloon-like organ called a swim bladder, which is filled with gas and acts like an internal lifebuoy, to keep the fish upright in the water.

Spinal cord inside backbone

Intestine

Heart

Liver

Ovary (female)

Anal fin

CARTILAGINOUS FISH

LIGHT LIVER
Instead of a swim bladder, cartilaginous fish have a large liver, in which digested nutrients are stored as oil – which is lighter than water. This is not as effective as a buoyancy aid, and many sharks need to keep moving, or they will sink.

Stiff gill rakers sieve in clean water passing over gills

Gill filaments, through which oxygen in the water passes into the fish's blood

Bony support of gill arch

TUNA FISH GILL

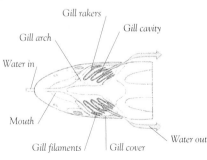

Gill rakers

Gill arch

Gill cavity

Water in

Mouth

Gill filaments

Gill cover

Water out

WATER FLOW
To obtain oxygen, the fish takes in a mouthful of water, while the gill cover shuts flat to stop water escaping. The fish then closes its mouth, forcing the water inside to flow past the gills. On its way out, the water pushes open the flap-like gill cover.

147

FISH BONES

ALL FISH HAVE internal skeletons.
Sharks and rays have skeletons
made of cartilage, but most
fish have skeletons
made of bone (bony
fish or teleosts).

First dorsal fin

*Cranium – supports
and protects
the brain*

*Upper
jaw*

Lower jaw

Pectoral fin

*Opercular bones form
the gill covers and protect
the delicate gills*

Pelvic fin

SKELETON PARTS
There are three main parts of a fish skeleton: the skull, which
contains the brain and suspends the jaw and gill arches; the
backbone or vertebral column, which bears spines and ribs,
and the "fin skeleton", the bones and rods which support
fins and tails.

SLOW SWIMMER
The trunkfish's backbone has long supporting rods for
its dorsal fin, which is near its tail. The trunkfish swims
slowly with its fins and tail, as its rigid, scaly body
makes it too stiff to flex in the normal way.

FISH FRAMEWORK

This well-preserved skeleton of an Atlantic cod is typical of teleosts, or "true" bony fish. Fish bones are of two main types. Cartilage bones form their shapes first in cartilage, which then changes into bone as the fish develops. Dermal bones develop from the dermal layers in the skin.

EVER GREEN

Marine garfishes have bright green skeletons, and the colour lasts even after boiling the bones!

MARINE GARFISH

Second dorsal fin

Interneurals – support the fins along the back

Lepidotrichs (fin rays) support all dorsal and anal fins

Spine

Front anal fin

Rear anal fin

Tail vertebrae

Interhaemals – support fin along the underside

Caudal fin (tail)

SHARK'S VERTEBRA

The basking shark is the world's second largest fish, next to the whale shark. Being a shark, its skeleton is made mainly of cartilage. This is the central portion or centrum of a vertebra, which is strengthened by a network of mineral-laced fibres.

SAILFISH

AN OCEAN LIFE

Great oceanic fishes have powerful muscles, and need a strong backbone. This sailfish vertebra has large projecting flanges for stability and muscle anchorage. This fish can reach speeds of up to 96 km/h (60 mph).

Large projecting flanges

149

COLOUR FOR SURVIVAL

MANY FISH USE colour for survival tactics, and have evolved almost every imaginable hue and pattern, for various reasons. Colour is an excellent means of camouflage or defence, or of advertising a territory, whether it be in the open sea, in rivers or lakes, or on a coral reef.

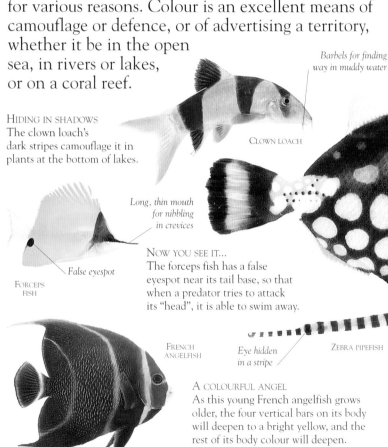

Barbels for finding way in muddy water

CLOWN LOACH

HIDING IN SHADOWS
The clown loach's dark stripes camouflage it in plants at the bottom of lakes.

Long, thin mouth for nibbling in crevices

False eyespot

FORCEPS
FISH

NOW YOU SEE IT...
The forceps fish has a false eyespot near its tail base, so that when a predator tries to attack its "head", it is able to swim away.

FRENCH
ANGELFISH

Eye hidden in a stripe

ZEBRA PIPEFISH

A COLOURFUL ANGEL
As this young French angelfish grows older, the four vertical bars on its body will deepen to a bright yellow, and the rest of its body colour will deepen.

150

Eye hidden by head stripe

Eyespot

LOTS TO LOOK AT
The threadfin butterfly fish, which lives in warm Australian seas, is a highly patterned and coloured fish. It has a white mustard-lined forehead, zig-zags on the front half of the body, and a false eyespot on the rear of the dorsal fin.

THREADFIN BUTTERFLY FISH

DIRTY DEALER
Scattered darker scales on the Cuban hock's body and fins give it a slightly "dirty" appearance, aiding camouflage.

CUBAN HOCK

CLOWN TRIGGERFISH

REGAL TANG

CONFUSING CLOWN
The contrasting patterns of the clown triggerfish confuse predators, making it less likely to be attacked.

INTO THE BLUE
The regal tang starts life mostly yellow, but turns blue gradually.

BLUE-RINGED ANGELFISH

STRIPY CAMOUFLAGE
The zebra pipefish hides horizontally in the stems of waterweed. Its stripes blend in with the weed, disguising it from predators.

LOOK AT ME!
The electric-blue bands of this blue-ringed angelfish give a strong visual signal to members of the same species.

151

SKATES AND RAYS

IT IS HARD TO BELIEVE that flat, slow-moving skates and rays, which live on the bed of the sea, are related to fast, streamlined sharks. However, the anatomy of rays and sharks is very similar: for example, both have cartilaginous skeletons, and up to seven gill slits.

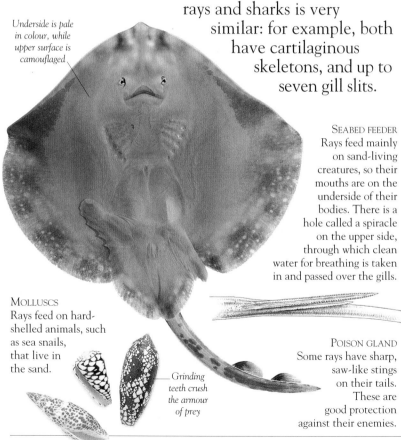

Underside is pale in colour, while upper surface is camouflaged

SEABED FEEDER
Rays feed mainly on sand-living creatures, so their mouths are on the underside of their bodies. There is a hole called a spiracle on the upper side, through which clean water for breathing is taken in and passed over the gills.

MOLLUSCS
Rays feed on hard-shelled animals, such as sea snails, that live in the sand.

Grinding teeth crush the armour of prey

POISON GLAND
Some rays have sharp, saw-like stings on their tails. These are good protection against their enemies.

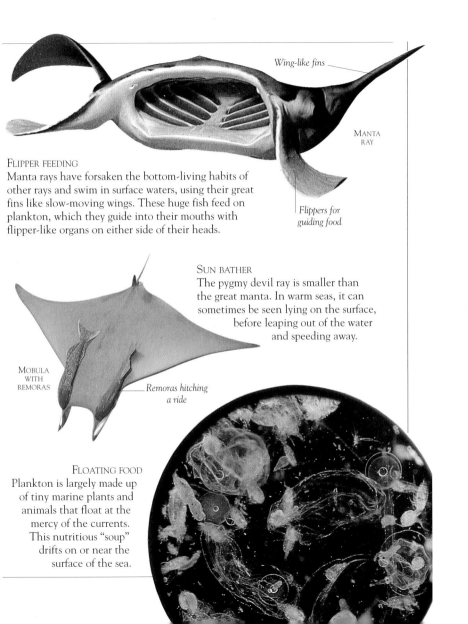

Wing-like fins

MANTA
RAY

FLIPPER FEEDING
Manta rays have forsaken the bottom-living habits of
other rays and swim in surface waters, using their great
fins like slow-moving wings. These huge fish feed on
plankton, which they guide into their mouths with
flipper-like organs on either side of their heads.

*Flippers for
guiding food*

SUN BATHER
The pygmy devil ray is smaller than
the great manta. In warm seas, it can
sometimes be seen lying on the surface,
before leaping out of the water
and speeding away.

MOBULA
WITH
REMORAS

*Remoras hitching
a ride*

FLOATING FOOD
Plankton is largely made up
of tiny marine plants and
animals that float at the
mercy of the currents.
This nutritious "soup"
drifts on or near the
surface of the sea.

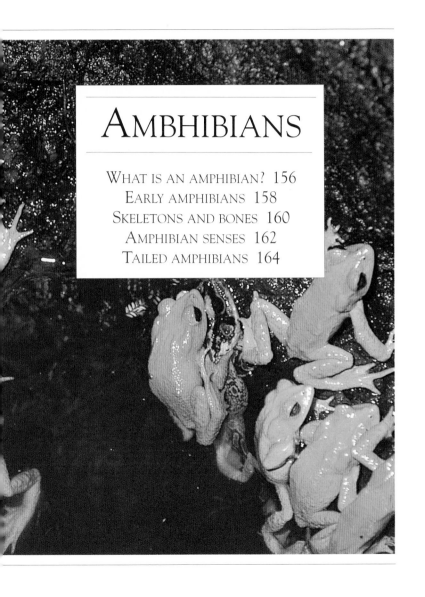

AMBHIBIANS

WHAT IS AN AMPHIBIAN?

AMPHIBIANS ARE DIVIDED into frogs and toads, salamanders, sirens, and the worm-like caecilians. They are vertebrates, and are cold-blooded, which means that their body temperature varies with their surroundings. Amphibians have no hair, feathers, or surface scales on their skin, and can breathe through their skin, as well as their lungs.

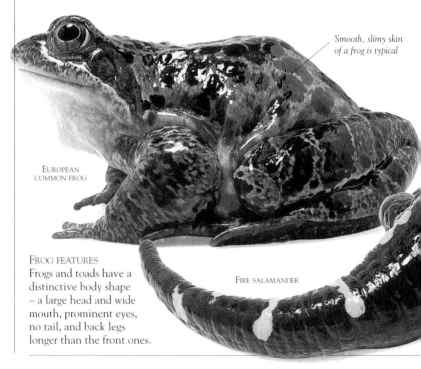

Smooth, slimy skin of a frog is typical

EUROPEAN
COMMON FROG

FIRE SALAMANDER

FROG FEATURES
Frogs and toads have a distinctive body shape – a large head and wide mouth, prominent eyes, no tail, and back legs longer than the front ones.

NOT AMPHIBIANS
Lizards and snakes are
reptiles, although
they look similar to
some amphibians.
Reptiles can be easily
distinguished by their dry, scaly skin.
Some tadpoles may look like small fish,
but the lack of scales and body fins
shows that they are quite different.

TEGU LIZARD

Typical dry, scaly
skin of a reptile

AMPHIBIAN ODDITY
The body rings on a caecilian
make it look like a worm, but
the shark-like head and
needle-sharp teeth
show it is not!

The smooth,
damp skin of a
salamander is
typical of many
amphibians.

A SPECIFIC SHAPE
Newts and salamanders have
narrower heads with smaller eyes and
mouths than frogs and toads. The body is
also longer and more lizard-shaped,
and there is always a well-developed tail.

157

EARLY AMPHIBIANS

THE FIRST AMPHIBIANS appeared some 360 million years ago. They evolved from fishes with fleshy fins that looked like legs, and had fish-like features. These amphibians may have been attracted onto land by a good food supply, and relatively few enemies to prey on them. Most amphibians had become extinct by the Triassic period, leaving only a few to evolve into modern amphibians.

SKELETON OF ICHTHYOSTEGA

FISH-LIKE AMPHIBIAN
Ichthyostega was an early amphibian from the Devonian period in Greenland. It had some fish-like features, but also had legs suitable for walking.

RECONSTRUCTION OF ICHTHYOSTEGA

SWAMP DWELLER
This skeleton is of *Eryops*, a crocodile-like amphibian that lived in swamps in Texas, USA, about 270 million years ago. These terrestrial creatures used their strong limbs to move around.

SKELETON OF ERYOPS

*Wide, flat skull, like
modern frogs*

FOSSIL SANDWICH
This fossil is the only
known specimen of
Triadobatrachus, which
was found in France,
dating from the Triassic
period about 210 million
years ago. It has a wide,
flat, frog-like skull, but
contains more vertebrae
than modern frogs do,
and also has a bony tail
and short hind legs.

Short tail

KEEPING WELL
Well-preserved fossil frog
skeletons like *Rana pueyoi*
show how little some
groups have changed in
the last 25 million years.

*Body shape
of fossil
salamander
is like that
of modern
hellbender*

*Short, stout legs
supporting heavy body*

LONG LOST RELATIVE
This fossil salamander was found in
Switzerland and is about eight million
years old. It is a close relative of the
hellbender salamander, the only living
member now found in the southeastern USA.

159

SKELETONS AND BONES

AMPHIBIANS HAVE SIMPLE SKELETONS with fewer bones than other modern vertebrates and many fewer than their fishy ancestors. This shows an evolutionary trend in amphibians – towards reducing the number of bones in the skull and spine (backbone).

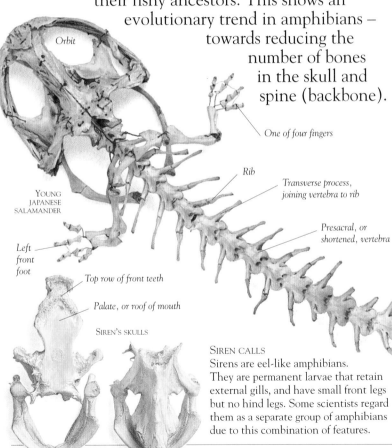

Orbit

One of four fingers

YOUNG
JAPANESE
SALAMANDER

Rib

Transverse process, joining vertebra to rib

Presacral, or shortened, vertebra

Left front foot

Top row of front teeth

Palate, or roof of mouth

SIREN'S SKULLS

SIREN CALLS

Sirens are eel-like amphibians. They are permanent larvae that retain external gills, and have small front legs but no hind legs. Some scientists regard them as a separate group of amphibians due to this combination of features.

Heart

Large orbit, or eye socket

Transverse process (no rib)

Liver

Stomach

Long ankle bone

CHARACTERISTIC FEATURES
This North American bullfrog skeleton shows some distinctive features of modern frogs, including two extra long ankle bones, that enable the legs to fold for jumping.

Sacral vertebra

SEEN IN TECHNICOLOUR
This anatomical preparation of a frog was injected with red dye to show up the arteries, which carry oxygenated blood, and blue to show the veins which carry oxygen-depleted blood.

SALAMANDER STYLE
This skeleton has some characteristic salamander features – it has about 16 to 22 presacral vertebrae, one sacral vertebra, and 18 to 20 vertebrae in the tail.

Tail vertebra

Compact, narrow skull

Rib

One of five toes

Sacral vertebra (wider processes, no ribs)

Left hind foot

TRUE AMPHIBIANS
Caecilians' lack of eyes and limbs, small skull, and extra rib-bearing vertebrae are an adaptation to a life spent burrowing.

161

AMPHIBIAN SENSES

AMPHIBIANS HAVE THE FIVE basic senses of touch, taste, sight, hearing, and smell. But they can also detect ultraviolet and infrared light, and the Earth's magnetic field. Through touch, amphibians can feel temperature and pain, and respond to irritants, such as acids in the environment. As cold-blooded animals with porous skin, amphibians need to respond quickly to external changes.

AFRICAN
CLAWED TOAD

Lateral line,
or plaque

Lateral line

THE PRESSURE'S ON
Aquatic frogs, newts, salamanders, sirens, and amphibian larvae have a lateral line sense system for detecting pressure changes from moving or stationary objects in the water.

FEELING HOT?

In hot or drying conditions, amphibians lose body water by evaporation. They control their body temperature by basking in the sun if too cold, or going into the shade if too hot. By tucking in its legs, the painted reed frog reduces the amount of body area exposed to the sun.

PAINTED REED FROG

RED-EYED TREEFROG

ORIENTAL FIRE-BELLIED TOAD

EYE SEE

Eye colour and pupil shape are variable in frogs. The red-eyed treefrog has vertical, cat-like pupils for night vision or quick response to rapidly changing light conditions. The fire-bellied toad has heart-shaped pupils.

AMERICAN BULLFROG TADPOLE

Ear of American bullfrog

LISTEN UP

Hearing is one of the most important senses in frogs. The size of, and distance between, a frog's ears are related to the wavelength and frequency of the sound of the male's call.

TAILED AMPHIBIANS

SALAMANDERS, NEWTS, AND SIRENS
make up a group of about 360
species of tailed amphibians,
which, like frogs and toads, have
adopted a wide range of lifestyles.
Some live on land in damp areas,
although they may go into the
water to breed. Some lungless
salamanders even live in trees.
Others spend their whole lives
in water. Caecilians are found
only in the tropics, and
burrow in soft earth or
mud, often near water,
or else swim in rivers
and streams.

*Short hind legs – toes
more equal in size
than in frogs*

Well-developed tail

TIGER SALAMANDER

*Tip of crest
on male's tail
only grows
during mating
season*

SHY AWAY
"Salamander"
is a term generally
used to refer to land-based
amphibians with tails, although newts
and sirens are also members of this family. Land-dwelling
salamanders are shy and live mostly in damp, hidden areas.

Longer body than frogs and toads

A LIFE IN THE WATER
Sirens are distinct from salamanders – they have lungs as well as gills and are permanent aquatic larvae (they never leave the water).

One of four toes on hind foot

LESSER SIREN

Gills

One of five toes on hind foot

Newts are semi-aquatic salamanders, that return to the water to breed

MALE GREAT CRESTED NEWT

165

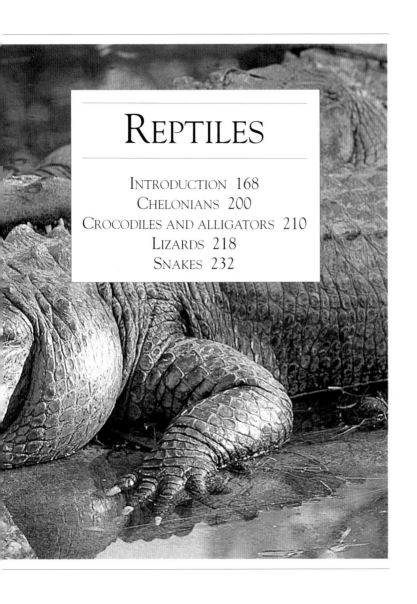

REPTILES

PAINTING OF MEDUSA

WHAT IS A REPTILE?

LIKE FISH, amphibians, birds, and mammals, reptiles are vertebrates (have backbones). But what makes them different from fish and amphibians is that they are basically land animals – they do not have to live in or keep returning to water. And unlike birds and mammals, they are cold-blooded. That is, their bodies remain at the same temperature as their surroundings.

MEDUSA
Throughout history, reptiles have been feared. Medusa, a monster from Greek mythology, had snakes for hair.

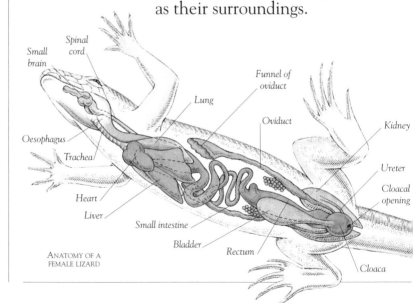

Small brain

Spinal cord

Small intestine

Oesophagus

Trachea

Heart

Liver

Lung

Bladder

Rectum

Funnel of oviduct

Oviduct

Kidney

Ureter

Cloacal opening

Cloaca

ANATOMY OF A FEMALE LIZARD

Long tail for balance

SEEN FROM
THE OUTSIDE
Lizards are typical
reptiles. The Thai water
dragon, shown below, is
found in Southeast Asia.
It has scaly skin that is
waterproof – thus retaining
moisture inside the reptile's body.

Eye

GLASSY STARE
Snakes and some
lizards do not have
movable eyelids. Instead,
the eye is covered with a
transparent membrane, called the
spectacle or brille, that protects
the eye from damage.

Long toes for
support

Scaly skin

THAI WATER DRAGON

EGG LAYERS
Some reptiles
produce active
young, but most
species lay eggs.
Here a young rat-
snake is hatching.

RATSNAKE

INSIDE A REPTILE
Most reptiles have a three-
chambered heart (a crocodile
heart has four chambers, like
our own). The cloaca, a chamber
at the rear of the gut, is used
by the bladder when excreting
and by the reproductive system
during mating.

AN EXTRA EYELID
Crocodiles have
three eyelids.
There are two
above and below
the eye. An extra
see-through lid
covers the eye
from the inner
corner to protect
the surface of the
eye under water.

REPTILE GROUPS

REPTILES FIRST APPEARED about 340 million years ago, during the Carboniferous period (see diagram). Their ancestors were amphibians, but the first reptiles could breed without having to return to water. Today, four main groups, or orders, remain: turtles and tortoises (chelonians), snakes and lizards, crocodilians, and tuataras.

GIANT SEASNAKE

PALAEOPHIS
Snakes first appeared in the late Jurassic. *Palaeophis* was an ancient seasnake.

MODERN PYTHON
These vertebrae are from a python that is four times smaller than *Palaeophis*.

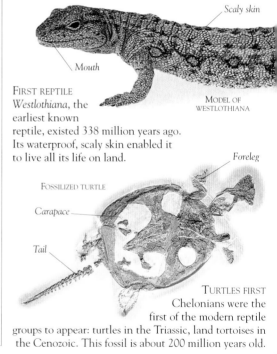

Scaly skin

Mouth

FIRST REPTILE
Westlothiana, the earliest known reptile, existed 338 million years ago. Its waterproof, scaly skin enabled it to live all its life on land.

MODEL OF WESTLOTHIANA

Foreleg

FOSSILIZED TURTLE

Carapace

Tail

TURTLES FIRST
Chelonians were the first of the modern reptile groups to appear: turtles in the Triassic, land tortoises in the Cenozoic. This fossil is about 200 million years old.

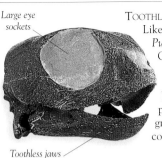

Large eye sockets

Toothless jaws

TOOTHLESS TURTLE

Like modern turtles, *Puppigerus*, a Cenozoic sea turtle, had toothless jaws. It used its beak to feed on plants such as sea-grass in shallow coastal waters.

REPTILE GROUP FACTS

• Rhynchocephalians were common in the Triassic. Today, the only ones left are tuataras.

• Mammal-like reptiles appeared in the Permian. During the Triassic they gave rise to the first mammals.

Semi-sprawling stance

Five-toed feet

REPTILE EVOLUTION

This diagram shows the evolution of reptiles. The column on the left shows when they existed and how many millions of years ago that was.

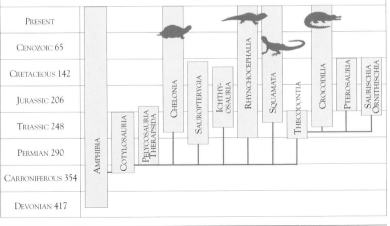

	AMPHIBIA	COTYLOSAURIA	PELYCOSAURIA THERAPSIDA	CHELONIA	SAUROPTERYGIA	ICHTHY-OSAURIA	RHYNCHOCEPHALIA	SQUAMATA	THECODONTIA	CROCODILIA	PTEROSAURIA	SAURISCHIA ORNITHISCHIA
PRESENT												
CENOZOIC 65												
CRETACEOUS 142												
JURASSIC 206												
TRIASSIC 248												
PERMIAN 290												
CARBONIFEROUS 354												
DEVONIAN 417												

PREHISTORIC REPTILES

THE FIRST REPTILES encountered no competition for the wide range of land habitats available. Over millions of years they adapted to every possible type of lifestyle and diet. Some of them even learned to fly. Others returned to living in the sea.

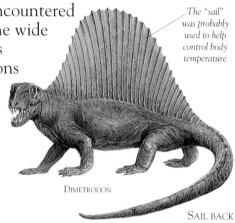

The "sail" was probably used to help control body temperature

DIMETRODON

SAIL BACK
Dimetrodon was a mammal-like reptile of the Permian period. Its relatives were the ancestors of modern mammals.

Fangs and sharp cheek-teeth for eating flesh

CYNOGNATHUS

Sharp claws

REPTILE DOG
Cynognathus lived in the early Triassic period. It was about 2 m (7 ft) long and looked like a large dog. Scientists have discovered that it probably had hair.

172

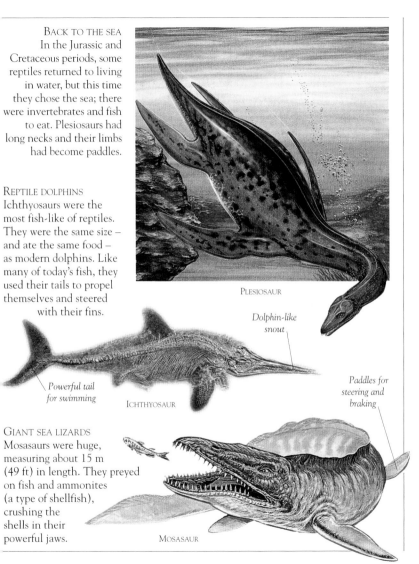

BACK TO THE SEA
In the Jurassic and
Cretaceous periods, some
reptiles returned to living
in water, but this time
they chose the sea; there
were invertebrates and fish
to eat. Plesiosaurs had
long necks and their limbs
had become paddles.

REPTILE DOLPHINS
Ichthyosaurs were the
most fish-like of reptiles.
They were the same size –
and ate the same food –
as modern dolphins. Like
many of today's fish, they
used their tails to propel
themselves and steered
with their fins.

PLESIOSAUR

Dolphin-like
snout

Powerful tail
for swimming

ICHTHYOSAUR

Paddles for
steering and
braking

GIANT SEA LIZARDS
Mosasaurs were huge,
measuring about 15 m
(49 ft) in length. They preyed
on fish and ammonites
(a type of shellfish),
crushing the
shells in their
powerful jaws.

MOSASAUR

173

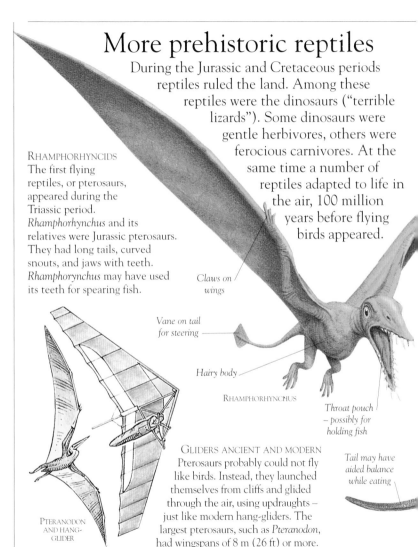

More prehistoric reptiles

During the Jurassic and Cretaceous periods reptiles ruled the land. Among these reptiles were the dinosaurs ("terrible lizards"). Some dinosaurs were gentle herbivores, others were ferocious carnivores. At the same time a number of reptiles adapted to life in the air, 100 million years before flying birds appeared.

RHAMPHORHYNCIDS
The first flying reptiles, or pterosaurs, appeared during the Triassic period. *Rhamphorhynchus* and its relatives were Jurassic pterosaurs. They had long tails, curved snouts, and jaws with teeth. *Rhamphorynchus* may have used its teeth for spearing fish.

Claws on wings

Vane on tail for steering

Hairy body

RHAMPHORHYNCHUS

Throat pouch – possibly for holding fish

GLIDERS ANCIENT AND MODERN
Pterosaurs probably could not fly like birds. Instead, they launched themselves from cliffs and glided through the air, using updraughts – just like modern hang-gliders. The largest pterosaurs, such as *Pteranodon*, had wingspans of 8 m (26 ft) or more.

Tail may have aided balance while eating

PTERANODON AND HANG-GLIDER

174

Strong neck to support
the huge head

Skin stretched
between elongated
fingers and the body,
forming wings

Tyrannosaurus
moved around on its
massive hind legs

TYRANNOSAURUS

LIZARD TYRANT
Standing taller than a
giraffe and weighing about
100 tonnes (98 tons),
Tyrannosaurus was a two-
legged carnivore with teeth up
to 18 cm (7 in) long.

Tough hide
helped protect
against predators

Bony club to
deter predators

EUOPLOCEPHALUS

EUOPLOCEPHALUS
Ankylosaurs, such as *Euoplocephalus*, needed
protection from their carnivorous relatives. The
tanklike ankylosaurs developed an armoured
covering of bony plates and knobs. Some
of them had clublike tails.

GENTLE GIANTS
Brachiosaurus
and its relatives
were huge, but only
ate vegetation. Its long
neck, balanced by a
long tail, enabled it to
reach into high branches
inaccessible to other creatures.

Massive legs to
support the body's
great weight

PREHISTORIC FACTS

• *Brachiosaurus* would
have eaten 400 kg
(882 lb) of food a day.

• Large carnivorous
dinosaurs may have
been warm-blooded.

• The fastest dinosaurs
could run at up to
80 km/h (50 mph).

BRACHIOSAURUS

SCALY SKIN

REPTILES TYPICALLY have skins covered in overlapping, horny scales. These act as a waterproof covering and help to retain precious body moisture. In some reptiles, the scales form an armoured protection. As a reptile grows, its old skin becomes too small and starts to wear out. A new skin replaces it.

ARMOURED ALLIGATOR
Like all crocodilians, this Chinese alligator is covered in large, tough, partly ossified (turned into bone) scales. As it grows, the scales flake off and are replaced by new ones.

SECTION THROUGH SKIN

Scales

Upper layer of skin (epidermis)

Lower layer of skin (dermis)

Scales form in the epidermis. They are made mostly of keratin – the same substance found in hair and nails.

The new segments are added where the tail joins the rattle

End segments may break off if the rattle gets very long

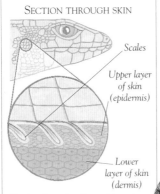

WARNING RATTLE
A rattlesnake's rattle is made up of hollow pieces of keratin formed at the end of the tail. A new segment is added when the snake sheds its skin.

The rattle warns off attackers

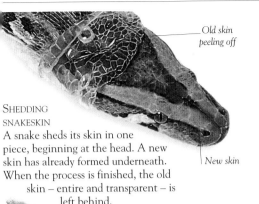

Old skin
peeling off

New skin

SHEDDING SNAKESKIN

A snake sheds its skin in one piece, beginning at the head. A new skin has already formed underneath. When the process is finished, the old skin – entire and transparent – is left behind.

A SHED SNAKESKIN

SCALY SKIN FACTS

• A reptile grows throughout its life.

• The crests and spines sported by some lizards are formed from scales.

• Turtle shells are made of bony plates covered in horny material.

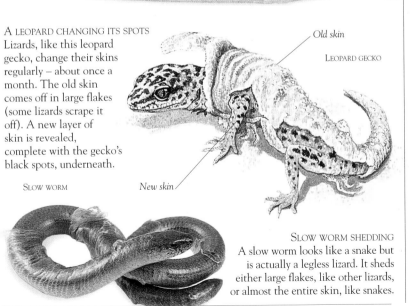

A LEOPARD CHANGING ITS SPOTS

Lizards, like this leopard gecko, change their skins regularly – about once a month. The old skin comes off in large flakes (some lizards scrape it off). A new layer of skin is revealed, complete with the gecko's black spots, underneath.

Old skin

LEOPARD GECKO

SLOW WORM

New skin

SLOW WORM SHEDDING

A slow worm looks like a snake but is actually a legless lizard. It sheds either large flakes, like other lizards, or almost the entire skin, like snakes.

177

COLD-BLOODED CREATURES

REPTILES ARE DESCRIBED as cold-blooded. This does not mean that their blood is always cold. But, unlike birds and mammals, they do not make their own heat by using the chemical reactions in their bodies. Instead, a reptile relies on heat from the outside, and its body temperature goes up or down according to the external temperature.

Reptiles warm up by basking in the sun

CHILLING OUT
To cool, a reptile finds shade, or angles its body to expose the smallest possible area to the sun.

AGAMA LIZARD

COLD-BLOODED FACTS
• Scientists call "cold-blooded" animals poikilotherms or ectotherms.

• Reptiles need a high body temperature for digestion to take place. If a snake eats when it is not warm enough, it has to regurgitate its meal.

WARMING UP
When a reptile starts to get too cold, it warms itself by basking in the sun, presenting as much of its body as possible to the sun's rays. By moving regularly between sun and shade, a reptile is able to maintain an almost constant body temperature.

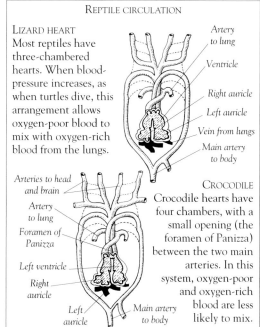

REPTILE CIRCULATION

LIZARD HEART
Most reptiles have three-chambered hearts. When blood-pressure increases, as when turtles dive, this arrangement allows oxygen-poor blood to mix with oxygen-rich blood from the lungs.

Artery to lung

Ventricle

Right auricle

Left auricle

Vein from lungs

Main artery to body

Arteries to head and brain

Artery to lung

Foramen of Panizza

Left ventricle

Right auricle

Left auricle

Main artery to body

CROCODILE
Crocodile hearts have four chambers, with a small opening (the foramen of Panizza) between the two main arteries. In this system, oxygen-poor and oxygen-rich blood are less likely to mix.

DIGGING IN
Shade is difficult to find in the desert. A sand viper solves this problem by wriggling its body down into the sand. If it did not do this it would literally fry in the heat.

Open-mouthed cooling is called gaping

Like all reptiles, the crocodile cannot sweat to lose heat

Water evaporates from mouth

OPEN-MOUTHED COOLING
One way of cooling is to let water evaporate from the body. A crocodile lies with its mouth open to let water evaporate from its mouth. American crocodiles lie in burrows when they get too hot. Other species cool down in water.

INTRODUCTION

179

SENSES

MOST REPTILES have eyes
and ears. Snakes and
lizards also "taste"
their surroundings
using their tongues.
The tuatara, and
many lizards, also have a
light-sensitive organ on
their heads, which may be
important to temperature
regulation and to reproduction.

Scaly skin contains sensors that detect touch, pain, heat, and cold

Notched iris with vertical slit

Heat-sensitive pit helps snake to calculate direction and distance of prey

SLIT EYES

A gecko is mostly
active at night and its
eyes are very sensitive.
In daylight, the iris of
each eye closes to a slit,
stopping too much light
reaching the retina.
Notches in the iris
allow the animal to see.

HEAT SENSITIVE

On either side of its
head, a pit viper has a
heat-sensitive pit that
can detect the body
heat given off by
warm-blooded prey.
The pits can sense
temperature changes as
small as 0.001°C
(0.002°F), enabling
the snake to strike
accurately, even at night.

TEGU SENSES

A tegu lizard's well-developed eyes are designed for use in daylight and are protected by movable eyelids. Its eardrums are visible as small patches on the sides of its head, behind the jaws. Its flicking, forked tongue is used, in conjunction with its Jacobson's organ, to "taste" the air.

SWIVELLING EYES

To see without being seen, a chameleon remains perfectly still, while swivelling its eyes to see in almost any direction. The eyes swivel independently of each other.

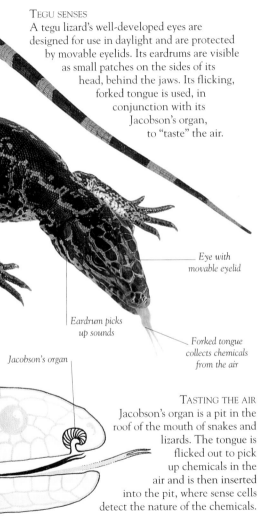

Eye with movable eyelid

Eardrum picks up sounds

Jacobson's organ

Forked tongue collects chemicals from the air

TASTING THE AIR

Jacobson's organ is a pit in the roof of the mouth of snakes and lizards. The tongue is flicked out to pick up chemicals in the air and is then inserted into the pit, where sense cells detect the nature of the chemicals.

SENSES FACTS

• A chameleon can use one eye to hunt and the other to watch out for predators.

• Most snakes "hear" by feeling vibrations through the ground; however, most lizards hear airborne sounds.

181

MOVEMENT

THE LEGS OF A typical reptile, such as a lizard, protrude sideways from its body. Heavier reptiles may require considerable physical effort to lift their bodies off the ground. Larger, land-based reptiles tend to move slowly, but smaller, lighter ones can be fast-moving and agile. Some reptiles, notably snakes, have dispensed with legs altogether.

GECKO

STICKY FEET
Geckos are small and light, and able to move rapidly. Pads on their feet have millions of tiny hooks that enable them to cling to smooth surfaces, even glass.

Fringe-like scales on feet

SANDFISH

SWIMMING IN SAND
A sandfish (a type of skink) has fringe-like scales on its feet to help it move on sand. It can also dive into the sand, wriggling like a snake.

SIDEWINDING
Some desert snakes move over the sand by looping their bodies sideways and moving in a series of sideways steps, known as sidewinding.

SIDEWINDER

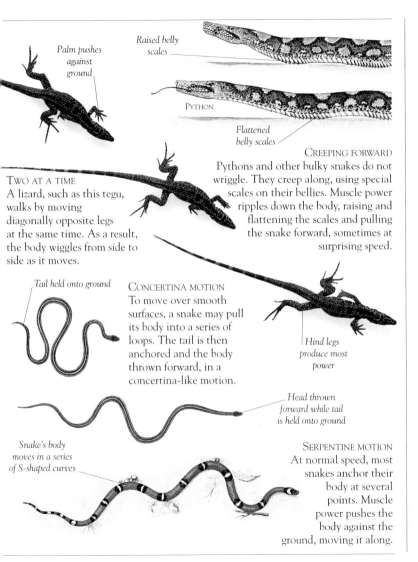

Palm pushes against ground

Raised belly scales

PYTHON

Flattened belly scales

CREEPING FORWARD
Pythons and other bulky snakes do not wriggle. They creep along, using special scales on their bellies. Muscle power ripples down the body, raising and flattening the scales and pulling the snake forward, sometimes at surprising speed.

TWO AT A TIME
A lizard, such as this tegu, walks by moving diagonally opposite legs at the same time. As a result, the body wiggles from side to side as it moves.

Tail held onto ground

CONCERTINA MOTION
To move over smooth surfaces, a snake may pull its body into a series of loops. The tail is then anchored and the body thrown forward, in a concertina-like motion.

Hind legs produce most power

Head thrown forward while tail is held onto ground

Snake's body moves in a series of S-shaped curves

SERPENTINE MOTION
At normal speed, most snakes anchor their body at several points. Muscle power pushes the body against the ground, moving it along.

183

Flying reptiles

Reptiles have never learned to fly like bats or birds. The first "flying" reptiles, the pterosaurs of the Triassic period, were gliding animals rather than fliers, and the same is true of the modern species that have taken to the air. Nevertheless, the ability to glide can be very useful in escaping quickly from predators or simply moving swiftly from one tree branch to the next in the search for food.

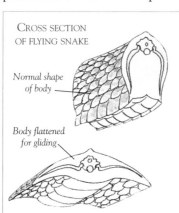

CROSS SECTION OF FLYING SNAKE

Normal shape of body

Body flattened for gliding

A flying snake turns itself into a wing by pushing out its ribs and holding in its belly, so that the body becomes flattened.

FLYING DRAGON
The "wings" of the flying dragon of Southeast Asia are flaps of skin supported by elongated ribs. They normally lie folded against the body, but can be spread out wide for gliding flights.

Six or seven pairs of ribs support skin flaps

Limbs spread out to help steering

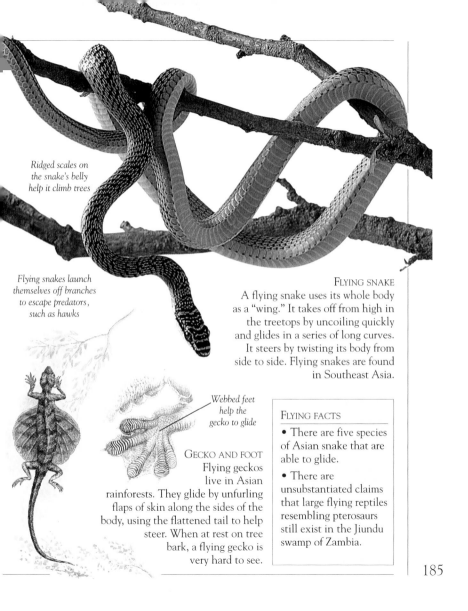

Ridged scales on the snake's belly help it climb trees

Flying snakes launch themselves off branches to escape predators, such as hawks

Webbed feet help the gecko to glide

FLYING SNAKE
A flying snake uses its whole body as a "wing." It takes off from high in the treetops by uncoiling quickly and glides in a series of long curves. It steers by twisting its body from side to side. Flying snakes are found in Southeast Asia.

GECKO AND FOOT
Flying geckos live in Asian rainforests. They glide by unfurling flaps of skin along the sides of the body, using the flattened tail to help steer. When at rest on tree bark, a flying gecko is very hard to see.

FLYING FACTS
• There are five species of Asian snake that are able to glide.

• There are unsubstantiated claims that large flying reptiles resembling pterosaurs still exist in the Jiundu swamp of Zambia.

185

COURTSHIP

LIKE ALL ANIMALS, reptiles need to attract members of
the opposite sex in order to reproduce. They do this
in various ways: by signals, colourful displays, or eye-
catching ornaments, such
as frills or crests.

Male's head

SNAKES MATING

Mating may
take several
hours

SNAKE CHARMERS
Once a male snake has attracted
a female he stimulates her
into mating by
rubbing his
chin along her
back. She then allows
him to intertwine her
body with his. This
enables their cloacal openings to
meet so that the pair can mate.

Tails
intwertwined

A CLASH OF SHELLS
Tortoise mating,
especially in large species
such as these Galápagos
tortoises, is a laborious
affair. The males roar
during mating.

All anoles have
very long tails

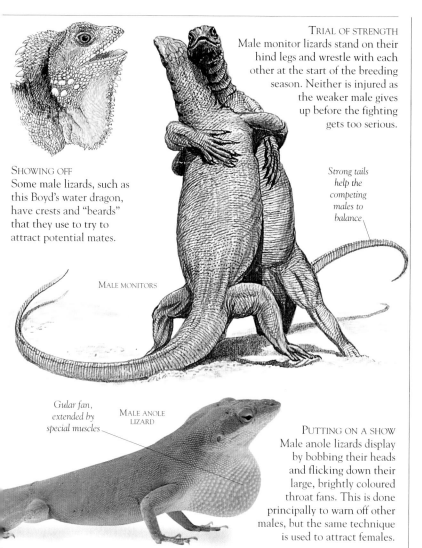

TRIAL OF STRENGTH
Male monitor lizards stand on their hind legs and wrestle with each other at the start of the breeding season. Neither is injured as the weaker male gives up before the fighting gets too serious.

SHOWING OFF
Some male lizards, such as this Boyd's water dragon, have crests and "beards" that they use to try to attract potential mates.

Strong tails help the competing males to balance

MALE MONITORS

Gular fan, extended by special muscles

MALE ANOLE LIZARD

PUTTING ON A SHOW
Male anole lizards display by bobbing their heads and flicking down their large, brightly coloured throat fans. This is done principally to warn off other males, but the same technique is used to attract females.

187

NESTS AND EGGS

ANIMALS THAT TAKE CARE of their young generally have fewer offspring than those that leave their young to fend for themselves. Some reptiles, such as the marine turtles, lay thousands of eggs, but because they abandon them only a few hatchlings reach maturity. A crocodile, on the other hand, guards not only her eggs but also her young for some time after they hatch. So a higher percentage of eggs and young survive.

ALLIGATOR NEST

ROTTEN NEST
A female American alligator builds a mound of mud and decaying vegetation, in which she lays 15 to 80 eggs. The heat produced by the rotting material incubates the eggs for two to three months.

ON GUARD
The estuarine, or saltwater, crocodile of Southeast Asia and northern Australia builds a mound of leaves for her eggs. She builds her nest near water and shade so she can keep cool as she guards her offspring against predators, including lizards, herons, mongooses, turtles, and other crocodiles.

The mother uncovers the eggs when they hatch

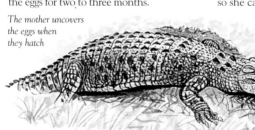

The female covers the nest with her body

SAFE IN MOTHER'S MOUTH
After baby Nile crocodiles have hatched, their mother gathers as many as she can in her mouth and carries them to the safety of a pool, making several trips to complete the task. She remains to defend her offspring.

Baby crocodiles

GREEN TURTLE LAYING EGGS

NO SAFETY IN NUMBERS
A marine turtle lays up to 200 eggs, burying them in a nest in the sand. If the nest remains undiscovered, the eggs hatch 6 to 10 weeks later, but the hatchlings fall prey to crabs, seabirds, and other predators on the way to the sea.

LIVE BIRTH
A rattlesnake keeps her eggs inside her body until they hatch, which greatly improves their chances of survival. Approximately 10 to 20 young are born, measuring about 30 cm (11¼ in) in length. The mother abandons them soon after birth.

RATTLESNAKE AND YOUNG

189

More nests and eggs

Reptile eggs have shells that retain moisture, so they can be laid on land. Most reptile eggs have soft, leathery shells, but some, such as a crocodile's, have hard shells. In most cases the eggs hatch outside the mother's body, although a few reptiles produce live young. In some cases the eggs hatch just before laying, in others the embryos obtain nourishment from their mother through a placenta.

GALÁPAGOS TORTOISE

Porous shell

Amnion

Bag-like allantois collects waste

ALLIGATOR

Embryo

Yolk sac

Chorion – tough layer surrounding egg

HOUSE SNAKE

CHAMELEON

CALABAR GROUND PYTHON EGG

ALL SHAPES AND SIZES

The shell of a reptile egg allows oxygen to reach the developing embryo. The embryo lies protected inside a membrane called the amnion, and receives its nourishment from the yolk sac. Reptile eggs vary widely in size, shape, and texture.

GARDEN LIZARD

EGG TOOTH

As it grows inside the egg, a young lizard or snake develops a sharp "egg tooth" on the tip of its upper jaw. When the time for hatching arrives, the animal escapes from the shell by using the egg tooth to cut its way out.

Egg tooth

HOW A SNAKE HATCHES

Just before a snake hatches, the yolk sac is drawn into the snake's body and the remaining yolk is absorbed into its intestine. Then, using its egg tooth, the snake cuts a slit large enough to push its head through. It may remain like this for up to two days before finally emerging from the egg. When it is fully hatched, the snake may be up to seven times longer than the egg from which it came.

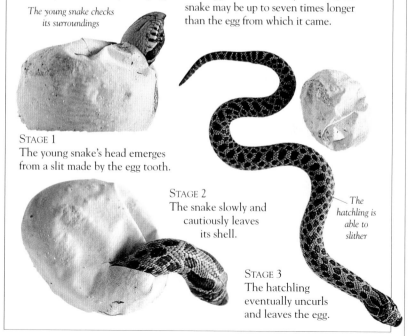

The young snake checks its surroundings

STAGE 1
The young snake's head emerges from a slit made by the egg tooth.

STAGE 2
The snake slowly and cautiously leaves its shell.

STAGE 3
The hatchling eventually uncurls and leaves the egg.

The hatchling is able to slither

191

DEADLY ENEMIES

MOST REPTILES are predators, but they are also preyed upon by other animals. Sometimes reptiles eat other reptiles. Eggs and young are especially vulnerable and in many cases adults, too, have their enemies. Even the largest and most dangerous reptiles may fall victim to human hunters.

The secretary bird tramples its reptile prey to death

SECRETARY BIRD
This African bird hunts tortoises, snakes, and lizards, flushing them from grass by stamping its feet. It uses its wings as a shield against venomous snakes.

The mongoose has lightning reactions

ENEMY FACTS

• When they are away from water, Nile crocodiles are vulnerable to attack by lions.

• The giant tortoises of Mauritius and Reunion Island were wiped out by hunters in the late 1700s.

Faced with a mongoose, a cobra looks fierce but its chances are slim

LEGENDARY ENEMIES
The mongoose is the only mammal that includes poisonous snakes in its diet. Although smaller than some of its prey, it is very courageous and is immune to snake venom. When tackling a snake, such as a spitting cobra, it bites the head of its prey with lightning speed.

SNAKE EATS SNAKE

Kingsnakes, some of which are also known as milk snakes, feed on small mammals, lizards, frogs, and other snakes. Kingsnakes, which squeeze their prey, are not afraid to tackle venomous snakes, such as copperheads.

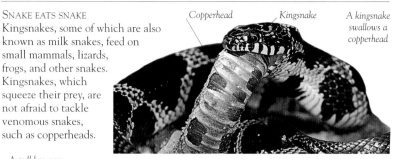

Copperhead *Kingsnake*

A kingsnake swallows a copperhead

A gull has easy pickings when a turtle nest hatches

GULL GAUNTLET

Young turtles hatch out from eggs buried high on the beach. They immediately head for the sea, but in doing so, they run the gauntlet of a number of predators. Seabirds, such as gulls, gather in large numbers to feast on the hatchlings, and many of them never reach the safety of the water.

HATCHLINGS AND GULL

Cobras are protected in India, but they are still caught so that that their venom can be collected (see page 97)

HUMANS AND REPTILES

Humans hunt reptiles for various reasons – for food, for their skins, or simply because they are poisonous. Humans have also reduced the natural habitat of many species. A combination of these factors has brought some species to extinction and made others very rare.

SOUTH INDIAN VILLAGERS DISPLAY A LIVE COBRA

BATTLE FOR SURVIVAL

SURVIVAL IN THE ANIMAL WORLD means not only being able to find something to eat, but also avoiding being eaten by other animals. Large reptiles deter predators by their sheer size, but smaller species have to use a range of strategies, including camouflage, warning colours, mimicry, and bluff.

Skin cells draw pigments from below to change skin colour

PARSON'S CHAMELEON

SLOW BUT SURE
In the branches of trees, a chameleon hides from prey and predators alike. Its movements are very slow, so as not to attract attention, and it adjusts its colouring to blend in with its surroundings.

CHANGING COLOUR
A chameleon does not only change colour to camouflage itself. It may also darken in heat or sunlight, or to indicate a change of mood – an angry chameleon turns black.

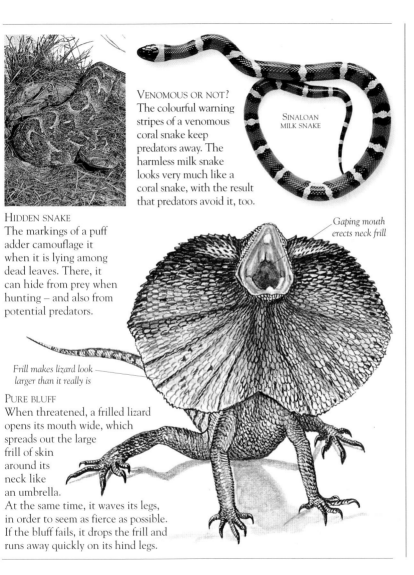

VENOMOUS OR NOT?
The colourful warning stripes of a venomous coral snake keep predators away. The harmless milk snake looks very much like a coral snake, with the result that predators avoid it, too.

SINALOAN MILK SNAKE

Gaping mouth erects neck frill

HIDDEN SNAKE
The markings of a puff adder camouflage it when it is lying among dead leaves. There, it can hide from prey when hunting – and also from potential predators.

Frill makes lizard look larger than it really is

PURE BLUFF
When threatened, a frilled lizard opens its mouth wide, which spreads out the large frill of skin around its neck like an umbrella. At the same time, it waves its legs, in order to seem as fierce as possible. If the bluff fails, it drops the frill and runs away quickly on its hind legs.

195

Defence strategies

Reptiles have evolved many ways to avoid being eaten. Small lizards often use speed to escape, and many species retreat into underground burrows or rock crevices. Some use water as a means of escape. When cornered, many lizards, particularly large ones like monitors, will turn to face their attackers. Two lizards, the Gila monster and the beaded lizard, are venomous.

The snake lies absolutely still

Mouth gapes and tongue hangs out

PLAYING DEAD
When it cannot escape, a grass snake turns over, curls up, then lies still. It is playing dead, hoping its attacker will go away.

STINKING STINKPOT
The stinkpot turtle is the reptile equivalent of the skunk. It produces such an unpleasant smell that predators avoid it.

As it loses speed, the basilisk drops into the water and must swim

SURVIVAL FACTS

• Horned lizards squirt blood at their attackers from their eyes.

• Some skinks have a bright blue tail that attracts predators away from vital body parts.

BASILISK

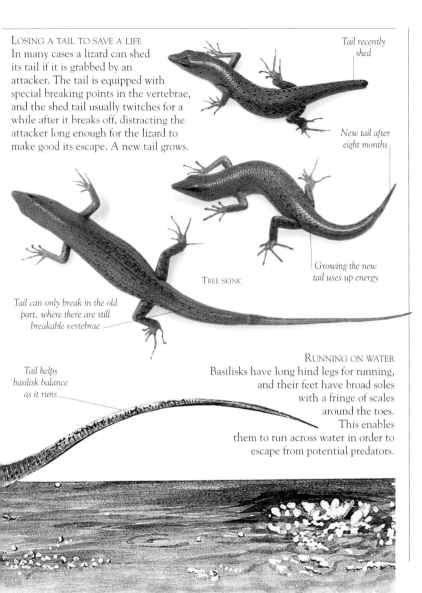

LOSING A TAIL TO SAVE A LIFE
In many cases a lizard can shed
its tail if it is grabbed by an
attacker. The tail is equipped with
special breaking points in the vertebrae,
and the shed tail usually twitches for a
while after it breaks off, distracting the
attacker long enough for the lizard to
make good its escape. A new tail grows.

Tail recently shed

New tail after eight months

TREE SKINK

Growing the new tail uses up energy

Tail can only break in the old part, where there are still breakable vertebrae

Tail helps basilisk balance as it runs

RUNNING ON WATER
Basilisks have long hind legs for running,
and their feet have broad soles
with a fringe of scales
around the toes.
This enables
them to run across water in order to
escape from potential predators.

LIVING IN WATER

ALTHOUGH REPTILES EVOLVED as land animals, many species have become adapted to living in water, where food is often plentiful. For these species, swimming is more important than walking, and many are equipped with paddles instead of feet. But they are still air-breathing animals and so have special adaptations enabling them to cope with a watery environment.

GOGGLE EYES
Crocodilians, like this caiman, lie submerged in the water, waiting for prey. The eyes and nostrils are placed high on the head, so that only these parts show above the water.

The spectacled caiman has a bony ridge between its eyes, resembling the frame of a pair of glasses

SNORKELLING TURTLE
The matamata turtle of Brazil waits for its prey on the river bed. It pokes its nostrils out of the water to breathe, without moving – and so avoids disturbing the fish.

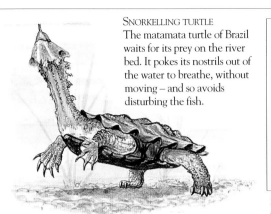

WATER FACTS

• Sea turtles excrete salt absorbed in sea water from their eyes, which is why they seem to cry.

• To prevent water getting into its lung, a sea snake closes off its nostrils with a special sponge-like tissue.

Sea snakes are very poisonous

Powerful tail moves the snake forward

The four paddles propel the turtle

PADDLE TAIL
A sea snake is virtually helpless on land but is an excellent swimmer. Its tail is flattened vertically to form a powerful, oar-like paddle.

WEB-FOOTED SLIDER
Freshwater chelonians, such as terrapins, have webbed feet for swimming. The red-eared slider has a habit of sliding back into the water if disturbed.

PADDLE FEET
A marine turtle can tolerate high levels of carbon dioxide in its blood and so can swim under water for long periods.

REPTILES

CHELONIAN ANATOMY

CHELONIANS are reptiles whose bodies are protected by shells. The shells are made up of the plastron which protects the belly, and the carapace, which covers the back. There are between 250 and 300 species of chelonian. Some live in salt water, others in fresh water, and yet others on land. Water dwellers are usually called turtles or terrapins, while land dwellers are known as tortoises.

FROM THE OUTSIDE
The red-eared terrapin is a typical chelonian. It has a carapace made up of several layers. The outer layer consists of horny shields, known as scutes.

INSIDE A CHELONIAN
The internal anatomy of a chelonian is similar to that of other vertebrates. A three-chambered heart lies between a pair of lungs. The gut, bladder, and oviduct all lead to a chamber known as the cloaca (meaning "sewer").

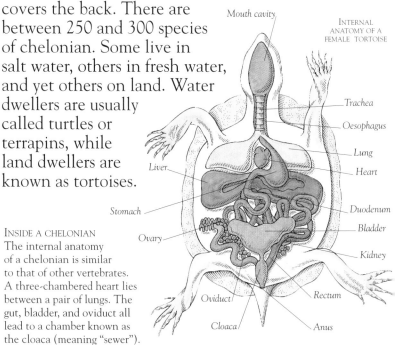

Carapace

INTERNAL ANATOMY OF A FEMALE TORTOISE

Mouth cavity

Trachea

Oesophagus

Lung

Heart

Liver

Stomach

Ovary

Oviduct

Cloaca

Duodenum

Bladder

Kidney

Rectum

Anus

FUSED VERTEBRAE

The carapace is made up of about 50 bony plates formed in the skin. The shell has an outer layer of horny shields and an inner one of bone. The vertebrae, with the ribs and the two limb girdles, are fused to the carapace. This has resulted in the limb girdles being inside the ribs.

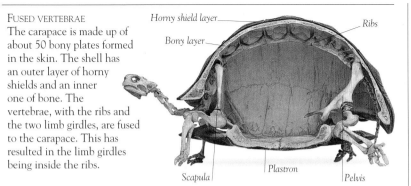

Horny shield layer

Bony layer

Ribs

Scapula

Plastron

Pelvis

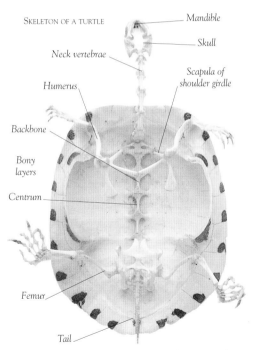

SKELETON OF A TURTLE

Mandible

Skull

Neck vertebrae

Scapula of shoulder girdle

Humerus

Backbone

Bony layers

Centrum

Femur

Tail

FLEXIBLE NECK

Inside the horny outer layer, the carapace is made of several layers of bone. The eight neck vertebrae are very flexible. The upper limb bones are short, with enlarged ends to take the weight of the animal's body and shell.

CHELONIAN FACTS

• Some female turtles produce eggs four years after mating.

• All chelonians lay eggs on land, even the marine turtles.

• Some turtles can live for more than a year without food.

MARINE TURTLES

TURTLES INVADED the world's seas and oceans during the Triassic period, some 200 million years ago. Today there are seven species, six of which are grouped together in the one family, the Chelonidae. The leatherback turtle is classified by itself in another family, called the Dermochelyidae.

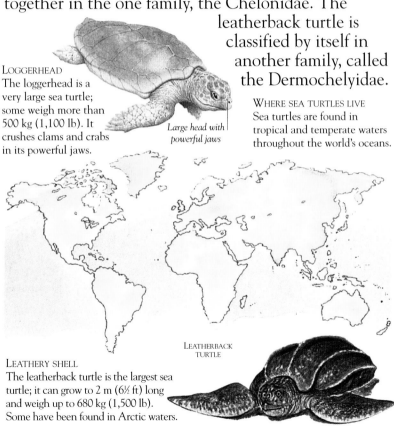

LOGGERHEAD
The loggerhead is a very large sea turtle; some weigh more than 500 kg (1,100 lb). It crushes clams and crabs in its powerful jaws.

Large head with powerful jaws

WHERE SEA TURTLES LIVE
Sea turtles are found in tropical and temperate waters throughout the world's oceans.

LEATHERBACK
TURTLE

LEATHERY SHELL
The leatherback turtle is the largest sea turtle; it can grow to 2 m (6½ ft) long and weigh up to 680 kg (1,500 lb). Some have been found in Arctic waters.

IMMUNE TO POISON
Hawksbill turtles are found near coral reefs. They feed on invertebrates, such as sponges, many of which contain poisons. These do not affect the turtles but may kill anyone who eats them.

NESTING TOGETHER
Ridley turtles come ashore in large numbers to nest together on certain beaches. Each female digs a hole in which she lays about 100 eggs. Olive ridleys live in the Atlantic, Indian, and parts of the Pacific Oceans.

CHELONIAN FEET

The limbs of marine turtles are very different from those of land and freshwater chelonians. Land tortoises have large, clawed feet. Freshwater turtles have webbing between the toes. The limbs of marine turtles have evolved into flippers.

LAND TORTOISE

Large claws for digging in soil

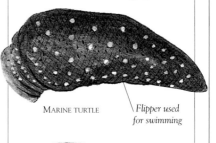

MARINE TURTLE

Flipper used for swimming

FRESHWATER TURTLE

Turtles in danger

Sea turtles are among the world's most vulnerable animals. They are relatively slow moving and easy to catch, and their nest sites are mostly well known – for example, Kemp's ridley turtles only nest on one beach in Mexico. Turtle products are much in demand, and large numbers of turtles are killed. In addition, their overall rate of reproduction is slow; although a green turtle may lay 1,000 eggs in one season, only a few survive into adulthood.

TURTLE EXPLOITATION

Turtles are large, meaty animals and in many places are hunted for food; green turtles are especially prized, particularly for turtle soup. When polished, the shell of a green turtle is a popular tourist souvenir. Pieces of turtle shell are also used in furniture-making.

END OF THE LINE
Green turtle eggs are popular as food. The nests are easy to find as the females leave an obvious trail to the nest.

GREEN TURTLE EGGS

TURTLES FOR SALE
Rows of stuffed turtles provide an income for a local trader. Trade in wild turtles is banned under the provisions of international agreements on trade in endangered animal products. Some trade in specially bred animals is allowed.

STUFFED TURTLES

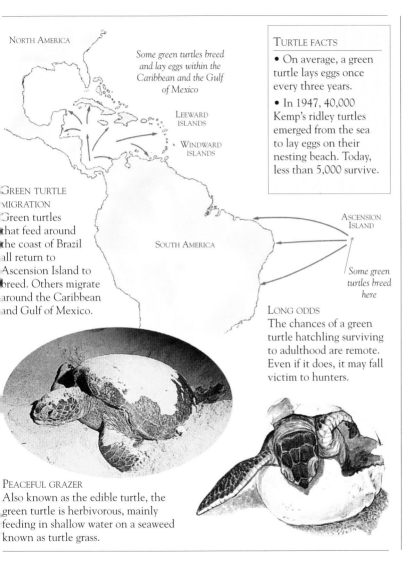

NORTH AMERICA

Some green turtles breed and lay eggs within the Caribbean and the Gulf of Mexico

LEEWARD ISLANDS

WINDWARD ISLANDS

TURTLE FACTS

• On average, a green turtle lays eggs once every three years.

• In 1947, 40,000 Kemp's ridley turtles emerged from the sea to lay eggs on their nesting beach. Today, less than 5,000 survive.

GREEN TURTLE MIGRATION
Green turtles that feed around the coast of Brazil all return to Ascension Island to breed. Others migrate around the Caribbean and Gulf of Mexico.

SOUTH AMERICA

ASCENSION ISLAND

Some green turtles breed here

LONG ODDS
The chances of a green turtle hatchling surviving to adulthood are remote. Even if it does, it may fall victim to hunters.

PEACEFUL GRAZER
Also known as the edible turtle, the green turtle is herbivorous, mainly feeding in shallow water on a seaweed known as turtle grass.

TURTLES AND TORTOISES

THE ORIGINS of the first chelonians are obscure because there is very little fossil evidence. However, it seems likely that their ancestors belonged to an early group of reptiles known as diadectomorphs that lived in swamplands. As some of them moved further onto the land, they acquired protective shells. Some ancestors of modern chelonians remained on land; others returned to the water.

Soft shell

Snorkel-like nose for breathing when underwater

SOFT KILLER
The shell of a soft-shelled turtle is covered in leathery skin instead of horny plates. Soft-shelled turtles are found in southern Asia, Africa, and North America. They live in rivers where they feed on water creatures, striking with lightning speed.

Fish being sucked in

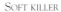

FISH SUCKER
Disguised as a rock, the matamata turtle of South America lurks on the river bed patiently waiting for a fish to swim close by. When its prey approaches, it expands its throat and sucks the fish into its gaping mouth.

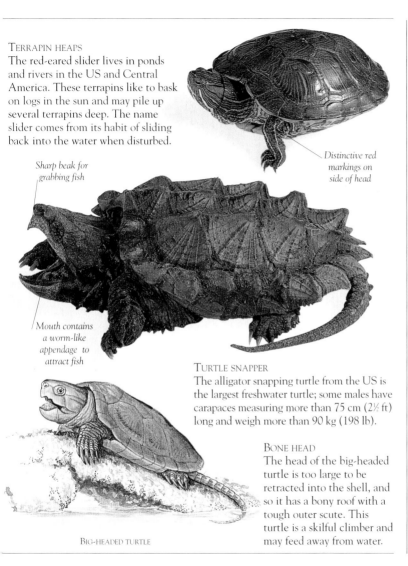

TERRAPIN HEAPS

The red-eared slider lives in ponds and rivers in the US and Central America. These terrapins like to bask on logs in the sun and may pile up several terrapins deep. The name slider comes from its habit of sliding back into the water when disturbed.

Sharp beak for grabbing fish

Distinctive red markings on side of head

Mouth contains a worm-like appendage to attract fish

TURTLE SNAPPER

The alligator snapping turtle from the US is the largest freshwater turtle; some males have carapaces measuring more than 75 cm (2½ ft) long and weigh more than 90 kg (198 lb).

BONE HEAD

The head of the big-headed turtle is too large to be retracted into the shell, and so it has a bony roof with a tough outer scute. This turtle is a skilful climber and may feed away from water.

BIG-HEADED TURTLE

207

More chelonians

Tortoises are among the most popular reptiles, being slow-moving, peaceful herbivores. Species of tortoise that have evolved in isolated places, where predators are few and competition for food is slight, may live to great ages and grow to vast sizes. Freshwater turtles are carnivorous and tend to be much more active.

RED-FOOTED TORTOISE

RED FEET
The red-footed tortoise is common in South America where it lives in rainforests. Large specimens can reach 50 cm (19½ in) in length.

PANCAKE TORTOISES
An African pancake tortoise's shell is light and flattened in shape, enabling it to move quickly and climb over rocks. It can also squeeze into small spaces when danger threatens.

PANCAKE TORTOISE

HINGE-BACK
The hinge-back tortoises of southern Africa have a hinge of cartilaginous tissue that allows the back of the shell to drop and protect the animal's rear. Hinge-backs sometimes share their burrow with lizards.

STARRED CAMOUFLAGE
The starred tortoise is found in India and Sri Lanka. It is well camouflaged; its shell blends in with dry grassland. Less than 25 cm (9½ in) long, it crawls slowly, at little over 0.2 km/h (⅛ mph).

STARRED TORTOISE

Sturdy legs

Shell may be up to 30 cm (1 ft) long

SNAKE-NECK
The snake-necked turtles of Australia live in rivers, where they hunt freshwater animals. However, like all chelonians, they leave the water to lay eggs in a nest on dry land. When threatened, they fold the head back into the shell.

Neck is nearly as long as the shell

SNAKE-NECKED TURTLE

GALÁPAGOS TORTOISE

GALÁPAGOS GIANT
The lumbering giant tortoises of the Galápagos Islands weigh up to 90 kg (198 lb). They were originally present in large numbers, but predation by humans, dogs, and pigs, plus competition for food with goats, have brought about a severe decline in numbers.

CROCODILE ANATOMY

CROCODILES AND ALLIGATORS are the only surviving reptiles from the archosaurs – the group to which the dinosaurs belonged. They are large animals with an armoured skin that covers the whole body. They are usually found in freshwater rivers and lakes in warm regions of the world. Some species enter saltwater as well.

CROCODILE-
BONE
FIGURINE

Powerful tail

CROCODILE BONE
Animal bones have often been used to make ornaments. This Egyptian figurine was carved from a crocodile bone.

NILE CROCODILE
The Nile crocodile is found in many parts of Africa, although its range has been much reduced due to hunting. It often swims out to sea, and so is also found in Madagascar.

ANATOMY FACTS

• A crocodile's skin is composed of partly ossified (converted into bone) horny plates.

• Crocodilians propel themselves through the water with their powerful tail.

SKELETON
Like all crocodilians, a caiman has a long skull, with nostrils and eyes set high. The body is long with two pairs of short legs held out sideways from the body.

Hind feet with four toes

Tail vertebrae

210

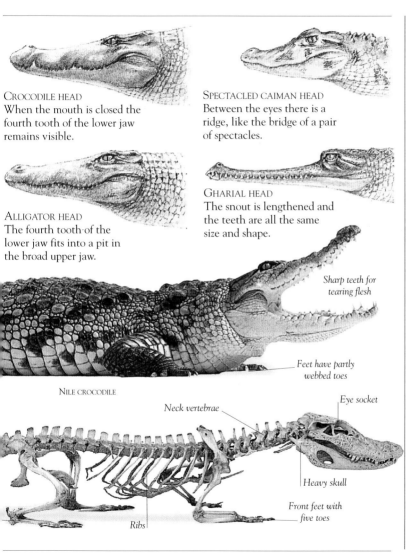

CROCODILE HEAD
When the mouth is closed the fourth tooth of the lower jaw remains visible.

SPECTACLED CAIMAN HEAD
Between the eyes there is a ridge, like the bridge of a pair of spectacles.

ALLIGATOR HEAD
The fourth tooth of the lower jaw fits into a pit in the broad upper jaw.

GHARIAL HEAD
The snout is lengthened and the teeth are all the same size and shape.

Sharp teeth for tearing flesh

Feet have partly webbed toes

NILE CROCODILE

Neck vertebrae

Eye socket

Heavy skull

Front feet with five toes

Ribs

CROCODILES

CROCODILES ARE FOUND in many tropical parts of the world. Large species include the American crocodile and the Nile crocodile, which reach about 6 m (20 ft) in length, and the saltwater crocodile, which can exceed 7 m (23 ft). Smaller species include the mugger of Sri Lanka and India, and Johnston's crocodile of Australia.

Prominent tooth

SKULL
A crocodile's skull is almost solid bone. The jaws are long, for holding prey, but the teeth cannot slice or chew, only tear.

SALTWATER TRAVELLER
The estuarine or saltwater crocodile can be found in coastal waters, in the brackish waters of estuaries, and some way inland up freshwater rivers. It is a strong swimmer, and sometimes travels long distances by sea.

Eye socket

CROCODILE SKULL
(TOP VIEW)

Female guards young in mouth

SHARING A MEAL
In Africa, crocodiles feed mostly on antelopes, which are seized as they come near the water to drink. However, other animals are also taken and crocodiles will feed on animals that have died, such as this zebra.

LYING IN WAIT
Even large animals, such as wildebeest, may fall victim to a crocodile attack. With a sudden rush the crocodile grabs the prey in its jaws and drags it into the water to drown.

UNLIKELY PARTNERS
As a crocodile lies with its mouth open, to keep cool, a spur-winged plover picks food from between its teeth. This looks dangerous for the bird, but the crocodile may benefit from having its teeth cleaned and the plover's cry warns the crocodile of danger.

ESTUARINE
CROCODILE

Crocodiles

An adult crocodile swallows stones, which accumulate in its stomach. The stones do not break up food, but scientists believe that they may act as ballast, allowing the animal to remain submerged under the water.

CROCODILE SKIN

NILE CROCODILE

CRACKING EGGS
When her eggs are about to hatch, the female uncovers them. She may gently crack them to help the young emerge.

SHOES AND HANDBAGS
Formerly many wild crocodiles and alligators were hunted for their skins, used for making shoes, handbags, and suitcases. Wild crocodiles are now protected, but are still illegally killed.

CROCODILE FACTS

• A saltwater crocodile arrived at the Cocos Islands in the Indian Ocean, having swum 1,100 km (684 miles).

• The ancient Egyptians worshipped a crocodile-headed god named Sebek.

ESTUARINE CROCODILE

CROCODILE TEARS
The estuarine crocodile gets rid of the excess salt it swallows with its food by excreting it via the tear glands in its eyes.

THE GHARIAL

The family Gavialidae contains just one species, the gharial, or Indian gavial. The Gavialidae is thought to have arisen during the Cretaceous period, some 100 million years ago. The modern gharial has rather weak limbs and spends nearly all its life in water, using its oar-like tail for swimming. It lives in India's Ganges, Mahanadi, Chambl, and Brahmaputra rivers, the Karnali River in Nepal, and the Koladan and Maingtha rivers in Southeast Asia.

GHARIAL SKULL (TOP VIEW)

Holes allow space for jaw muscles to expand when feeding

Eye socket

Nasal opening

LONG SNOUT
The main characteristic of the gharial is its long snout. At the tip it widens into an oval area that bears the nostrils; in males this region is bulbous. Each jaw contains more than 50 sharp teeth.

NO PROTECTION
For a long time, the gharial was protected from hunters because it was sacred to the Hindu god Vishnu. Today, however, it is illegally hunted for its skin.

FISH FEEDER
The gharial feeds entirely on fish. It lies in wait, moving its head from side to side to cover a large area, and catches its prey with a sudden jerk of its head.

ALLIGATORS AND CAIMANS

ALLIGATORS AND CAIMANS have shorter snouts than crocodiles, and they live solely in freshwater. There are two species of alligator, the American alligator and the rare Chinese alligator. The six species of caiman are all found in the Americas, ranging from Mexico down through much of South America.

SECURE FUTURE
American alligators were once killed in large numbers for their skins, but since they became a protected species in the 1960s, their populations have recovered. Today, they are the only crocodilians not endangered in the wild.

AMERICAN ALLIGATOR

Males bellow during breeding season to attract females

SKULL
An alligator's skull is shorter and broader than a crocodile's. The fearsome jaws can carry young with surprising delicacy.

HUNTED DOWN
American alligators are opportunist feeders, taking whatever they can, including fish, snakes, turtles, mammals, and waterbirds snatched from low branches.

CAIMAN ENEMIES

Adult spectacled caimans have few natural enemies, apart from anacondas, which can devour caimans up to 2 m (6½ ft) long, and egg-thieves such as tegu lizards, which raid their nests.

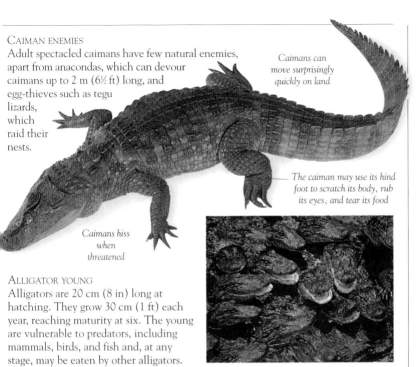

Caimans can move surprisingly quickly on land

The caiman may use its hind foot to scratch its body, rub its eyes, and tear its food

Caimans hiss when threatened

ALLIGATOR YOUNG

Alligators are 20 cm (8 in) long at hatching. They grow 30 cm (1 ft) each year, reaching maturity at six. The young are vulnerable to predators, including mammals, birds, and fish and, at any stage, may be eaten by other alligators.

YOUNG ALLIGATORS

Adults may catch raccoons and small deer

ALLIGATOR FACTS

• The English word "alligator" comes from the Spanish for lizard, "el largato".

• The Chinese alligator is nearly extinct in the wild due to hunting and the destruction of its habitat.

LIZARD ANATOMY

THE FIRST LIZARDS appeared 200 million years ago, in the Triassic period. They fed on insects and looked similar to modern lizards. Typically, a lizard has a broad head, a long, slender body with limbs held out sideways, and a long tail. However, there are more specialized forms, such as chameleons and legless lizards.

ANATOMY OF A FEMALE LIZARD

Heart

Lungs

Ovary

Intestine

Opening of cloaca

INTERNAL ANATOMY
A lizard's body is symmetrically arranged both externally and internally. As in nearly all reptiles, the heart has three chambers and the gut, oviduct, and ureter empty into a common chamber, the cloaca.

UNUSUAL LIZARD
A chameleon does not have the flexible spine of most lizards. In addition, its legs are proportionately longer, and it can raise its body higher than other lizards.

Spine is less flexible than other lizards'

Prehensile tail for gripping onto branches

CHAMELEON SKELETON

Broad body with many ribs

Toes designed for grasping

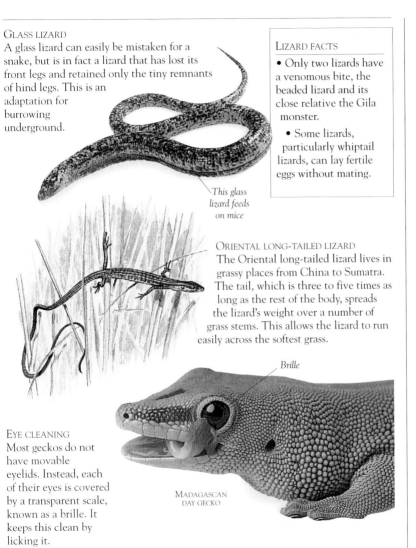

GLASS LIZARD
A glass lizard can easily be mistaken for a snake, but is in fact a lizard that has lost its front legs and retained only the tiny remnants of hind legs. This is an adaptation for burrowing underground.

This glass lizard feeds on mice

LIZARD FACTS
• Only two lizards have a venomous bite, the beaded lizard and its close relative the Gila monster.

• Some lizards, particularly whiptail lizards, can lay fertile eggs without mating.

ORIENTAL LONG-TAILED LIZARD
The Oriental long-tailed lizard lives in grassy places from China to Sumatra. The tail, which is three to five times as long as the rest of the body, spreads the lizard's weight over a number of grass stems. This allows the lizard to run easily across the softest grass.

Brille

EYE CLEANING
Most geckos do not have movable eyelids. Instead, each of their eyes is covered by a transparent scale, known as a brille. It keeps this clean by licking it.

MADAGASCAN DAY GECKO

219

How lizards feed

SOME LIZARDS eat almost anything; others, such as the plant-eating Galápagos iguanas, have a specialized diet. Many lizards prey on insects, and some of them also eat vegetable matter. Some species prey on other animals, such as birds, small mammals, and other lizards.

VEGETARIAN
The Galápagos land iguana feeds only on plants, particularly the fleshy leaves and fruits of the prickly pear cactus. It deals with the spines by working the food around in its mouth until they break off.

GALÁPAGOS LAND IGUANA

CHAMELEON

Insect trapped in sticky mucus

Muscular tongue is as long as the lizard's body

STICKY TONGUE
A chameleon moves very slowly and deliberately towards its potential prey. When within range, it shoots out its long, muscular tongue at incredible speed. The insect is trapped on the end of the lizard's sticky tongue and drawn into its mouth.

EYED LIZARD

CATCHING INSECTS

The eyed lizard feeds on insects, small birds, rodents, other lizards, and some fruits. A large prey item is shaken rapidly to stun it and then passed to the back of the lizard's mouth. It is then crushed by the jaws in a series of rapid, powerful snaps.

The eyed lizard is native to southern Europe and North Africa

ANT EATER

Despite its fierce appearance, the Australian thorny devil, or moloch, lives solely on ants, which it eats in large quantities. It obtains much of its water from dew, which condenses on its spines and runs into its mouth.

THORNY DEVIL

KOMODO DRAGON

PREDATORY DRAGON

The huge Komodo dragon is a large monitor lizard found only on a few Indonesian islands. The lizard mostly eats carrion, but it is capable of catching and killing animals up to the size of a big deer.

FEEDING FACTS

• The caiman lizards of South America feed almost exclusively on marsh snails.

• The Galápagos marine iguana eats only seaweed, which it grazes from the seabed, sometimes diving for long periods to feed.

221

THE WORLD'S LIZARDS

BECAUSE THEY ARE COLD-BLOODED and use their environment to maintain body temperature, lizards prefer warm climates. Thus most species occur in tropical and subtropical regions. There are 17–26 recognized families (different experts have different opinions), the largest being the skinks (about 1,000 species), the geckos (800 species), and the agamids (300 species).

GECKO

Large toes with hooked pads

MARINE IGUANA

OCEAN-LOVING LIZARD
The Galápagos marine iguana uses its robust, flattened tail to swim in coastal waters. It has glands in its nose for excreting excess salt taken in from seawater.

HOUSE GUEST
Pads on the gecko's feet help it cling to any surface. Geckos can often be seen hunting for insects on walls in the tropics.

LIZARD FACTS

• Some lizards do live in temperate climates, for example the common lizard and slow worm of Britain.

• On some West Indian islands, there can be more than 20,000 anole lizards per hectare.

MADAGASCAN
DAY GECKO

FOREST
DWELLER
This gecko's bright green coloration is perfect camouflage for its home – the forests of Madagascar. Unlike most geckos, it hunts during the day.

IN THE JUNGLE

Some rainforest iguanas are slender animals with long toes. Males are often larger and more brightly coloured than the females. In some cases, the colours become more apparent during the breeding season.

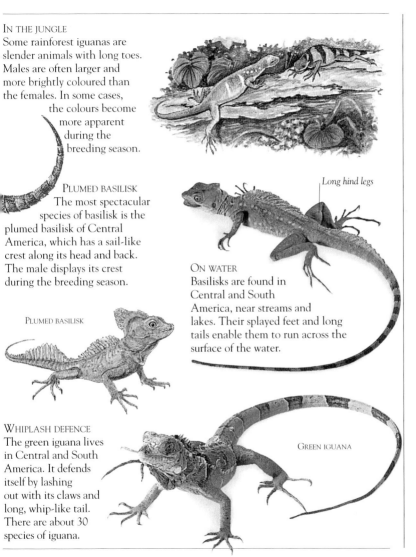

PLUMED BASILISK

The most spectacular species of basilisk is the plumed basilisk of Central America, which has a sail-like crest along its head and back. The male displays its crest during the breeding season.

PLUMED BASILISK

Long hind legs

ON WATER

Basilisks are found in Central and South America, near streams and lakes. Their splayed feet and long tails enable them to run across the surface of the water.

WHIPLASH DEFENCE

The green iguana lives in Central and South America. It defends itself by lashing out with its claws and long, whip-like tail. There are about 30 species of iguana.

GREEN IGUANA

223

The Agamid family

Agamids, of which there are about 300 species, are found in central, south, and Southeast Asia, Australia, and Africa. The only species found in Europe is the starred lizard, or hardun, which lives on some Greek islands, in North Africa, and in southwest Asia. Many species spend their lives in the branches of trees, but agamids have adapted to a wide range of habitats. Some species live at high altitudes; *Laudakia tuberculata* is found on Himalayan slopes at 3,300 m (10,800ft).

GARDEN LIZARD

BLOODSUCKER
Like a chameleon, the garden lizard, or blood-sucker, can change colour rapidly. It is found in India, Afghanistan, and China.

Large scales protect underside of jaw

BEARDED DRAGON
Some seven species of Australian lizard are known as bearded dragons because of the long, pointed scales on their throats.

BEARDED DRAGON

THORNY DEVIL

Spines provide excellent defence

HOT AND SPINY
The thorny devil, or moloch, is an Australian desert dweller. It allows its body to heat up to an almost lethal temperature so that it can spend as much time as possible feeding in the open.

SPINY TAIL
Spiny-tailed lizards tolerate very high temperatures and are among the hardiest lizards of the African Sahara. They feed on plants and insects and survive on the moisture they obtain from their food and from dew.

Channels between scales guide water condensed from the air towards the mouth

"Eyebrows" protect eyes from twigs and leaves

Spiny tail is used for defence and acts as a fat store

SPINY-TAILED LIZARD

Dorsal crest of pointed scales

PRICKLY NECK
The pricklenape agama lives high in the trees in mountain forests from China to Indonesia. Its name comes from the long, sharp spines on its neck. Its long toes have fringed scales that help it cling to branches.

PRICKLENAPE AGAMA

WATER DRAGON
The Thai water dragon lives mainly in trees beside rivers and lakes. It usually basks on a branch overhanging the water. When threatened by a predator, it simply drops from its branch into the water and swims away.

THAI WATER DRAGON

Long rear legs for rapid movement

More lizards of the world

Many lizards are specially adapted for particular environments.
A chameleon's body, for example, is greatly modified for living in
trees. The body is flattened from side to
side, a shape that helps the reptile
avoid the heat of the sun during the
hottest part of the day, but absorb
heat in the early morning and
late evening. It also helps to
camouflage the body and
makes it easier to balance
on the branches of trees.

CHAMELEON
Chameleons have pincer-like toes
for gripping branches. The largest
species, found in Madagascar, may
be over 60 cm (2 ft) in length.

TREE SKINK
Emoid skinks are found in
the Indo-Pacific region.
Many, including this one,
are tree-dwellers. The
long, slender body is
designed for scuttling
rapidly over tree branches.

Long tail helps balance

Chameleon species vary greatly in size

EMOID SKINK

Colour makes skink hard to see among trees

THREE HORNS
Jackson's chameleon
is found around
Mt. Kenya in Africa.
Males have horns or crests on
their heads. They use them in
fights with other males over territory.

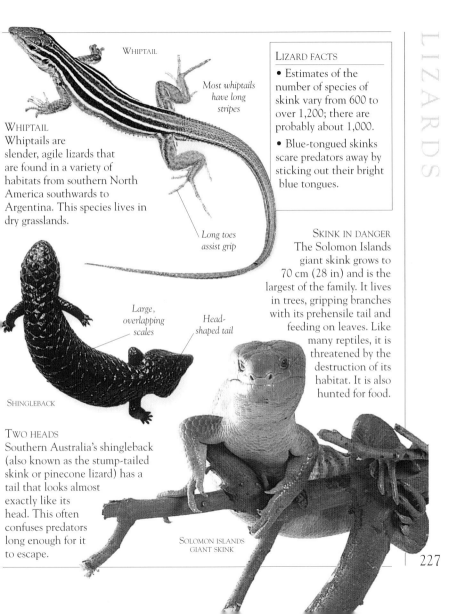

WHIPTAIL

Most whiptails have long stripes

WHIPTAIL
Whiptails are slender, agile lizards that are found in a variety of habitats from southern North America southwards to Argentina. This species lives in dry grasslands.

Long toes assist grip

LIZARD FACTS
• Estimates of the number of species of skink vary from 600 to over 1,200; there are probably about 1,000.

• Blue-tongued skinks scare predators away by sticking out their bright blue tongues.

Large, overlapping scales

Head-shaped tail

SHINGLEBACK

SKINK IN DANGER
The Solomon Islands giant skink grows to 70 cm (28 in) and is the largest of the family. It lives in trees, gripping branches with its prehensile tail and feeding on leaves. Like many reptiles, it is threatened by the destruction of its habitat. It is also hunted for food.

TWO HEADS
Southern Australia's shingleback (also known as the stump-tailed skink or pinecone lizard) has a tail that looks almost exactly like its head. This often confuses predators long enough for it to escape.

SOLOMON ISLANDS GIANT SKINK

Lizard protection

For a small animal that lives in the open, a scaly skin affords only limited protection, and so some lizards have additional protective features. Girdle-tailed lizards and their relatives are well armoured, and the armadillo lizard makes good defensive use of its spines. The beaded lizard and the Gila monster defend themselves with venom, while some monitor lizards find protection in their sheer size.

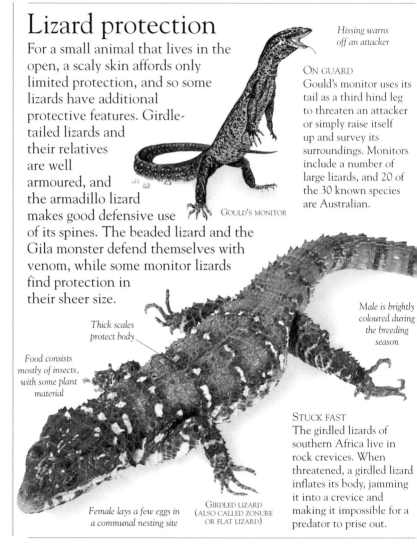

Hissing warns off an attacker

ON GUARD
Gould's monitor uses its tail as a third hind leg to threaten an attacker or simply raise itself up and survey its surroundings. Monitors include a number of large lizards, and 20 of the 30 known species are Australian.

GOULD'S MONITOR

Male is brightly coloured during the breeding season

Thick scales protect body

Food consists mostly of insects, with some plant material

STUCK FAST
The girdled lizards of southern Africa live in rock crevices. When threatened, a girdled lizard inflates its body, jamming it into a crevice and making it impossible for a predator to prise out.

Female lays a few eggs in a communal nesting site

GIRDLED LIZARD
(ALSO CALLED ZONURE OR FLAT LIZARD)

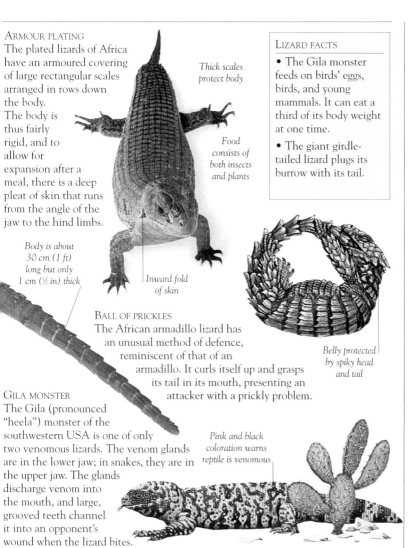

ARMOUR PLATING

The plated lizards of Africa have an armoured covering of large rectangular scales arranged in rows down the body. The body is thus fairly rigid, and to allow for expansion after a meal, there is a deep pleat of skin that runs from the angle of the jaw to the hind limbs.

Thick scales protect body

Food consists of both insects and plants

Body is about 30 cm (1 ft) long but only 1 cm (½ in) thick

Inward fold of skin

LIZARD FACTS

- The Gila monster feeds on birds' eggs, birds, and young mammals. It can eat a third of its body weight at one time.

- The giant girdle-tailed lizard plugs its burrow with its tail.

Belly protected by spiky head and tail

BALL OF PRICKLES

The African armadillo lizard has an unusual method of defence, reminiscent of that of an armadillo. It curls itself up and grasps its tail in its mouth, presenting an attacker with a prickly problem.

GILA MONSTER

The Gila (pronounced "heela") monster of the southwestern USA is one of only two venomous lizards. The venom glands are in the lower jaw; in snakes, they are in the upper jaw. The glands discharge venom into the mouth, and large, grooved teeth channel it into an opponent's wound when the lizard bites.

Pink and black coloration warns reptile is venomous

TUATARAS

THE TWO SPECIES OF TUATARA look like lizards, but they have a different structure to their skeleton and skull. Tuataras are the sole survivors of the rhynchocephalians, a group of primitive reptile that thrived between 100 and 200 million years ago during the Jurassic and Triassic periods.

Tuatara is Maori for "peaks on the back"

LIVING FOSSIL
Tuataras are called living fossils because they have changed little in 200 million years. All their closest relatives died out; no one knows why tuataras alone survived.

LONG LIFE
Male tuataras grow to about 61 cm (2 ft) long, while females are slightly shorter. Both sexes reach sexual maturity at the age of 20, and may live for another 100 years.

FOSSILIZED RELATIVE
Homoeosaurus, an extinct relative of tuataras, lived about 140 million years ago. Rhynchocephalians were widespread and successful at the time.

MALE TUATARA

Short, powerful legs for burrowing

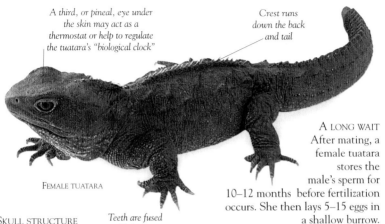

A third, or pineal, eye under the skin may act as a thermostat or help to regulate the tuatara's "biological clock"

Crest runs down the back and tail

FEMALE TUATARA

A LONG WAIT
After mating, a female tuatara stores the male's sperm for 10–12 months before fertilization occurs. She then lays 5–15 eggs in a shallow burrow.

SKULL STRUCTURE
The tuatara skull is very different from that of a lizard. It resembles a crocodile's in having two bony arches at the back. Most lizards have just one arch, while in burrowing lizards and snakes the arches have disappeared.

Teeth are fused with the jaws

Two bony arches

Tuatara have large, wedge-shaped teeth at the front

TUATARA SKULL

ISLAND HOME
Tuataras are found on a few small islands off the coast of New Zealand. They live in burrows (which they often share with seabirds) and are active at night, when they come out to search for insects and earthworms. They grow very slowly.

TUATARA FACTS
• Eggs hatch 15 months after laying – the longest incubation period of any reptile.

• A tuatara breathes very slowly, about once every seven seconds, and can hold its breath for nearly an hour.

231

SNAKE ANATOMY

SNAKES ARE PROBABLY descended from burrowing lizards that gradually lost their legs as they adapted to an underground life. Today's snakes do not generally live underground, but they have retained their ancestral form and found new ways of getting around.

RHINOCEROS VIPER

VENOMOUS RHINO
Like all snakes, the deadly African rhinoceros viper has a long, legless body. Its name comes from the rhino-like "horns" (actually long scales) on its nose.

INSIDE A SNAKE
A snake's body is long and thin, so the stomach, liver, kidneys, and ovaries are greatly elongated, as is the right lung; the left lung is very small. The intestines form a long tube straight down the body.

SNAKE FACTS

• The longest snakes have skeletons with some 400 vertebrae.

• King cobras may be able to detect some airborne sounds.

• Some snakes use part of the windpipe as an extra lung.

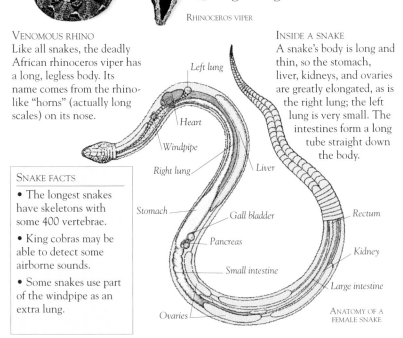

Left lung

Heart

Windpipe

Right lung

Liver

Stomach

Gall bladder

Pancreas

Small intestine

Ovaries

Rectum

Kidney

Large intestine

ANATOMY OF A
FEMALE SNAKE

SNAKE SKELETON

A snake has a very long, flexible backbone, made up of at least 180 vertebrae. All the neck and trunk vertebrae have strong ribs, which are not attached at the front so that the snake is free to swallow large items of food.

Neck vertebrae

Trunk vertebrae

Skull

Tail vertebrae

Ribs

PYTHON SKELETON

Backward-pointing teeth help move prey down the gullet

SNAKE SKULL AND JAWS

Joints loosely held together by ligaments

Lower jaw bones are not joined

SNAKE SKULL

The upper jaw is loosely attached to the rest of the skull, and the two halves of the lower jaw are separated. This makes a wide opening possible for swallowing prey whole.

TEMPTATION

Because of their slithery nature, snakes have long been regarded as evil. In the Bible, a snake tempted Eve to eat from the Tree of Knowledge, destroying her innocence and causing her and Adam to be banished from the Garden of Eden.

THE SERPENT TEMPTS EVE

CONSTRICTORS

BOAS AND PYTHONS are constricting snakes – they kill by wrapping prey so tightly in their strong body coils that the animal suffocates. Their victims are usually mammals, but many constrictors kill birds as well, and some are known to prey on other reptiles.

The coils tighten each time the rat breathes out

BALL PYTHON

DEADLY SQUEEZE
This West African ball python is killing its prey, a rat, by coiling itself around the animal's chest and gradually tightening its grip. Soon, the rat will not be able to inhale, and it will die from suffocation.

BIRDS
BEWARE
Tree boas hunt birds by creeping up on them as they roost in the branches of trees; mammals are also eaten. The emerald tree boa lives in the lush rainforests of the Amazon basin.

EMERALD TREE BOA

PRIMITIVE SNAKES
Scientists call pythons, boas, and some other species "primitive" because these snakes have tiny claws where the hind legs and hips of their lizard ancestors once were. The claws lie on either side of the cloaca. Males use them to stimulate females into mating.

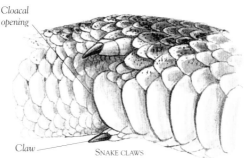

Cloacal opening

Claw

SNAKE CLAWS

HOW A CONSTRICTOR CONSUMES ITS PREY

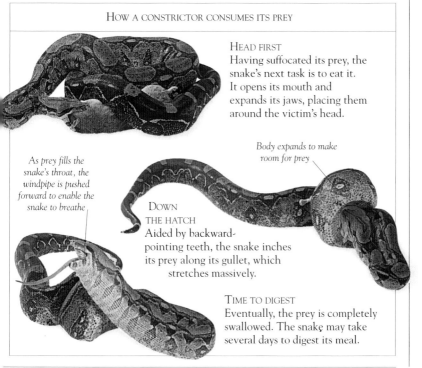

HEAD FIRST
Having suffocated its prey, the snake's next task is to eat it. It opens its mouth and expands its jaws, placing them around the victim's head.

Body expands to make room for prey

As prey fills the snake's throat, the windpipe is pushed forward to enable the snake to breathe

DOWN
THE HATCH
Aided by backward-pointing teeth, the snake inches its prey along its gullet, which stretches massively.

TIME TO DIGEST
Eventually, the prey is completely swallowed. The snake may take several days to digest its meal.

Boas

Most species of boa are found in the Americas and the Caribbean, although boas can also be found in Africa, Madagascar, Europe, and the Pacific region. These constrictors have adapted to a wide variety of habitats. Many spend their lives in trees, while a number of others live on the ground or burrow into it.

RUSCHENBERGER'S TREE BOA

RAINBOW COLOURS
The dazzlingly iridescent rainbow boa lives in the forests, woodlands, and grassy plains of northwestern South America. It feeds on small mammals and birds.

RAINBOW BOA

RED-TAILED BOA

BOA CONSTRICTOR
The red-tailed boa is one of 10 subspecies of boa constrictor. It grows to an average of 3 m (10 ft) in length (although snakes over 4 m [13 ft] have been seen), and lives in the semidesert plains of northwestern Peru.

RUSCHENBERGER'S TREE BOA
This snake is the largest of the four species of South American tree boa. The highly sensitive heat pits on the boa's lips enable it to hunt warm-blooded animals in total darkness, and even to catch bats on the wing.

SOLOMON ISLANDS GROUND BOA

BOA FACTS

• When a rubber boa is threatened, it rolls itself into a ball, hides its head among its coils, and presents its tail towards the intruder.

• Boas do not hatch from eggs. Instead, females give birth to live young.

SOLOMON ISLANDS GROUND BOA

Found in the rainforests and plantations of islands in the southwestern Pacific, this nocturnal snake lives and hunts on the ground. It is relatively inactive, and spends most of the time hidden under logs or leaf litter waiting to ambush prey.

AMAZON TREE BOA

AGILE TREE DWELLER

This South American tree boa, or garden boa, uses its prehensile tail to cling to the branches of trees. Although the Amazon tree boa is not venomous, it can inflict a painful bite.

RUBBER ROBBER

The North American rubber boa lives in woodlands and meadows, where it hunts among fallen logs, in crevices, or down burrows. It also climbs trees to steal young birds from their nests. This snake looks and feels rubbery, hence its name.

RUBBER BOA

More constrictors

Pythons, from Australasia, Africa, and Asia, and anacondas (aquatic boas), from South America, are some of the world's biggest snakes. On very rare occasions, anacondas, rock pythons, and reticulated pythons have been known to attack people. But eating such a huge meal is risky, since the snake is defenceless for at least a week while it digests its food.

Distinctive "piano key" lip markings

D'ALBERTIS PYTHON

HUNTER IN THE TREES
D'Albertis python, which can reach 2.4 m (8 ft) long, hunts small mammals at night. It lives in New Guinea and on neighbouring islands in a range of habitats, but it prefers damp environments such as monsoon forests and rainforests.

RETICULATED PYTHON

LARGEST PYTHON
The reticulated python of Southeast Asia is well camouflaged for life on the forest floor. It may grow to 10 m (33 ft) in length, making it the longest snake in the world. It feeds on mammals, lizards and the occasional snake.

SHORT AND BLOODY
The blood python, or short-tailed python, gets its name from its colourful camouflage markings. It is also known as the short python because its tail is much shorter than those of other species. It lives in wet places on the central and southern Malay peninsula and on the islands of Borneo and Sumatra.

BLOOD PYTHON

HUNTED FOR ITS SKIN

The Indian python lives in a wide range of habitats, feeding on mammals, birds, and reptiles. It is now an endangered species because people have slaughtered it for its skin and destroyed much of its natural habitat.

Skin is used to make belts and shoes

INDIAN PYTHON

ANACONDAS

YELLOW ANACONDA

SWAMP SNAKE

The yellow anaconda lives in swamps and marshes and on the banks of rivers and streams in Brazil, Bolivia, Paraguay, and Argentina. At 3.5 m (11½ ft) in length, it is about half the size of the common anaconda.

RECORD HOLDER

The common anaconda is probably the world's largest snake, being heavier than its rival for the title, the reticulated python. The average adult length is about 6 m (20 ft), although individuals of over 8 m (26 ft) have been seen. It is found in Trinidad and many parts of tropical South America.

COMMON ANACONDA

COLUBRID SNAKES

ABOUT THREE-QUARTERS of the world's snakes – over 2,000 species – belong to the colubrid family. Some are venomous, but a large number are completely harmless. Among the harmless ones are kingsnakes, water snakes, ratsnakes, egg-eating snakes, and the grass snake.

CALIFORNIA KINGSNAKE

VARIABLE PATTERNS
The colours and patterns of California kingsnakes vary greatly – individuals may be cross-banded or have stripes running down the body. Kingsnakes eat a wide range of small animals, including venomous snakes.

Markings look similar to a coral snake's

CALIFORNIA MOUNTAIN KINGSNAKE

COLUBRID FACTS

• The Japanese ratsnake, or Aodaisho, is considered to be an earthly form of a fertility goddess called Benzai-ten.

• Scientists call colubrids "typical" snakes.

MOUNTAIN KINGS
California mountain kingsnakes prey on small animals, including rodents, lizards, and nestling birds. When not hunting, they often hide under stones, logs, or piles of leaves. They come from the west coast of the USA.

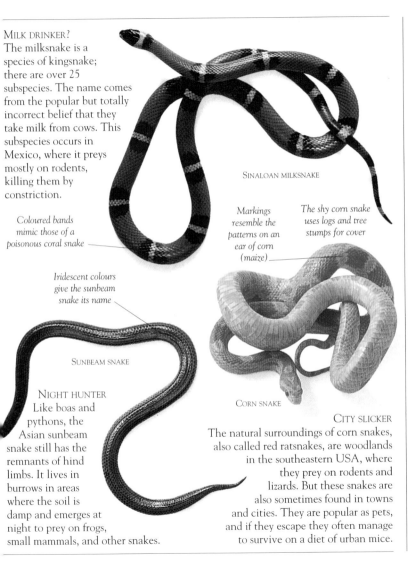

MILK DRINKER?
The milksnake is a species of kingsnake; there are over 25 subspecies. The name comes from the popular but totally incorrect belief that they take milk from cows. This subspecies occurs in Mexico, where it preys mostly on rodents, killing them by constriction.

Coloured bands mimic those of a poisonous coral snake

SINALOAN MILKSNAKE

Markings resemble the patterns on an ear of corn (maize)

The shy corn snake uses logs and tree stumps for cover

Iridescent colours give the sunbeam snake its name

SUNBEAM SNAKE

CORN SNAKE

NIGHT HUNTER
Like boas and pythons, the Asian sunbeam snake still has the remnants of hind limbs. It lives in burrows in areas where the soil is damp and emerges at night to prey on frogs, small mammals, and other snakes.

CITY SLICKER
The natural surroundings of corn snakes, also called red ratsnakes, are woodlands in the southeastern USA, where they prey on rodents and lizards. But these snakes are also sometimes found in towns and cities. They are popular as pets, and if they escape they often manage to survive on a diet of urban mice.

241

More colubrid snakes

Non-venomous colubrid snakes kill either by constriction or by overpowering and swallowing the victim. For defence, they usually rely on camouflage and the ability to escape quickly. Many will try to scare off attackers by vibrating their tails against leaves. Bullsnakes inflate their bodies to make a prolonged aggressive hiss, while red-tailed racers puff themselves up to appear more formidable.

MOELLENDORFF'S
RATSNAKE

Flower-like patterns give this snake its Chinese name

COLUBRID FACTS

• When threatened ratsnakes vibrate their tails, they are often mistaken for rattlesnakes.

• In the USA, farmers sometimes use bullsnakes to catch rats and mice in barns.

FLOWERY SNAKE
Moellendorff's ratsnake, known poetically as the "hundred flower snake" in Chinese, comes from southeastern China, where it feeds on rodents and birds.

VIPERINE
WATERSNAKE

Markings look like an adder's

HARMLESS VIPER
The viperine watersnake from Spain has warning markings that resemble those of a venomous adder. It is actually completely harmless, although it may launch mock strikes with its mouth closed. A good swimmer, it feeds on fish and frogs.

BAT CATCHER
The fast-moving red-tailed
racer lives in the rainforests of
Southeast Asia. It preys on
birds and small mammals,
including bats, which it
snatches as they fly out to
feed. The victims are
suffocated by the snake's
muscular coils. When
threatened, it inflates
its body to look larger
than normal.

RED-TAILED
RACER

SPECIAL SPIKES
The egg-eating
snake's backbone
has about 30
ventral spikes, which
are used for breaking
up eggs inside the
snake's body.

EGG-EATER'S SPINE — *Ventral spikes*

EGG-EATER
Egg-eating snakes are virtually
toothless and have unusually
elastic skins.
This enables
them to
swallow a whole
egg, which is crushed
inside the body. About
15 minutes later, the
snake ejects the shell
remains from its mouth.

*Egg may be up to three
times the size of the
snake's mouth*

AFRICAN EGG-EATING SNAKE

243

VENOMOUS SNAKES

VENOM – a poisonous fluid produced by an animal – is widely used for killing or incapacitating prey. Snake venom, which is a very complex substance, serves two main purposes. First, the poison quickly subdues a prey animal, thus reducing the risk to the snake of injury from retaliation. At the same time, chemicals within the venom start to break down the prey's tissues, making digestion easier.

KING COBRA

FIXED FANGS
Cobras have fixed fangs at the front of the mouth, as do kraits, sea snakes, coral snakes, the taipan, and the tiger snake.

WARNING RATTLE
A rattlesnake is a typical front-fanged snake. As it opens its mouth the snake rotates its fangs forwards, ready to inject venom. The snake's first line of defence is to vibrate its rattle. If that does not deter the attacker, it delivers a deadly bite.

Fangs are in forward position, ready to strike

Fangs normally lie flat inside the mouth

Rattle warns off predators

RATTLESNAKE

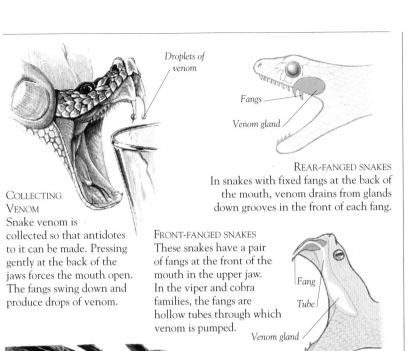

Droplets of venom

Fangs

Venom gland

COLLECTING VENOM

Snake venom is collected so that antidotes to it can be made. Pressing gently at the back of the jaws forces the mouth open. The fangs swing down and produce drops of venom.

REAR-FANGED SNAKES

In snakes with fixed fangs at the back of the mouth, venom drains from glands down grooves in the front of each fang.

FRONT-FANGED SNAKES

These snakes have a pair of fangs at the front of the mouth in the upper jaw. In the viper and cobra families, the fangs are hollow tubes through which venom is pumped.

Fang

Tube

Venom gland

VARIABLE VIPERS

The bush vipers of Central Africa are found in rainforests, open woodland, and swamps. Their coloration is extremely variable and may be anything from pale green to reddish brown.

VENOMOUS FACTS

• The king cobra is the only snake that builds a nest in which to place its eggs.

• The eastern diamondback is the largest rattlesnake. It can grow to about 2.5 m (8 ft).

REAR-FANGED SNAKES

SNAKES WITH FANGS in the back of their mouth are found in both the Old and New Worlds and, as with other groups of snakes, they vary greatly in colour, size, and habitat. They are not as efficient as front-fanged snakes at injecting venom, and so most species are harmless to humans. Large rear-fanged snakes, however, can be dangerous.

Large, light-grey eyes with vertical pupils resemble those of cats

FOREST DWELLER
The false coral snake preys on lizards, small mammals, and other small snakes. It is found in the forests of Central America, from Venezuela to Costa Rica.

FALSE CORAL SNAKE

Colours are similar to those of the more dangerous coral snakes

MANGROVE SNAKE
In the mangrove swamps of the Malay Peninsula, this long snake – adults grow to over 2 m (6½ ft) – preys on a wide variety of small animals. Its large head and mouth enable it to swallow birds' eggs and even squirrels.

LIZARD HUNTER
The blunt-headed tree snake is found in trees and shrubs from southern Mexico to Bolivia and Paraguay. It is active by night and feeds mostly on lizards such as anoles and geckos.

PARROT
SNAKE

*Gaping mouth
is a warning
to enemies*

BLUNT-HEADED TREESNAKE

BOLD BITER
When threatened, a parrot snake raises its head and opens its mouth. This is no idle threat, since parrot snakes are very aggressive and will bite readily. They hunt lizards and amphibians in the dense foliage of the rainforests of Central and South America.

TREE-TOP KILLER
The green catsnake lives in the forests of Southeast Asia. It hunts at night for lizards, other snakes, and small mammals, which it easily subdues with a combination of venom and constriction.

*Slender and camouflaged
for life in the tree-tops*

GREEN
CATSNAKE

More rear-fanged snakes

Many rear-fanged snakes use weak venom to kill small animals such as lizards or frogs. Sometimes the venom is specific to a particular prey – the venom of a snake that usually eats frogs may be more toxic to frogs than to other animals, such as mice. Some rear-fanged species have stronger venom. The boomslang and the African twigsnake, for example, occasionally kill people.

HOG-NOSED BURROWER
The Madagascan giant hognose snake eats birds and small mammals. It shelters in rock crevices, beneath debris, or in burrows that it digs itself. It lives in grassland and grows to about 1.5 m (5 ft).

When threatened, this snake flattens its neck like a cobra and hisses loudly

MADAGASCAN GIANT HOGNOSE SNAKE

SONORAN LYRE SNAKE

REAR-FANGED FACTS

• The mussurana first constricts its prey, then injects venom into it.

• The Australasian brown tree snake, introduced into Guam, has caused the decline of many native birds.

LYRE HEAD
Lyre snakes get their name from the lyre-shaped marking on the head. They live in rocky places in California, Arizona, and Mexico, feeding on lizards, small birds, and mammals. They are nocturnal.

FROG-EATER

The American cat-eyed snake spends most of its time in trees and hunts at night for frogs and lizards. It often feeds on eggs laid on leaves by frogs. Cat-eyed snakes are found from the US down into northern South America.

AMERICAN CAT-EYED SNAKE
EATING FROGS' EGGS

Vine snake hangs from a branch, waiting for prey

VINE CREEPER

The green vine snake's camouflage allows it to creep unseen among vines and branches. Ranging from southern Mexico to Argentina, it eats frogs, mice, and lizards, and is particularly skilled at catching birds. In some areas, it waits by flowers for hummingbirds to arrive to feed.

GREEN
VINE SNAKE

BOOMSLANG

The agile African boomslang moves with speed and grace through woodland, scrub, savanna, and swamp. It uses its quick-acting venom to kill chameleons and birds. The name boomslang is Afrikaans for "tree snake".

249

FRONT FANGS

FRONT-FANGED SNAKES, such as cobras, can inject venom into almost any animal, making them among the most dangerous of all reptiles. As with all venomous snakes, their venom is normally used for killing or disabling prey, but it is equally effective as a defence. However, most snakes usually prefer to escape rather than attack a predator.

HORUS
The Egyptian sky god, Horus, demonstrates his dominion over reptiles by grasping snakes and standing on a crocodile.

RED SPITTING COBRA

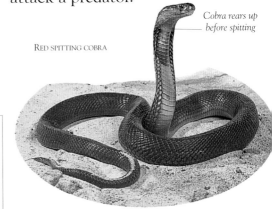

Cobra rears up
before spitting

COBRA FACTS

• Every year, thousands of Asian cobras are killed for their skins.

• The king cobra is the world's largest venomous snake – individuals exceeding 5 m (16½ ft) in length have been recorded.

VENOM SPITTER
A spitting cobra has a very effective method of defence. When threatened, and with no means of escape, it rears up and squirts a jet of poison into the attacker's eyes, causing severe pain and even permanent blindness.

FALSE-EYE MARKING
Some cobras have an eye-
like marking on the back
of their hood that
warns off aggressors.
In Chinese and
monocled cobras it
resembles a monocle;
in the Indian cobra it
looks more like spectacles.

CHINESE COBRA

*Some snake
charmers remove
the cobra's fangs*

*Cobras follow
the instrument's
movements*

*"Eye" is meant to
deter attackers*

*Cobras are active
at dawn and dusk*

SNAKE CHARMER
AND COBRAS

HOODED MENACE
All cobras have a hood,
created by spreading the
neck ribs as the front of the
body is raised off the ground.
This characteristic is
particularly well developed
in Asian species, such as the
monocled, or Thai, cobra.
The snake raises the hood to
scare off enemies.

*A cobra can
move forward
while keeping its
front raised*

CHARMED SNAKES
Snake charmers in Asia and North Africa
have long induced cobras to "dance" to their
tunes. The snakes, however, are deaf and are
probably reacting to the swaying movements
of the instrument, not to the music.

*The hood is
spread as the
body is raised*

MONOCLED,
OR THAI, COBRA

251

Vipers

With their long, hollow fangs, vipers
and their close relatives, the pit vipers,
are among the most dangerous snakes
in the world. When one of these
snakes opens its mouth to bite, it
swings its fangs downwards and
forwards, ready to stab the victim.
The snake has absolute control over
the movement of its fangs – it can even
choose to erect them one at a time.

RECORD RANGE
The adder has the greatest
range of any land snake. It is
found throughout Europe
and Asia, as far north as the
Arctic circle and eastwards
through northern China to
the Pacific coast.

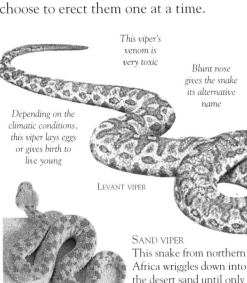

*This viper's
venom is
very toxic*

*Blunt nose
gives the snake
its alternative
name*

*Depending on the
climatic conditions,
this viper lays eggs
or gives birth to
live young*

LEVANT VIPER

LEVANT
VIPER
Levant, or blunt-nosed,
vipers, of which there are
seven subspecies, are
found in dry, rocky places
from Georgia southwards
to northern Israel, Iraq,
Iran, and a few of the
Greek islands.

SAND VIPER
This snake from northern
Africa wriggles down into
the desert sand until only
its eyes are visible. From
this hidden position it
strikes out with lightning
speed to ambush lizard prey.

SAHARAN SAND VIPER

YELLOW PERIL
The eyelash viper has spiny scales above its eyes that resemble eyelashes. This tree-dwelling pit viper is found in rainforests from southern Mexico southwards to Ecuador and western Venezuela. It varies in colour from brown or green to lemon yellow.

EYELASH VIPER

LOOKS LIKE A VIPER...
The death, or deaf, adder looks and behaves like a viper, but is related to the cobras, coral snakes, and kraits. It lives in grassland, forest, and mountain valleys in Australia and New Guinea.

DEATH ADDER

Grey-and-brown colouring for camouflage in dry grass

ALL PUFFED UP
A good swimmer, the puff adder occurs in sub-Saharan Africa and Morocco, where it is found in all habitats except desert. It preys on a wide variety of animals and, like all vipers, it prefers to lie in wait for its victims. The puff adder's venom is highly toxic.

PUFF ADDER

Rattlesnakes

The distinctive features of these well-known, front-fanged snakes are the warning rattle at the end of the tail and the heat-sensitive pits on their heads (they are pit vipers). Rattlesnakes, all of which are found in the Americas, are under threat, mainly from excessive slaughter by hunters, together with the continued spread of agriculture and urban development. All rattlesnakes give birth to live young.

SOUTHERN PACIFIC RATTLESNAKE

ADAPTABLE
The southern Pacific rattlesnake is found in rocky and sandy environments. An adaptable species, it can also survive in urban and agricultural areas. It preys mainly on rodents.

NEOTROPICAL RATTLESNAKE

RATTLESNAKE FACTS

• Organized hunts called "rattlesnake roundups" in the US have wiped out many local populations.

• Western diamondbacks always return to the same den to hibernate.

NEOTROPICAL RATTLESNAKE
This snake lives in savanna grasslands and woodlands from Mexico down into South America. Like all rattlesnakes it gives birth to live young, producing up to 47 offspring. It does not always rattle a warning before it strikes.

RODENT CATCHER

Black-tailed rattlesnakes are found in Mexico, Arizona, and Texas, usually in rocky places and sometimes in woodland and open grassland. They may be active at any time of the day, and they prey on small rodents.

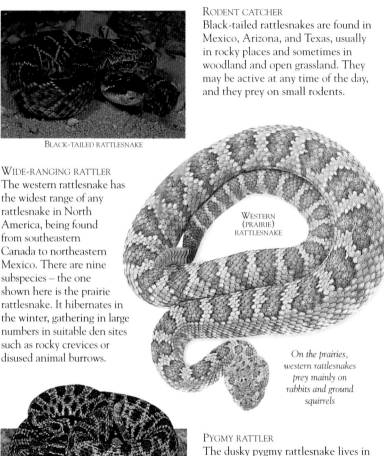

BLACK-TAILED RATTLESNAKE

WIDE-RANGING RATTLER

The western rattlesnake has the widest range of any rattlesnake in North America, being found from southeastern Canada to northeastern Mexico. There are nine subspecies – the one shown here is the prairie rattlesnake. It hibernates in the winter, gathering in large numbers in suitable den sites such as rocky crevices or disused animal burrows.

WESTERN (PRAIRIE) RATTLESNAKE

On the prairies, western rattlesnakes prey mainly on rabbits and ground squirrels

DUSKY PYGMY RATTLESNAKE

PYGMY RATTLER

The dusky pygmy rattlesnake lives in dry, sandy places near water. It is active at any time of the day or night, and it preys on small animals, including snakes, lizards, and large insects. It grows to only about 50 cm (20 in) in length.

Other front-fanged snakes

Front-fanged snakes that have fixed fangs include tiger snakes, taipans, kraits, and seasnakes. Unlike true vipers and pit vipers, these snakes cannot stab their prey with their fangs and must actually bite. The cottonmouth and its close relatives, the moccasin and the copperhead, are pit vipers and are thus members of the Crotalinae, the viper subfamily that includes the rattlesnakes.

COMMON SEA KRAIT

SEA SERPENT
The sea krait is found on mangrove-fringed coasts and coral reefs in southern Asia. Highly venomous, it poses no threat to people, since it does not bite. It lays its eggs on land; true seasnakes give birth to live young at sea.

TIGER SNAKE

TOXIC TIGER
The venom of southern Australia's tiger snake is highly toxic – just 3 mg is enough to kill a human. It feeds mainly on frogs, but also kills small mammals and lizards. The tiger snake is quick to attack if disturbed.

NEVER FATAL
The American copperhead is found in open woodland, where it feeds on mice, birds, frogs, and insects. Contrary to popular belief, its bite is never fatal, although this has not stopped the widespread killing of these snakes.

Copperheads hibernate in communal dens

COPPERHEAD

WETLAND PREDATOR

The cottonmouth, also called the water moccasin, is an impressive-looking, heavy-bodied snake that lives in swamps and marshes in the US states of Alabama, Georgia, and Virginia. Its prey includes fish, frogs, and small mammals.

COTTONMOUTH

Taipans shelter in mammal burrows, rock crevices, or under piles of forest litter

TAIPAN

DO NOT DISTURB

The taipan is a large, slender snake found in northern Australia and southern New Guinea. It shelters when not hunting, and, whenever possible, it will retreat when disturbed. If cornered, however, it becomes fearsomely aggressive.

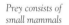
Prey consists of small mammals

Taipan is one of Australia's most dangerous snakes

COMMON KRAIT

The common, or blue, krait is a highly venomous snake found in the dry woodland plains and meadows of Bangladesh, India, and Sri Lanka. It hides during the day and at night hunts rodents, lizards, and other snakes.

FRONT-FANGED FACTS

• Young cottonmouths use the bright tip of their tail to lure prey.

• A bite from a krait is fatal in over 75 per cent of cases.

• Some species of sea snake are considered to be a delicacy in the Far East.

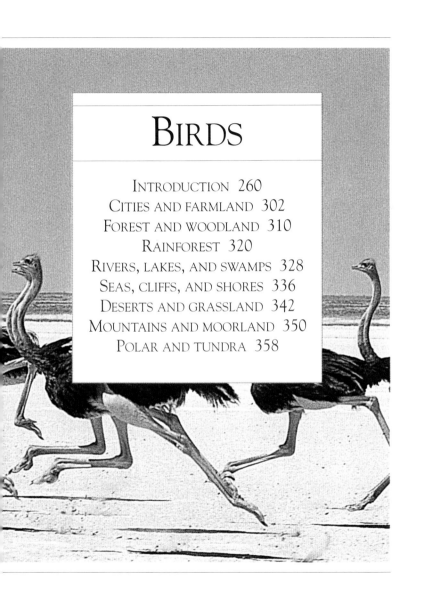

BIRDS

WHAT IS A BIRD?

BIRDS ARE DIFFERENT from all other animals because they have feathers – usually over a thousand of them. They also have two wings, a strong bill, no teeth, scaly legs and feet, and three or four toes with claws on the end. Most birds can fly, and they are the largest, fastest, and most powerful flying animals. Like us, birds breathe air, have a skeleton inside their bodies, and are warm-blooded. Unlike us, birds lay eggs.

JUVENILE STARLING FEATHER

ADULT STARLING FEATHER

FEATHERS
Birds' feathers are light, yet strong and flexible. The feathers of young birds are often a different colour from those of the adults.

Secondary flight feathers

Primary flight feathers

Rump

Upper tail coverts

Under tail coverts

Wing coverts

Ankle

Tail

STARLING

STARLING EGGS

EGGS
A bird's egg is a survival capsule that protects and nourishes a baby bird while it develops inside. When it is ready to hatch, the baby bird has to force its way out.

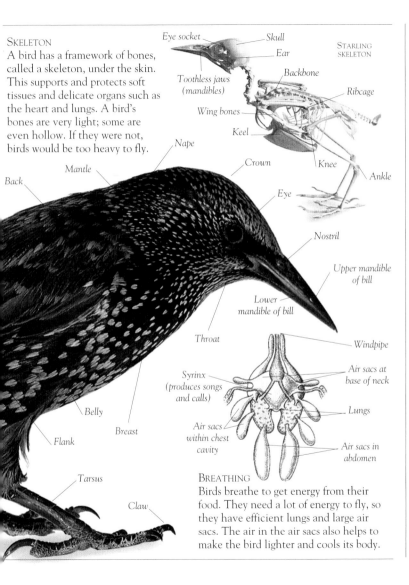

SKELETON
A bird has a framework of bones, called a skeleton, under the skin. This supports and protects soft tissues and delicate organs such as the heart and lungs. A bird's bones are very light; some even hollow. If they were not, birds would be too heavy to fly.

STARLING SKELETON

Eye socket
Skull
Ear
Toothless jaws (mandibles)
Backbone
Ribcage
Wing bones
Keel
Nape
Crown
Knee
Ankle
Back
Mantle
Eye
Nostril
Upper mandible of bill
Lower mandible of bill
Throat
Windpipe
Syrinx (produces songs and calls)
Air sacs at base of neck
Belly
Lungs
Air sacs within chest cavity
Breast
Flank
Air sacs in abdomen
Tarsus

BREATHING
Birds breathe to get energy from their food. They need a lot of energy to fly, so they have efficient lungs and large air sacs. The air in the air sacs also helps to make the bird lighter and cools its body.

Claw

261

Types of birds

The huge variety of birds alive today – over 9,500 species – evolved from reptile-like creatures that climbed trees about 150 million years ago. Reptile scales developed into bird feathers, although there are still scales on a bird's legs. Now, there are birds of all shapes and sizes, from huge ostriches to tiny wrens. Some of the main types of bird are shown here.

PIGEON

PIGEONS
Most pigeons and doves have rather small heads, plump bodies, dense, soft feathers and a powerful straight flight. They live all over the world.

ARCHAEOPTERYX
The earliest known bird was *Archaeopteryx*, which means "ancient wing". It may not have been able to fly well, but it had feathers similar to those of modern birds.

ANCIENT BIRD FACTS

• Birds are thought to be living descendants of the dinosaurs, some of which are now known to have been feathered.

• Unlike modern birds, *Archaeopteryx* had teeth.

• *Dromornis stirtoni*, the heaviest bird, was about four times heavier than an ostrich.

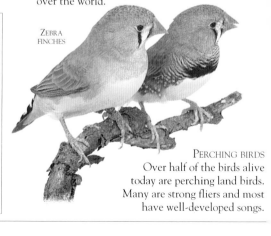

ZEBRA FINCHES

PERCHING BIRDS
Over half of the birds alive today are perching land birds. Many are strong fliers and most have well-developed songs.

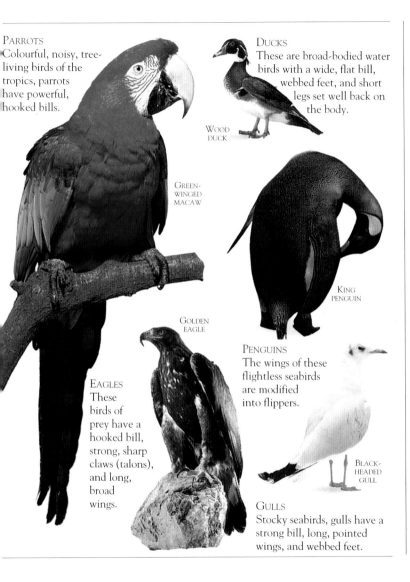

PARROTS
Colourful, noisy, tree-living birds of the tropics, parrots have powerful, hooked bills.

GREEN-WINGED MACAW

DUCKS
These are broad-bodied water birds with a wide, flat bill, webbed feet, and short legs set well back on the body.

WOOD DUCK

KING PENGUIN

GOLDEN EAGLE

EAGLES
These birds of prey have a hooked bill, strong, sharp claws (talons), and long, broad wings.

PENGUINS
The wings of these flightless seabirds are modified into flippers.

BLACK-HEADED GULL

GULLS
Stocky seabirds, gulls have a strong bill, long, pointed wings, and webbed feet.

Bird senses

Birds rely mainly on their eyes and ears to find food or a mate, to fly, and to escape from danger. Their eyes are so large that there is not much room for them to move in the skull. Instead, birds have flexible necks and move the whole head to see things. Most birds have a poor sense of smell.

SIGHT

A bird's huge eyes are often as big as its brain. Much of the brain deals with the information picked up by the eyes. Like us, birds see in colour, but they may have better eyesight than we have.

Large eyes to spot danger coming

PIED AVOCET

The avocet uses its sense of touch to catch small water creatures.

TOUCH

Some birds, such as the avocet, have a well-developed sense of touch in the tongue and bill tip. Nightjars have bristles around their broad bills to help them sweep moths into their mouths as they fly at night.

WOODCOCK EYES
To watch for danger, woodcocks have eyes on the side of their head. This helps them to see all around, but there are two blind spots behind and in front of the head.

Binocular vision (can see with both eyes)

Blind spot

Monocular vision (can see with one eye)

Binocular vision

HEARING
Birds hear a greater frequency of sound – more sounds per second – than we can. Their ears are hidden under the feathers at the sides of the head. Good hearing is especially important to birds that hunt in the dark.

A bird breathes and smells through two openings in its bill.

BROWN KIWI

SMELL
Most birds seem to have a poor sense of smell, but there are a few exceptions. The kiwi smells food with nostrils at the tip of its long bill. The vultures of the Americas can detect the smell of rotting dead animals from some distance. Some seabirds can pick up scents carried by the wind.

265

FEATHERS

A BIRD'S BODY is almost completely covered with
feathers, although many birds have bare legs. Feathers
keep the bird warm, give it shape, colour and pattern,
and help most birds to fly. Some birds have
special display feathers. Feathers carry
out so many important jobs they need
to be kept in good condition.

What is a feather?

Vane

There are three main types of
feather – flight, body, and down.
Feathers grow out of pits or follicles
in a bird's skin, like the hairs all
over our skin. They can be easily
smoothed because of the way the
parts of the feather hook together.

*Smooth,
curved shape
for flight*

*Shaft or
rachis*

Barbules

Hook

Barb

BARBS AND BARBULES
Each side of a feather consists
of parallel barbs, held in place
by tiny hooks on side branches
called barbules. There are many
thousands of barbules on
a flight feather.

MACAW
FLIGHT
FEATHER

FEATHER STRUCTURE
Feathers have a central
shaft with a vane or web on
either side. They are made of
a strong, flexible material
called keratin, which also
forms our hair and nails.

266

FLIGHT FEATHERS
Found in the wings, flight feathers provide a large surface area over which air can flow. The wings' special aerofoil shape (see p.273) lifts the bird into the air, and controls the way it twists and turns in flight.

PEACOCK
DOWN
FEATHER

Short shaft

REGENT
PARROT
FLIGHT
FEATHERS

Long shaft

AFRICAN
GREY PARROT
BODY FEATHER

*Inner fluffy
part to keep
bird warm*

Quill

DOWN FEATHERS
The soft down feathers trap warm air next to the body and are very important in young birds. The barbs are long and soft and the barbules do not hook together so the feather stays fluffy.

FEATHER FACTS
- Swans have 25,000 feathers, sparrows 3,500, and humming-birds fewer than 1,000.

- The male crested argus pheasant has the longest and largest tail feathers of any wild bird at 173 cm (5.7 ft) long, 13 cm (5.1 in) wide.

- Grebes eat their own feathers, which form a soft lining in the gut and prevent damage from sharp fish bones.

BODY FEATHERS
Overlapping like tiles on a roof, body feathers act as a weatherproof jacket. The inner part has softer barbs and the barbules have no hooks.

267

Feather colour

The colours of feathers are produced in two main ways. One is by chemical pigments laid down in the feather as it grows. The other is by the feathers' microscopic structure affecting the way they reflect the light. Colours help birds of the same species to recognize each other, attract mates, threaten rivals, or camouflage themselves.

SHINING COLOURS
The feathers forming the "eyes" of a male peacock's fan are iridescent – they change colour as they move. Their barbules split the light falling on them into different colours. The colours you see depend on the angle from which you view the feathers.

"Eye"

FLAMINGO
FEATHERS

FOOD COLOUR
The colour of flamingo feathers comes from a pink pigment in the shrimps and other small water creatures which the birds sieve from the water.

PEACOCK
FEATHERS

LIGHT COLOURS
These macaw feathers
are blue above and
brownish below. This
effect is caused by the
way light is reflected
from them.

MACAW
FEATHERS

*Tropical birds
often have
brightly coloured
feathers.*

PIGMENT COLOURS
This parakeet feather
has red, orange,
yellow, and dark
brown colours. The
melanin pigment
produces black and
brown colours.
The carotenoid
pigment causes red,
orange, and yellow.

PARAKEET
FEATHER

269

Looking after feathers

Birds must take great care of their feathers
and spend a few hours each day preening
(cleaning and tidying
their plumage). They
use the bill to pull
ruffled feathers
into shape, and
may also take
water or dust
baths. Many
birds spread
a special oil
over their
feathers to
keep them
waterproof.

YELLOW
CANARY
PREENING

PREENING
To preen its feathers, a bird draws
each one carefully through its bill.
This fits the barbs and barbules back
into place – like pulling up a zip –
and cleans and smooths the feathers.
Preening also removes parasites,
such as feather lice, which live on
feathers and eat them.

*Most birds use
their feet to
preen their head
feathers.*

*The oil used for preening
comes from a special
preen gland at the base of
the tail, on the rump.*

270

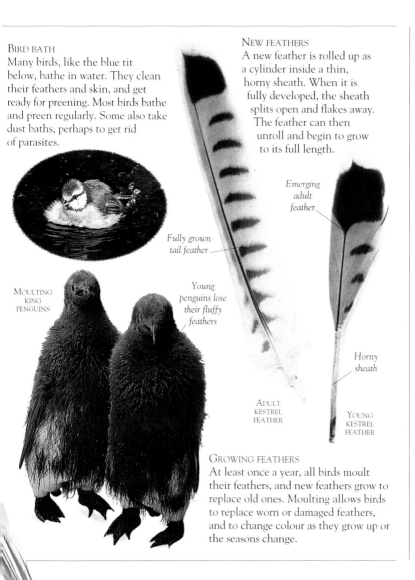

BIRD BATH

Many birds, like the blue tit below, bathe in water. They clean their feathers and skin, and get ready for preening. Most birds bathe and preen regularly. Some also take dust baths, perhaps to get rid of parasites.

NEW FEATHERS

A new feather is rolled up as a cylinder inside a thin, horny sheath. When it is fully developed, the sheath splits open and flakes away. The feather can then unroll and begin to grow to its full length.

Emerging adult feather

MOULTING KING PENGUINS

Fully grown tail feather

Young penguins lose their fluffy feathers

Horny sheath

ADULT KESTREL FEATHER

YOUNG KESTREL FEATHER

GROWING FEATHERS

At least once a year, all birds moult their feathers, and new feathers grow to replace old ones. Moulting allows birds to replace worn or damaged feathers, and to change colour as they grow up or the seasons change.

271

HOW BIRDS MOVE

TO FIND FOOD and escape danger, birds walk, run, hop, wade, swim, and dive. Most birds can also fly. They have light bones, powerful flight muscles, and an efficient respiratory system. A few birds cannot fly. Some of these flightless birds run very fast indeed.

Flight

Birds flap their wings up and forwards, then down and backwards. The wings' downstroke pushes the air back, and the bird moves forwards. Air flowing over and under the wings creates the lifting force.

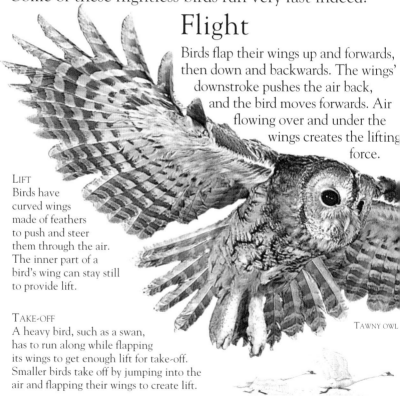

LIFT
Birds have curved wings made of feathers to push and steer them through the air. The inner part of a bird's wing can stay still to provide lift.

TAKE-OFF
A heavy bird, such as a swan, has to run along while flapping its wings to get enough lift for take-off. Smaller birds take off by jumping into the air and flapping their wings to create lift.

TAWNY OWL

COMING IN TO LAND

To land, birds slow down in mid-air, then drop gently to the ground, onto a perch, or the surface of water, spreading out their wings and tail like brakes. Heavy birds land into the wind to help slow themselves down.

Strong legs to absorb impact of landing

Wings and tail spread to increase air resistance and drag

BLUE-AND-WHITE FLYCATCHER

CURVED WINGS

A bird's wing is an aerofoil shape – curved on top and slightly hollow underneath. The air flows faster over the top, creating low air pressure, while air pressure underneath stays much the same. The difference in pressure produces lift.

Finger-like feathers to push and steer through the air

MUTE SWAN

Neck stretched out and feet tucked up to streamline bird's body

FLIGHT FACTS

• Common swifts may stay in the air for up to four years without landing.

• Some hummingbirds beat their wings up to 200 times a second.

• A Rüppel's griffon vulture was recorded flying at a record height of 11,277 m (37,000 ft).

• Diving peregrine falcons can reach speeds of 180 km/h (112 mph).

Flight patterns

Different types of bird have differently shaped wings. The way wings are used in flight depends on a bird's lifestyle. To save energy, some birds like seagulls and vultures soar on rising air, while smaller birds glide between flaps of the wings. Ducks and other heavy birds flap their wings all the time they are in the air. Some, such as hummingbirds and kestrels, can hover in one spot.

Feathers spread apart on upstroke for air to slip through wing

FLIGHT PATH
Small birds, like this minla, have a bounding, undulating flight. Bigger birds such as cranes, ducks, and geese tend to fly in straight lines.

RED-TAILED MINLA

Eagles thermalling

Hot air rising

Seabirds have powerful flight muscles.

GLIDING AND SOARING
Seabirds glide upwards on air currents rising from waves or over cliffs. Some large birds, such as eagles, vultures, and storks, also use natural currents of rising hot air to lift them higher into the air. These currents are called thermals.

GLIDING IN A THERMAL

274

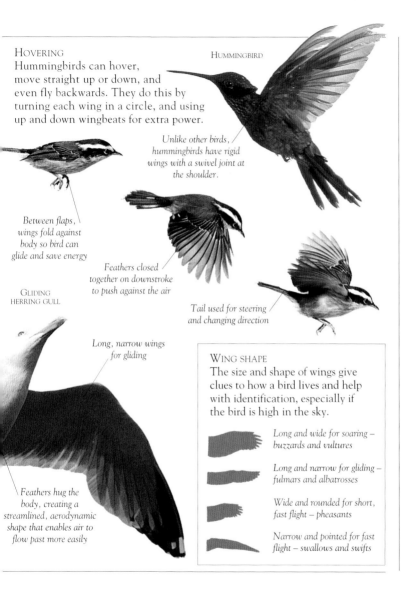

HOVERING

Hummingbirds can hover, move straight up or down, and even fly backwards. They do this by turning each wing in a circle, and using up and down wingbeats for extra power.

HUMMINGBIRD

Unlike other birds, hummingbirds have rigid wings with a swivel joint at the shoulder.

Between flaps, wings fold against body so bird can glide and save energy

GLIDING
HERRING GULL

Feathers closed together on downstroke to push against the air

Tail used for steering and changing direction

Long, narrow wings for gliding

Feathers hug the body, creating a streamlined, aerodynamic shape that enables air to flow past more easily

WING SHAPE

The size and shape of wings give clues to how a bird lives and help with identification, especially if the bird is high in the sky.

Long and wide for soaring – buzzards and vultures

Long and narrow for gliding – fulmars and albatrosses

Wide and rounded for short, fast flight – pheasants

Narrow and pointed for fast flight – swallows and swifts

275

CASSOWARY
AND CHICK

Flightless birds

A few birds have given up flying altogether. Some of them are so good at swimming or running that they do not need to fly. Many flightless birds, such as ostriches, rheas, or emus, are very large birds that can run faster than their enemies, or can defend themselves so we that they do not need to fly away. Some flightless birds live on remote islands where there are few enemies from which they need to escape.

DEFENCE
With powerful legs and dagger-like claws, birds such as cassowaries do not need to fly away. Cassowaries even attack people, lashing out with strong feet and sharp nails.

GALAPAGOS
CORMORANT

WINGS
Flightless birds usually have small, weak wings which are not strong enough for flight. The Galapagos cormorant uses its wings to help it balance on land

FLIGHTLESS FACTS

• The heaviest bird ever was the flightless *Dromornis stirtoni*. It died out 25,000 years ago.

• Ostriches are nearly seven times too heavy to fly. They have the biggest legs of any bird, over 1.2 m (4 ft) long.

• The Inaccessible Island rail, the world's smallest flightless bird, is the size of a newly hatched farm chick.

BIRDS IN DANGER
The kakapo is the heaviest of the parrots. Like many flightless birds, kakapos are threatened by cats and rats that people have introduced to their island homes.

KAKAPO

GREATER
RHEA

FAST RUNNERS

Running away from danger can be just as effective as flying. Rheas can sprint faster than a horse, reaching speeds of 50 km/h (31 mph), and are also good swimmers. Rheas are related to ostriches and emus and follow a similar lifestyle, but they live on the South American grasslands, rather than on the grasslands of Africa or Australia.

Fluffy wings used for display, not flight

Long neck to see over tall grasses

HUMBOLDT
PENGUIN

FAST SWIMMERS

Penguins are so well suited to their life in the sea that they look more like fish when they swim. They use their wings as flippers for swimming while their feet and tail steer like a rudder.

Large leg muscles provide power when running

Three strong toes on each foot for defence and for running fast

277

LEGS AND FEET

BIRDS USE their legs and feet for moving around and, in some bird groups, for holding food. The size and shape of their feet depend on where they live and how they feed.

Three toes point forward and one back.

Stringy, elastic tendons

PERCHING
Birds that perch can sleep without falling off a branch. They bend their legs, pulling the tendons tight and drawing in the toes. This locks their feet tightly round the perch.

TAWNY OWL TALON

TALONS
Birds of prey, such as owls and eagles, have strong, sharp, curved claws called talons. They use these to catch, carry, and often kill prey.

Long toes that spread wide

WATTLED JACANA

Lobe of skin along each toe

WIDE TOES
Some water birds, such as coots, have lobes of skin on each toe. When spread, the lobes push aside the water for faster swimming and help stop the coot from sinking into mud.

COOT TOES

LONG TOES
Jacanas or lily trotters have very long, thin toes. These spread the weight of the bird over a bigger area so it can "trot" across lily pads on the ponds and lakes where it lives.

SPEED

Ostriches have long legs and strong toes to run at speeds of up to 72 km/h (45 mph). They only have two toes on each foot; most birds have three or four.

BLUE
FRONTED
PARROT

WEBBED FEET

Water birds, such as ducks, geese, and flamingos have webs of skin between their toes. The webs work like paddles when the bird is in water. They also spread its weight when the bird walks on soft, marshy ground.

GRIPPING TOES

The two outer toes of a parrot's foot point backwards, and the two inner toes point forwards. This gives parrots a very powerful grip for climbing through the trees. It also allows them to hold food up to the bill.

Two toes forward, two toes back

LEGS OF
FLAMINGO

279

COLLARED
SUNBIRD SIPPING
NECTAR

FOOD AND FEEDING

BIRDS SPEND MUCH of their time
finding food, whether pecking at
berries and nuts, or snapping up fish or
small mammals. They rely mainly on their
eyes and ears to find food, and their bill or
claws to catch it. A few birds steal their food
from other birds. Some birds eat plants; others
eat animals (alive or dead) or have a mixed diet.

Hunting and fishing

Meat-eating birds often target young,
weak, or unfit prey. They may lie in wait
to ambush their quarry, or chase after it
through air or water. Most of these birds
hunt by day; a few, such as most
owls, hunt at night.

GREAT WHITE
PELICAN

GOLDEN
EAGLE

BIRDS OF PREY
Many birds of
prey, such as this
golden eagle, soar
high in the sky to
search for food,
then swoop down to
seize and crush their
prey with their sharp talons. However,
nine out of ten attacks are unsuccessful
and the prey manages to escape.

*Prey is either
seized with the
bill-tip, or trapped
in the pouch, and
then swallowed.*

UMBRELLA FISHING
Some birds have developed their own special techniques for catching food. The black heron shades the water with its wings. This cuts out reflections and makes it easier for the bird to see fish.

Great white pelicans eat about 1.2 kg (2 ½ lb) of fish a day.

SNAKE HUNTERS
Secretary birds are unusual because they search for their prey on foot. They have tough scales on their legs for protection from the snakes' bites. They pin prey to the ground with sharp claws.

SECRETARY BIRDS

Sharp, hooked bill to pull and tear at food

EGYPTIAN VULTURE

Bare skin on face to avoid soiling feathers

FISHING IN GROUPS
Great white pelicans usually fish in groups. The birds gather in a circle on the water, lifting their wings and plunging their bills into the water to drive the fish into the middle of the circle. Then they scoop up the fish.

USING TOOLS
A few birds use tools to find and deal with their food. Egyptian vultures throw or drop stones on to ostrich eggs to break open the thick shells.

281

What birds eat

Birds have healthy appetites. They need to eat large amounts of food to give them enough energy to fly, keep warm, build nests, and lay eggs. Some birds eat only one kind of food, while others, such as starlings, crows, and jays eat almost anything. Birds such as vultures eat carcasses, the dead bodies of animals.

HELMET BIRD

MICROSCOPIC SEAFOOD
A drop of seawater teems with tiny plants such as diatoms and animals such as crab larvae. This plankton floats about the oceans and is a vital part of the diet of many seabirds.

ACORN

SEEDS

RASPBERRIES

HIBISCUS FLOWER

FLOWERS, FRUITS, AND SEEDS
The sweet liquid called nectar produced by flowers is a high-energy food for birds such as hummingbirds. Many birds eat the fruits and seeds that develop when the flowers are pollinated.

GRASS

CABBAGE LEAF

CONIFER

GRASS AND LEAVES
A few birds, such as geese and grouse, eat grass and leaves. These can be hard to digest and poor in nutrients, so the birds have to eat a lot of this sort of food to get the energy they need.

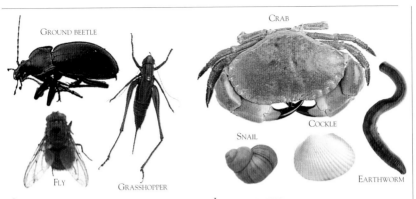

GROUND BEETLE

FLY

GRASSHOPPER

CRAB

SNAIL

COCKLE

EARTHWORM

INSECTS
Adult insects are more abundant in warmer weather, but caterpillars and grubs survive colder periods buried in soil or under bark. Insects are a body-building food, vital for young birds.

INVERTEBRATES
Invertebrates such as crabs and shellfish are an important source of food on the seashore, where there are few insects. Garden and woodland birds, such as thrushes, eat juicy earthworms.

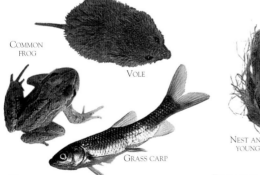

COMMON FROG

VOLE

GRASS CARP

NEST AND YOUNG

VERTEBRATES
Birds that feed on vertebrates (animals with backbones) have to work hard for their meals. The animals they hunt do their best to run, swim or slither away, and often succeed in escaping.

EGGS AND YOUNG
Some birds eat the eggs and helpless young of other birds. For example, skuas pounce on puffin and penguin chicks, while magpies may steal eggs and young birds from the nest.

283

Bird bills

A bird uses its bill like a hand to carry out all sorts of tasks, from catching and holding food to preening its feathers and building a nest. Parrots also use their bills to help them climb. The size and shape of a bird's bill depends mainly on what it eats and where it finds its food.

YELLOW-HEADED PARROT

FLAMINGO

FRUIT-AND-NUT EATERS
A parrot uses its muscular tongue to hold a nut, seed, or fruit in its bill so that it can split the hard skin or inedible husk with the chisel-like edge of its lower mandible. It also uses its feet to hold food.

A flamingo dips its bill upside down in the shallow water.

Bee-eaters beat stinging insects against a branch to get rid of the stings.

WHITE-THROATED BEE-EATER

FILTER-FEEDER
The upper mandible of the flamingo's bill filters out tiny seeds, algae, shrimps, and other invertebrates from the water. The lower mandible and the piston-like tongue move up and down to pump water through comb-like fringes on the inside and edges of the bill.

INSECT EATERS
Birds that feed on insects have thin, pointed bills to probe under bark and stones. Birds that eat flying insects have wide, gaping bills to scoop them up as they fly.

BLACK-CROWNED
NIGHT HERON

*Bill used to
seize fish*

GOULDIAN
FINCH

*Powerful bill that is
broad at the base and
pointed at the tip.*

FISH EATERS

Some fish-eating birds, such as herons, have a long, narrow bill that can rapidly snap shut around prey. Others, including cormorants, have a hooked bill to grip slippery fish firmly.

SEED EATERS

To crack open seeds, seed-eating birds such as finches have cone-shaped bills. The hawfinch's bill is so strong it can even crush cherry stones.

SCARLET-CHESTED
SUNBIRD

*Flaps over
nostrils keep out
flower pollen*

NECTAR EATERS

Various kinds of smaller bird feed on nectar. Sunbirds and hummingbirds push their needle-like bills into flowers and lick up the sweet nectar.

*Powerful
hooked bill to
tear up food*

GOLDEN
EAGLE

MEAT EATERS

Often called birds of prey, these include eagles, owls, and falcons. They use their bills to pull apart animals they kill into bite-sized chunks. Owls swallow small animals, such as voles and mice, whole.

COURTSHIP

BEFORE MATING, male birds usually court the
females. Some males grow more colourful
or elaborate feathers for the breeding
season. They may give singing or
dancing displays. Some show off
nest-building or
hunting skills.

YELLOW-
THROATED
LAUGHING
THRUSH

TERRITORY
Many birds nest in an area, or
territory, that has enough food for
their young when they hatch out. Male
birds sing in their territory to attract a
mate and keep away other males.

*Laughing thrushes
make loud,
cackling sounds.*

MALE
PIN-TAILED
WHYDAH

MALES AND FEMALES
Male and female birds of
the same species often
look different. The
male is usually more
colourful, but the
dull colours of
the female
help
camouflage
her on the
nest.

*Female bird
duller, with
short tail*

*Long tail
feathers used in
display flight to
impress females*

FEMALE
PIN-TAILED
WHYDAH

MALE
PEACOCK

*Male's tail is small; it is
the feathers overlying it
that form the fan*

DISPLAY
The male
peacock spreads
out his long, colourful
feathers in a shimmering
fan to impress a female.
After the breeding season, the
long fan feathers fall out.

RED-CROWNED
CRANES

*The "eyes"
attract female
peacocks.*

DANCING
Some birds dance together
before they mate. Cranes jump
up and down in the air with
their partners. Great crested
grebes perform a series of
dances, including head-shaking.

287

NESTS AND EGGS

ALL BIRDS LAY EGGS and most build nests
to keep eggs and young safe and warm.
Birds know instinctively how to
build a nest, and female birds
usually do most of the work. Nests
vary from a shallow scrape in the
ground and simple cup shapes, to
more elaborate constructions.

NEST BOX

Building a nest

Birds use a wide range of
nesting materials and may
make hundreds of trips to
collect material. Nest materials must both
support the nest and keep the young warm.
Nest boxes encourage birds to nest in
gardens or woods with few
natural tree holes.

WAGTAIL
NEST

PEBBLE NEST
Oystercatchers lay their
eggs in a shallow dip, or
scrape, on the shoreline.
Their eggs are difficult to
see among the pebbles.

TWIGS
Most hedgerow and
woodland birds use twigs
and sticks to support
their nests as these are
readily available.

FEATHERS
Birds may use feathers –
3,000 or more in the case
of long-tailed tits – to
make a warm nest lining.

To make the cup shape, birds turn round and round.

MOSS
Moss traps warm air in the nest and stops heat loss. It helps to keep both eggs and young birds warm.

STRING
Birds sometimes collect household materials when nest-building. Pieces of string have been found in many nests.

MUD
Some nests are lined with wet mud mixed with saliva and droppings. When it dries, it forms a hard and strong lining.

GRASS
Grass is a flexible nest material. It is used by many birds because it is easy to weave into differently shaped nests.

MUD NEST
Swallows and martins collect hundreds of little pellets of wet mud with their bills and stick them together to form a nest.

Woodpeckers have chisel-like bills.

TREE NEST
Woodpeckers dig nest holes in rotten trees with their strong beaks. Many other birds use existing tree holes. The nests inside the holes are usually lined with grass or feathers.

HOUSE MARTIN NEST

289

Unusual nests

From woven purses and saliva cups to mud ovens and compost heaps, some birds' nests are quite unusual and elaborate. They may be a strange shape, such as the trumpet-like weaver bird nests. Birds need a lot of practice to perfect the technique of making a complex nest.

PENDULINE TIT NEST

Strong and lightweight basket

False entrance

WOVEN NEST
A male West African weaver bird knotted grasses to weave this nest. The entrance tunnel stops snakes and other enemies from getting inside.

PURSE NEST
The penduline tit weaves a hanging nest from grasses, leaves, and moss. A false entrance leads to an empty chamber and dead end.

WEAVER NEST

THATCHED COTTAGE
Each colony of the sociable weaver bird of South Africa builds a huge "haystack" that is up to 4 m (13 ft) deep and 7.2 m (24 ft) across. Up to 300 pairs then build their nests under the protection of this thatched roof.

NEST FACTS

• The biggest tree nest ever found belonged to a bald eagle. It was 2.9 m (9.5 ft) wide and 6.1 m (20 ft) deep.

• A bee hummingbird's nest is no bigger than a thimble.

• A mallee fowl's nest is a "compost heap" of rotting vegetation.

• A hammerkop nest may be made of over 10,000 sticks.

BASKET NEST

Reed warblers join their nest to several reed stems. This helps to hold the nest steady as the wind blows. The nest is made from grass, reed fibres, and feathers.

Nest is joined to reeds

TAILOR BIRD ON NEST

REED WARBLER NEST

SEWING BIRD

The tailorbird sews a pocket of leaves to support its nest. Its sharp bill makes holes along the edges of the leaves. Then the bird pulls spider or insect silk or plant material through the holes to "stitch" the leaves together.

HUNG UP

Many birds suspend nests from branches, to make it difficult for predators to reach them. The Baltimore orioles that built this nest used string to hang it up, and also in the construction of the nest.

BALTIMORE ORIOLE NEST

291

All kinds of eggs

Birds lay eggs because they would be too heavy to fly if they carried their young around inside them. Some birds lay one large clutch (set of eggs) in a season, while others lay several smaller clutches. Birds such as snowy owls lay extra clutches if there is plenty of food. No two eggs have exactly the same markings. The colour and shape depends on where the eggs are laid and how much camouflage they need.

SECTION THROUGH
CHICKEN EGG

Strong shell

Egg white

Yolk sac

Developing chick

INSIDE AN EGG
A bird's egg contains a developing bird – an embryo – plus a store of food and a supply of air. Pores in the shell allow air to pass through from outside. The egg white supplies proteins, water, and vitamins.

EGG FACTS

• An average-sized ostrich egg has the same volume as 24 hen's eggs.

• Cuckoos can lay eggs in a few seconds; some birds take 1–3 minutes.

• About 80 species of bird lay eggs in the nests of other species.

• Grey partridges lay the biggest clutches among wild birds, up to 17 eggs.

• Many small eggs take under an hour to hatch.

BARN OWL
EGG

CURLEW
EGG

WHITE EGGS
Birds that nest in holes or burrows, such as owls or kingfishers, usually lay white eggs. They do not need to be camouflaged because they are hidden.

SPECKLED EGGS
Birds that nest in the open, where there is little cover, usually lay patterned eggs. The camouflage colours hide the eggs from enemies.

PALE EGG

SPECKLED EGG

DARK EGG

DISGUISE

Female cuckoos lay their eggs in the nests of other birds such as dunnocks, robins, wrens, or meadow pipits. The foster parents raise the cuckoo chick as their own. The cuckoo's egg often looks similar to those of the foster parents.

CUCKOO EGG

COLOURS IN A CLUTCH

The three eggs above were laid by a single snipe but come from different clutches. In one clutch, the eggs usually look similar.

GUILLEMOT EGG

EURASIAN ROBIN EGGS

BIG AND SMALL

Ostriches lay the largest eggs of any living bird. Each weighs up to 1.8 kg (3.9 lb) and is the size of an adult human's hand. The smallest hummingbird eggs, however, are only as big as peas.

PATTERNS

Common guillemot eggs show a variety of patterns and colours, possibly to help parent birds recognize them. The pear shape stops it rolling off cliff ledges.

HUMMINGBIRD EGGS

OSTRICH EGG

HATCHING AND GROWTH

MOST PARENT BIRDS SIT on their eggs to keep them warm so that the chicks inside can develop properly. This is called incubation. After the chicks hatch, the parents work hard feeding the chicks, keeping them warm and clean, and protecting them from enemies.

Egg to chick

In order to incubate, most birds develop patches of bare skin, brood patches, to let body warmth through

SWAN INCUBATING EGGS IN NEST

to the eggs. Small birds incubate eggs for about two weeks, eagles for six or seven weeks, and albatrosses and kiwis for up to 12 weeks.

First the chick pecks at shell to make a hole

Then chick cuts a circle

Chick pushes to widen crack

HATCHING
To break out of its shell, a baby bird chips away with a pointed "egg tooth" on top of its bill. This egg tooth disappears soon after hatching. Some clutches hatch together; others hatch at intervals of a few days.

*Helpless young
are usually born
in a nest*

BLUE TIT
NEST

HELPLESS CHICKS
Birds born naked,
blind, and feeble are
called altricial. They
grow at a very fast
rate, often eating
their own weight
each day. Songbirds,
such as thrushes and
chaffinches, are
born like this.

INDEPENDENT CHICKS
Some chicks are born
with feathers, and are
able to see and run soon after
hatching. They are called
precocial. Ducks, geese, and
terns are born like this.

*Wet and
bedraggled chick
struggles free*

*Dry and
fluffy
feathers*

SCALED QUAIL
CHICK

295

Growing up

Baby birds take a few weeks or a few months to grow up. Almost all rely on their parents to keep them warm and out of danger, and most chicks are fed by their parents as well. Small birds can make hundreds of feeding trips in a day; larger birds only two or three. Chicks that are born helpless grow faster than chicks that are born fluffy and alert.

RED KITE AND CHICKS

HEN AND CHICKS

BIRDS OF PREY
Kites, eagles, and other birds of prey tear up food for their chicks at first. As the chicks grow bigger, they learn to do this for themselves.

INDEPENDENT FEEDERS
Some baby birds, such as chickens, ducks, and geese, can feed themselves soon after hatching. At first, they peck at anything; then they watch their parents to find out what to eat.

PECKING SPOT
A herring gull chick pecks at a red spot on its parent's bill to make the parent cough up food. Herring gulls feed out at sea, so they swallow food to help them carry it long distances.

HERRING GULL

CRECHE OF YOUNG
KING PENGUINS

SAFETY IN NUMBERS

Young penguins cannot join their
parents in the water until they
have grown waterproof adult
feathers. The parent birds
leave them behind when they
go to sea to feed. When they
return, the adults regurgitate
partly digested fish for the
chicks, but there may be a
wait of days or even
weeks between meals.

*Young penguins huddle
together for warmth and
protection while their
parents are away.*

JUVENILE
STARLING

*A young starling
takes off unsteadily
for its first flight*

FIRST FLIGHT

Baby birds have to learn how to fly
as quickly as possible to avoid
predators and other dangers. They
flap their wings while they are in the
nest to exercise their muscles, and make
them strong. Taking off and landing is
not easy – many young birds crash-land.

MIGRATION

NEARLY HALF the world's birds migrate – to find food and water, to nest, or to avoid bad weather. They navigate by instinct, but use familiar landmarks, the Sun, the Moon, the stars, and the Earth's magnetic field to find their way. Migration journeys are often dangerous for birds and use up a lot of energy. Some small birds double their weight to provide enough fuel for travelling.

RED-BREASTED
GOOSE

NESTING
This goose is one of many birds that migrate to the Arctic tundra to nest in the brief summer when there is plenty of food available.

MIGRATION ROUTES

ARCTIC TERN
This is the champion bird migrant, flying from the Arctic to Antarctica and back each year. It spends summer in both polar regions.

AMERICAN GOLDEN PLOVER
This plover has the longest migration of all land birds. It breeds in northern Canada and flies to the Argentinian pampas for the winter.

V-FORMATION

Flying in a V-shaped formation helps birds to save energy on a long journey. The birds following the leader fly in the "slipstream" of the bird in front. When the leader tires, another bird takes over.

SNOW GEESE
MIGRATING

Snow geese breed in the Arctic tundra and migrate to the Gulf of Mexico for the winter.

MIGRATION FACTS

• Some American golden plovers cover 3,300 km (2,050 miles) in 35 hours.

• The ruby-throated hummingbird travels 3,200 km (2,000 miles) across the Americas.

• Most migrating birds fly below altitude of 1,500 m (5,000 ft).

MOUNTAIN MIGRATION

Some birds migrate short distances. The Himalayan monal pheasant migrates up and down the mountains with the seasons, moving to warmer, lower slopes in winter.

HIMALAYAN
MONAL
PHEASANTS

SHORT-TAILED SHEARWATER

Between breeding seasons off southern Australia, this bird flies in a figure-of-eight route from Australia to the North Pacific and back again.

WHITETHROAT

This small warbler breeds in Europe in spring and summer, and then migrates to Africa just south of the Sahara Desert for the winter.

WHERE BIRDS LIVE

FROM BUSY CITIES to frozen polar regions, birds have adapted to a range of habitats on every continent. Where birds live depends on the food they eat and their nesting requirements, as well as their competitors and predators. In many parts of the world, where people live has had a destructive influence on the distribution of birds.

NORTH
AMERICA

SOUTH
AMERICA

SEAS, CLIFFS, AND SHORES
Marine habitats are a huge feeding ground for many birds. They nest on shores around all continents.

DESERTS AND GRASSLAND
These dry, mainly hot habitats provide little shelter for birds. Food and water may be hard to find.

POLAR AND TUNDRA
In the Antarctic, Arctic, and tundra, it is cold and windy. Birds breed there in summer.

RIVERS, LAKES, AND SWAMPS
Lakes and rivers are fresh
water, while marshes and
swamps are fresh
or salt water.

FOREST AND WOODLAND
Conifers and broadleaved
trees grow in temperate
climates where there is
usually rain all year.

EUROPE

ASIA

AFRICA

AUSTRALASIA

ANTARCTICA

CITIES AND FARMLAND
Birds that have adapted to
live near people can take
advantage of the extra food
and the less severe climate.

MOUNTAINS AND MOORLAND
Moorlands occur in cool,
wet uplands. Mountains
have a variety of habitats.

RAINFOREST
These are mostly hot, wet
habitats near the Equator in
the Americas, Africa,
Southeast Asia and
northeastern Australia.

TOWNS, CITIES, AND FARMLAND

BIRDS HAVE LEARNED to live close to people, and eat the food we give them, as well as the plants, insects, or crops around our homes. Buildings, parks, waste-ground, meadows, orchards, and hedgerows provide ample nesting places for birds.

KESTREL

HUNTING BIRDS
Most birds of prey do not like living near people, but kestrels hunt along roadsides and sparrowhawks in parks.

HABITAT FACTS

• At night, a city is as much as 5°C (9°F) warmer than the surrounding countryside.

• Some starling roosts in cities have contained over one million birds.

• As few as one in ten captured wild birds may reach the pet shop alive.

• The African red-billed quelea is the world's worst agricultural bird pest.

BLUE BUDGERIGAR

CITY BIRDS
Birds such as geese fly over cities on migration routes, or land to feed and roost in city parks. Starlings roost in city centres at night because it is warmer than the countryside.

CAGED BIRDS
Many people keep birds such as budgerigars, canaries, and parrots in cages. They like their colours, their company, and their songs. People breed birds to create colours never seen in the wild.

BARN
SWALLOW
FEEDING
YOUNG

SONG THRUSH

NESTS IN BUILDINGS

Window ledges, attics,
barns and even chimney
pots make ideal nesting places for
birds used to nesting on cliffs, rocky
hillsides or trees. Barn swallows
used to nest in caves, but now
almost all nest inside buildings.

NESTS IN HEDGEROWS

Hedgerows are strips of trees
and shrubs where birds such as
the song thrush can nest safely.
Birds roost and feed in hedgerows,
which are an important refuge in
open areas of crops and grass.

SONG THRUSH NEST

HOMES AND STREETS

MANY BIRDS HAVE LOST their natural fear of people and live near our homes and in our cities, despite all the noise and pollution. These urban birds change their diet or the places they nest to take advantage of our leftover food scraps, the artificial habitats we build, and the warm climates we create.

HOUSE SPARROW
By following people from country to country, the fearless house sparrow has spread from Europe and Asia over about two-thirds of the world's land surface. It nests in buildings close to people.

The male has a grey crown and black bib.

BIRDS IN DANGER
Thousands of birds are taken from the wild every year. This has reduced numbers of some wild birds, especially parrots.

The house sparrow is bold and adaptable.

WHITE STORKS
In many parts of Europe, white storks are believed to bring good luck. They often nest on roofs and people may put up platforms to encourage them.

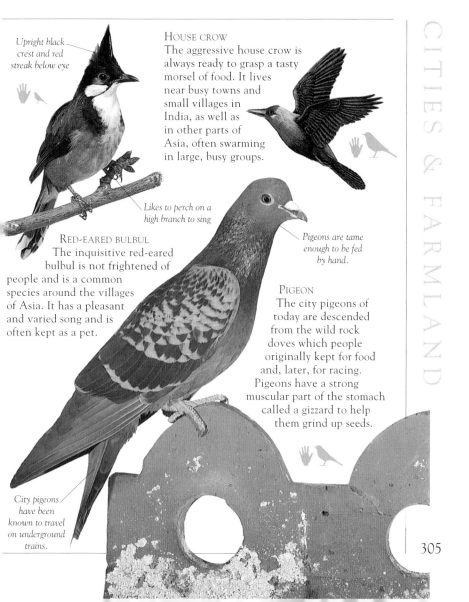

Upright black crest and red streak below eye

HOUSE CROW

The aggressive house crow is always ready to grasp a tasty morsel of food. It lives near busy towns and small villages in India, as well as in other parts of Asia, often swarming in large, busy groups.

Likes to perch on a high branch to sing

RED-EARED BULBUL

The inquisitive red-eared bulbul is not frightened of people and is a common species around the villages of Asia. It has a pleasant and varied song and is often kept as a pet.

Pigeons are tame enough to be fed by hand.

PIGEON

The city pigeons of today are descended from the wild rock doves which people originally kept for food and, later, for racing. Pigeons have a strong muscular part of the stomach called a gizzard to help them grind up seeds.

City pigeons have been known to travel on underground trains.

PARKS AND GARDENS

FROM TREES AND FLOWERBEDS to grassy lawns and garden ponds, parks and gardens contain a great variety of habitats for birds. People put up feeding tables, bird baths, and nesting boxes to encourage birds to live near houses. Unfortunately, pets, especially cats, often catch and kill garden birds.

BLACK-BILLED MAGPIE
This adaptable magpie visits suburban gardens. It eats a range of food, especially insects and plant matter, but also steals eggs and young from the nests of other birds.

Pale grey border

Red breast and face used in threat displays by adult robins

EURASIAN ROBIN
These birds are aggressive and males often set up territories in gardens. They sing loudly to keep away other male robins. In winter, both males and females defend feeding territories.

BLUE TITS

These bold, lively birds often visit gardens in winter to feed on nuts, seeds, and leftover food scraps put out by people. They can easily land on nut feeders and often use the nest boxes that people build and put up for them.

Blue tits are agile, acrobatic birds.

Cone-shaped bill typical of a seed eater

WATERFOWL IN PARKS

The artificial lakes in parks make a welcome feeding, resting, and nesting area for geese, ducks, and coots. Islands in the middle of lakes provide safe nesting places.

NORTHERN CARDINAL

These cardinals are frequent visitors to feeders in the backyards of North America. They often move around in pairs or family groups to feed on seeds that people leave out for them.

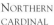

SUPERB STARLING

A common visitor to lawns, campsites, and hotels in East Africa, the superb starling is a tame bird, not frightened of people. It feeds mainly on the ground, pecking up seeds, fruit, and insects.

FIELDS AND HEDGEROWS

FARMLAND HAS TAKEN the place of woodlands, grasslands, and wetlands, but some birds have adapted to this habitat. They feed on crops, and nest in pastures, hedges, orchards, and farm buildings. However, their numbers have been reduced by intensive farming, including the removal of hedgerows and the use of poisonous pesticides.

GOLDFINCH
Flocks of goldfinches feed on weeds along the edges of fields. They are light enough to perch on thistle heads and eat the seeds.

FOLLOWING THE PLOUGH
Large flocks of birds, such as black-headed gulls, often follow a tractor ploughing a field. The birds feed on the insects and other invertebrates, such as worms, exposed by the plough.

Seagulls following the tractor

PHEASANT
The female common pheasant may nest in hedgerows, making a shallow scrape in the ground in which to lay her eggs. Pheasants wander over farmland, feeding mainly on grains, seeds, berries, and insects.

HOOPOE
The weeds and grasses under Mediterranean olive groves teem with invertebrates. Hoopoes probe the ground with long curved bills for worms and insects.

DUNNOCK
Sometimes called the hedge sparrow, the dunnock is not related to sparrows at all. It has a slim, insect-eating bill, rather than a seed-eating one. It nests in hedgerows, where it builds cup-shaped nests.

The chicks are well camouflaged, like their mother.

The grey head and underparts help to tell the dunnock from a sparrow

FOREST AND WOODLAND

Jays store acorns in autumn

JAY

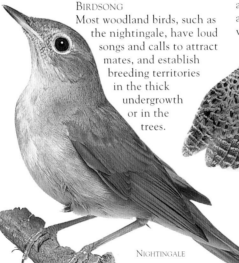

THIS KIND OF HABITAT provides birds with plenty of food and safe nesting places. A greater variety of birds live in the deciduous and eucalyptus woodlands than in the dark conifer forests, because of the warmer, wetter conditions.

FOOD AND FEEDING
Woodland birds feed on buds, berries, and seeds from the tree and shrubs. Some eat insects and small animals. Diets may vary with changes in season.

BIRDSONG
Most woodland birds, such as the nightingale, have loud songs and calls to attract mates, and establish breeding territories in the thick undergrowth or in the trees.

PHEASANT WING

WINGS
Many woodland birds have short, broad, rounded wings to help them rise fast into the air and avoid twigs and branches. Pheasants can fly quickly for short distances.

NIGHTINGALE

NESTS IN HOLES

Holes in trees are safe and warm places for birds such as redstarts to raise a family. In the nesting season, the adults frequently fly in and out with food for the growing young.

MALE
REDSTART

CAMOUFLAGED
WOODCOCK

FOREST FACTS

• The northern forest called the taiga is the largest in the world.

• There are over 600 species of eucalyptus in Australia.

• Up to half of all woodland birds nest in tree holes.

• The woodpecker family may have existed for 50 million years.

CAMOUFLAGE

Many woodland and forest birds are well camouflaged to protect them from predators. The dull, mottled colours of this woodcock hide it against the decaying leaf litter of the woodland floor.

DECIDUOUS WOODLAND

IN THESE temperate woodlands, a great variety of birds can live together because they feed at different levels, sharing out available food. In warm weather, the birds nest, raise their young, and eat as much as possible. In colder weather, the leaves fall off the trees, and some birds migrate to warmer places.

Thick skull

Long, curved claws to cling to tree trunks

WOODPECKER SKULL

Strong, stiff tail feathers for support

YELLOW-FRONTED WOODPECKER
This small woodpecker of Eastern Brazil hammers into decaying tree trunks to find insect larvae and make nesting holes. It licks up insects with its long, sticky, barbed tongue.

LONG-TAILED TITS
Long-tailed tits flit about on the edges of woodlands, pecking insects and spiders off the leaves and bark. Outside the breeding season, the tits huddle in small groups at night to keep warm.

GREEN WOOD HOOPOE
These birds probe tree trunks with their long, curved bills searching for food. They live in noisy family groups in African woodlands.

Long bill is used to find insect grubs or eggs, and spiders.

The bill is broad at the base to catch insects.

SPOTTED FLYCATCHER
Perching on exposed branches, spotted flycatchers dart out to snap up passing insects. In cold weather, they migrate to Africa, south of the Sahara, to find food.

Green wood hoopoes have high, cackling calls

WHIP-POOR-WILL
By day, this camouflaged nightjar sleeps on the woodland floor. At night, it flies near the ground catching insects.

313

The capercaillie is able to eat pine needles. This helps it survive through the hard winter. Comb-like fringes on its toes stop it sinking into snow.

CONIFEROUS FOREST

DARK CONIFEROUS FORESTS – the taiga – stretch across the top of the Northern Hemisphere, bordered by the tundra in the north and the more open deciduous woodlands farther south. The leaves stay on the trees all year round, but winters are bitterly cold and most birds leave for warmer places. In the short summer, they feed on seeds, berries or insects.

SISKIN
The restless and acrobatic siskin often hangs upside-down to pull the seeds out of pine and larch cones. Siskins are social birds and build nests high in conifer trees, where the young cannot easily be reached by enemies.

The siskin feeds on the seeds of pine, larch, alder and birch trees.

RED CROSSBILL

Crossbills use their scissor-like bills to lever apart the scales on the cones of pine, spruce, larch and other conifers to reach the seeds. Parent crossbills cough up partly digested pine seed to feed to their young.

PINE
CONES

Scales
opened by a
crossbill

BOHEMIAN WAXWING

These birds are named after the red, wax-like tips on some of their flight feathers. Waxwings eat berries or fruit in winter, and insects during summer. They migrate south in the autumn in large numbers.

Waxwings
have soft,
silky plumage

Male and
female birds
are similar
in colour

JUVENILE BALD EAGLE

Bald eagles breed in forests near water, where they hunt for fish and waterbirds. They do not grow the white feathers on the head and tail until they are four years old.

EUCALYPTUS WOODLAND

IN THE EVERGREEN eucalyptus woodlands of Australia, there is food and shelter for a variety of unique birds all year. The birds help to pollinate the trees and shrubs, and spread their seeds. In the rainy season, waterbirds gather in marshy areas on the borders of these woodlands.

Strong, hooked beak characteristic of parrot family

MALLEE FOWL
These birds build a huge mound of rotting vegetation covered with sand to keep their eggs warm. The male checks the temperature with his bill.

Plumage varies, but most have a yellow collar

RAINBOW LORIKEETS
Noisy flocks of rainbow lorikeets feed high in the trees. They crush the flowers of eucalyptus and other flowering trees to soak up the sticky mixture of nectar and pollen with their fringe-tipped tongues.

Large, broad-based bill to catch and swallow prey

Large head and bill with brown ear patch

LAUGHING KOOKABURRA
Named after its very noisy, chuckling calls, the laughing kookaburra is a giant kingfisher that rarely eats fish. Instead, it pounces on reptiles such as snakes, small mammals, birds, and invertebrates.

317

Feathers are fanned out to make owl look frightening

OWLS

MOST OWLS SLEEP by day and hunt by night. Their sharp hearing and keen eyesight help them catch prey such as mice and small birds. Many owls roost in trees and have brown feathers for camouflage.

SCOPS OWL

Almost impossible to spot because of its superb camouflage, the scops owl eats large insects. It raises its feathers to scare off its enemies.

In a complete pellet, animal fur and bones are all stuck together.

Owl mucus binds pellet together

OWL FACTS

- Order *Strigiformes*
- About 174 species
- Mainly nocturnal
- Birds of prey
- Eat birds, insects and small mammals
- Habitat: mainly woodland
- Nest in tree holes, or other birds' nests
- Eggs: white

OWL PELLETS

Once or twice a day, owls cough up pellets containing indigestible bits of their last meal, such as fur or bones. Pulling a pellet apart reveals what an owl has eaten.

BOOBOOK OWL

This small Australian owl gets its name from its double hoot. It feeds mainly on insects.

Large feet with hooked talons

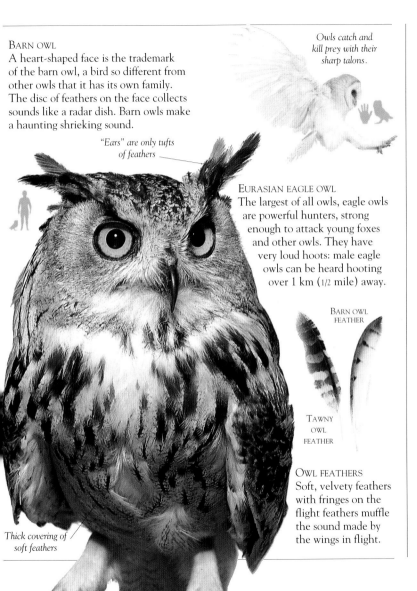

BARN OWL
A heart-shaped face is the trademark of the barn owl, a bird so different from other owls that it has its own family. The disc of feathers on the face collects sounds like a radar dish. Barn owls make a haunting shrieking sound.

Owls catch and kill prey with their sharp talons.

"Ears" are only tufts of feathers

EURASIAN EAGLE OWL
The largest of all owls, eagle owls are powerful hunters, strong enough to attack young foxes and other owls. They have very loud hoots: male eagle owls can be heard hooting over 1 km (1/2 mile) away.

BARN OWL
FEATHER

TAWNY
OWL
FEATHER

OWL FEATHERS
Soft, velvety feathers with fringes on the flight feathers muffle the sound made by the wings in flight.

Thick covering of soft feathers

319

RAINFORESTS

TROPICAL RAINFORESTS are the richest bird habitats. They provide a wealth of food and safe nesting places, and a warm, wet climate all year round. Rainforest birds usually have short, broad wings to twist and turn easily when flying through the trees. This unique habitat is under threat from forestry, mining, dams, and farming.

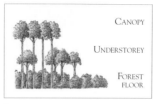

CANOPY

UNDERSTOREY

FOREST FLOOR

BIRDS OF PARADISE
Male birds of paradise have ornate and colourful feathers to attract females. Some tail feathers are very beautiful, like this tail feather from a Count Raggi's bird of paradise.

LAYERS OF LIFE
The birds live at different levels in the trees. In this way, they share the available food and nesting places, so a huge variety of birds can live close together.

SPREADING SEEDS
Fruit-eating birds such as aracaris (small toucans) and parrots help to spread the seeds of rainforest trees. They feed on fruits and pass the seeds in their droppings.

Wide tail helps the aracari to balance on branches

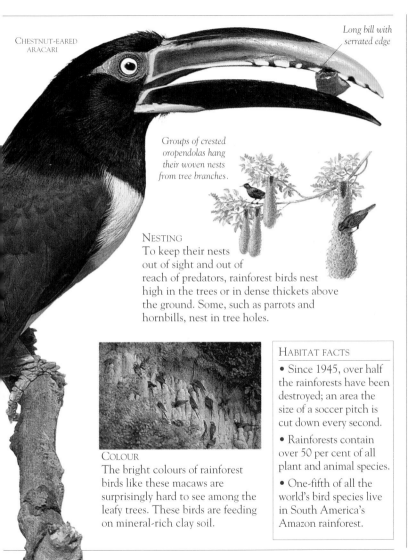

CHESTNUT-EARED
ARACARI

Long bill with
serrated edge

Groups of crested
oropendolas hang
their woven nests
from tree branches.

NESTING

To keep their nests
out of sight and out of
reach of predators, rainforest birds nest
high in the trees or in dense thickets above
the ground. Some, such as parrots and
hornbills, nest in tree holes.

COLOUR

The bright colours of rainforest
birds like these macaws are
surprisingly hard to see among the
leafy trees. These birds are feeding
on mineral-rich clay soil.

HABITAT FACTS

• Since 1945, over half
the rainforests have been
destroyed; an area the
size of a soccer pitch is
cut down every second.

• Rainforests contain
over 50 per cent of all
plant and animal species.

• One-fifth of all the
world's bird species live
in South America's
Amazon rainforest.

321

UNDER THE CANOPY

BENEATH THE GREEN ROOF of the forest is the dark, cool understorey of smaller trees, shrubs, and climbing plants, and below this, the leafy forest floor. There is less food and warmth at these lower levels than up in the canopy, so there are fewer birds. Large birds such as trumpeters and cassowaries stalk across the forest floor. In the understorey, hummingbirds and jacamars flit through the branches.

HOATZIN CHICK

HOATZIN
Groups of hoatzins live along riverbanks in the rainforests of South America. They are poor fliers and make short flights through the trees.

Chick has claws on its wings for climbing

DOUBLE-WATTLED CASSOWARY
This huge cassowary melts into the forest if it senses danger. Males make loud, booming calls during courtship. The horny casque on its head is probably a badge of rank and dominance.

SUNBITTERN
This bird is named after the sunset colours on its wings, visible during its courtship display. At other times, it is well camouflaged by the mottled grey and brown colours of its feathers.

Male not
displaying

Courtship
display of male

BLUE BIRDS OF PARADISE
The male blue bird of paradise
performs a dramatic upside-down
display to show off his iridescent
feathers to a female. He also utters a
weird buzzing noise that sounds rather
like an electric motor.

These birds live in
the middle or
upper levels of the
rainforest, rarely
coming down to
the ground.

ASIAN FAIRY BLUEBIRDS
Noisy fairy bluebirds move busily
through the trees searching for
fruit, such as figs. The metallic
blue of the male is not easy to see
in the shade of the trees.

Fairy bluebirds
often make sharp,
whistling calls.

IN THE TREETOPS

HIGH UP IN THE RAINFOREST CANOPY it is light and warm and there is plenty of food, especially fruits, seeds, and insects. Bird life includes large bird predators such as eagles which patrol the treetops looking for prey. Canopy birds, such as parrots and toucans, climb well and have strong feet for grasping branches.

Bare, orange-yellow face and bill

HARPY EAGLE

The huge harpy eagle is one of the most powerful birds of prey. It swoops into the canopy to seize monkeys (like this capuchin), birds, sloths, and reptiles. It can fly very fast through the branches.

LADY ROSS'S TURACO

This African turaco lives in small, noisy groups, usually high in the canopy. Although clumsy fliers, turacos are good at running along tree branches. They make a great variety of cackling and croaking calls.

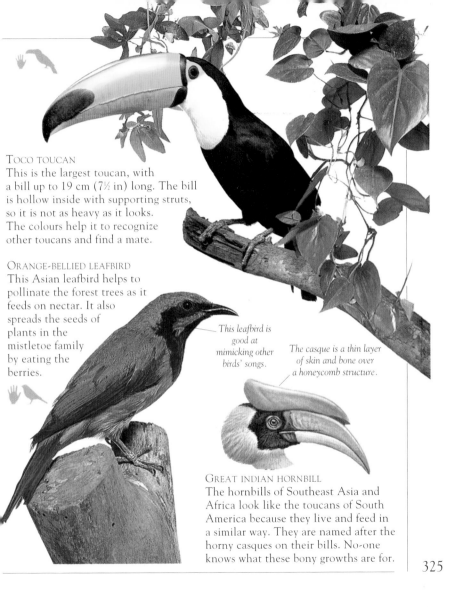

TOCO TOUCAN
This is the largest toucan, with a bill up to 19 cm (7½ in) long. The bill is hollow inside with supporting struts, so it is not as heavy as it looks. The colours help it to recognize other toucans and find a mate.

ORANGE-BELLIED LEAFBIRD
This Asian leafbird helps to pollinate the forest trees as it feeds on nectar. It also spreads the seeds of plants in the mistletoe family by eating the berries.

This leafbird is good at mimicking other birds' songs.

The casque is a thin layer of skin and bone over a honeycomb structure.

GREAT INDIAN HORNBILL
The hornbills of Southeast Asia and Africa look like the toucans of South America because they live and feed in a similar way. They are named after the horny casques on their bills. No-one knows what these bony growths are for.

325

PARROTS

MOST PARROTS are brightly coloured and live in tropical forests. They mainly fly around in flocks, making harsh, screeching calls. Many species are threatened by habitat destruction. There are three main groups: the lories, the cockatoos, and the parrots.

Narrow, tapering wings to fly fast through the trees

CANARY-WINGED PARAKEET
This small parrot's long tail helps it balance as it flies fast through the trees. Larger parrots usually fly more slowly. One parrot, the kakapo, cannot fly at all.

CHATTERING LORY
The chattering lory spends most of its time high in the trees feeding mainly on pollen and nectar. Lories have a brush-like tip to the tongue which soaks up their liquid diet.

LESSER SULPHUR-CRESTED COCKATOO
Cockatoos raise and lower their head crests when they are excited, frightened, or angry. They also do this when landing on a perch.

PARROT FACTS
- Family: *Psittacidae*
- About 330 species
- Diurnal
- Tropical land birds
- Eat fruits, seeds, nuts, and other plants; also some invertebrates
- Habitat: forest, scrub, grassland, and mountains
- Nest: usually tree hole, holes in banks or among rocks
- Eggs: white

326

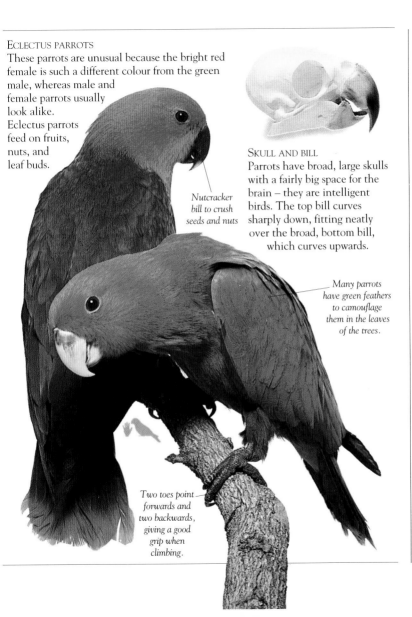

ECLECTUS PARROTS

These parrots are unusual because the bright red female is such a different colour from the green male, whereas male and female parrots usually look alike. Eclectus parrots feed on fruits, nuts, and leaf buds.

Nutcracker bill to crush seeds and nuts

SKULL AND BILL

Parrots have broad, large skulls with a fairly big space for the brain – they are intelligent birds. The top bill curves sharply down, fitting neatly over the broad, bottom bill, which curves upwards.

Many parrots have green feathers to camouflage them in the leaves of the trees.

Two toes point forwards and two backwards, giving a good grip when climbing.

327

RIVERS, LAKES, AND SWAMPS

WATERY HABITATS are home to a rich variety of birds, from ducks, coots, and rails to herons and storks. There is plenty of food for birds to eat, and safe nesting places in reeds and on riverbanks. Many birds rest and feed on lakes, marshes, and swamps during migration. But drainage schemes, dams, acid rain, and pollution from farms and factories threaten these habitats.

KINGFISHER DIVING

WEBBED FEET
Many waterbirds, such as Canada geese, have webbed feet to push the water aside as they swim. Long legs to wade in deep water, and long toes to walk over soft mud are other common features of waterbirds.

HUNTING FOR FISH
To catch fish, birds like this kingfisher dive into the water to seize their prey. Others, such as herons, stand still and catch fish that swim past. The pelican's technique is to scoop up fish from the surface.

CATCHING FISH
Birds need strong bills and feet to hold slippery prey. Merganser ducks have serrated edges to their bill to help them keep a grip on fish they catch.

CANADA GOOSE FOOT

HOODED MERGANSER SKULL

NORTHERN
SHOVELER

FILTER FEEDING
Ducks like the shoveler
filter tiny floating plants
and animals from water.
The shoveler has "combs"
on its bill to trap food.

CAMOUFLAGE
The dark, mottled colours of some
birds, such as the buff-banded
rail, help to
camouflage them
as they skulk
noiselessly through the reed
beds of marshes and swamps.

BUFF-
BANDED
RAIL

HABITAT FACTS

• Siberia's Lake Baikal
is the oldest freshwater
lake – at least 25
million years old.

• About six per cent
of the Earth's surface is
covered by marshes,
bogs, and swamps.

• One-fifth of all fresh
water on Earth flows
through the Amazon
River each day.

NESTING
Hiding a nest away from predators is a relatively
easy task in these habitats. Nesting materials
such as dried reeds are also easy to find. Some
birds even build floating
platforms of
vegetation for extra
security.

COOT
NESTING IN
REEDS

RIVERS AND LAKES

THESE FRESHWATER habitats are important for birds, especially in undisturbed areas free of pollution. Some birds prefer the still waters of ponds and lakes while others, such as dippers, are adapted to move in fast-flowing waters. Around the edge of the water are many places to nest and a variety of food for the young, including water insects.

GREY WAGTAIL
The busy grey wagtail patrols upland streams, darting out to snap up flying insects in its long bill. It has sharp claws to grip slippery rocks and wet branches.

WESTERN GREBES
The courtship dance of the western grebe is long and unusual. During the dance, a pair stands up tall and races fast across the water with heads tilted forwards.

Long legs to wade through deep water while feeding

Flamingos hold their bills upside down as they filter food from the water.

OSPREY

At the last moment, the feet swing forward to grasp the fish.

The osprey is a powerful hunter, plunging feet first into water to snatch fish from near the surface. It sometimes goes right under before pulling up into the air again. Strong claws and spines under the toes help it hold slippery fish.

All flamingos have some black feathers in their wings.

WHITE-CROWNED FORKTAIL
These Asian birds live by rocky streams, perching on boulders wagging their long tails. They have a loud, high-pitched whistle to communicate above the noise of the water.

Lesser flamingos are the smallest of the six species of flamingo.

Crop

LESSER FLAMINGOS
Flamingos live in noisy colonies, sometimes containing thousands of birds. They nest on mounds of mud, and both parents feed the young on a rich "milk" produced in the crop.

331

SWAMPS AND MARSHES

Permanently waterlogged swamps and seasonal marshes are often referred to as "wetlands". They can be freshwater or saltwater habitats. Fish-eating birds, such as egrets and pelicans, are common in wetlands, but a wide variety of birds manage to feed together by eating different kinds of food at different levels in the water.

SCARLET IBIS
Spectacular flocks of scarlet ibises feed, roost, and nest together in the tropical swamps of South America. Scarlet ibises feel in soft mud or under plants for insects, crabs, shellfish, frogs, and fish. Young scarlet ibises have grey-brown upperparts for a year while they mature into adults.

Long, thin, down-curved bill to probe for food

Slim body to slide easily through dense vegetation

BLACK CRAKES
These East African birds have long, widely spaced toes to stop them sinking into the mud and help them walk over floating water plants. Their short, thick bills are not long enough to probe in mud, so they peck small invertebrates and seeds off the surface.

BEARDED TIT
Active and acrobatic bearded tits or reedlings fly low over reed beds on their rounded wings. They feed on insects in warm weather, and seeds in cold weather. Both parents build the nest in the reeds and share the care of their young.

WHOOPING CRANES
Among the world's rarest birds, the whooping crane breeds only in one Canadian national park, and winters only on a few coastal marshes in Texas, U.S.A.

Male has black moustaches

A bird's "knee" is really its ankle, so it bends backwards, just like a person's ankle.

DUCKS

WEBBED FEET and broad, flat bills are a distinctive feature of ducks. These birds are good swimmers and strong fliers. There are two main types of duck – dabbling ducks, such as the mallard, that feed on the surface, and diving ducks, such as the pochard. Many ducks migrate to avoid cold weather.

FEMALE

MALE

DOWN FEATHERS
Female ducks pluck down feathers from their breasts and use them to line their nests and cover the eggs to keep them warm.

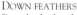

Short legs set well back on body

MANDARIN DUCKS
These ducks live near ponds and lakes surrounded by woods, and nest in tree holes. The male is more colourful than the female, except when he moults his feathers once a year.

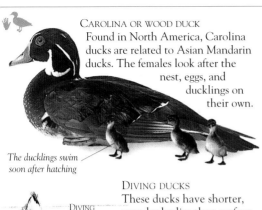

Carolina or Wood Duck

Found in North America, Carolina ducks are related to Asian Mandarin ducks. The females look after the nest, eggs, and ducklings on their own.

The ducklings swim soon after hatching

DIVING POCHARD

Diving ducks

These ducks have shorter, rounder bodies than surface-feeding ducks. Pochards can stay submerged for up to 30 seconds. Some species can dive for even longer.

Duck facts

• Family: *Anatidae* includes ducks, swans, and geese

• About 152 species

• Diurnal

• Waterfowl

• Eat water plants and water animals

• Habitat: wetlands, ponds, lakes, rivers, sea.

• Nest: near water, or in tree holes • Eggs: white or pale

Plumed whistling duck

Whistling ducks live in the tropics and look more like geese than ducks. They feed mainly on the surface.

MALE MALLARD

Webbed feet used like paddles for swimming

Wide, flat bill with comb-like fringes to sift food from water

Mallard duck

Mallards feed on the surface of the water or upend to reach plant and animal food a little way below the surface. Mallards are the ancestors of most domestic ducks.

335

SEAS, CLIFFS, AND SHORES

SOME SPECIALLY adapted birds spend most of their lives gliding over the open oceans. But they nest on shores and in the safety of cliff ledges, usually in large colonies. The rich feeding grounds of estuaries attract huge numbers of waders and wildfowl, especially on migration.

FLIGHT

Tubenoses such as fulmars have long, narrow wings to glide fast over the waves for long distances. However, they are not very good at walking, and are clumsy and ungainly on land.

FULMAR IN FLIGHT

Fulmars have tube-shaped nostrils above the bill. Albatrosses and petrels are also tube-nosed birds.

Fulmars have a stiff-winged flight, hardly bending their wings at all.

CURLEW   REDSHANK   LITTLE STINT   RINGED PLOVER

FEEDING

Finding food out at sea is not always easy, and seabirds spend most of their time looking for the next meal. Terns dive to take fish at or near the surface. Other seabirds, such as puffins, swim deeper underwater.

PUFFIN WITH CATCH

SHARING FEEDING PLACES

Waders avoid competion because their bills are different lengths, enabling them to feed at different levels in the mud. The curlew's long bill reaches worms in deep burrows, while the ringed plover picks insects off the surface.

HERRING
GULL EGGS

Most seabird eggs are more pointed at one end than the other.

CAMOUFLAGED EGGS
Birds such as gulls or terns have camouflaged eggs, as they nest in the open on beaches or dunes. The spots and other markings help the eggs to blend into the background so predators find it hard to see them.

GANNET
ON NEST

HABITAT FACTS

• Oceans cover about 70 per cent of the Earth's surface.

• The sea cools more slowly than the land, keeping coastal areas warmer in winter.

• The tidal range in open oceans is only about 50 cm (20 in).

• In 1 sq m (10 sq ft) of estuary there may be 50,000 crustaceans.

NESTING
Many seabirds nest in tightly packed colonies of thousands or even millions of birds. The vast numbers stimulate them to breed at the same time. Gannets nest close together in noisy, smelly colonies.

ESTUARIES AND SHORES

APART FROM CLIFFS, other areas along the shoreline, such as dunes and beaches, provide nesting areas for seabirds. And where rivers meet the sea, the shallow, muddy waters of estuaries teem with a wealth of food such as fish, worms, and shellfish. Estuaries are particularly important in cold weather, when inland feeding areas are frozen.

PURPLE SANDPIPER
Stocky purple sandpipers migrate south in colder weather to feed on rocky shores. They search the shoreline for food, finding their prey by sight rather than by touc

BLACK-NECKED STILT
This stilt has extremely long legs which allow it to feed in deeper water than other waders. It uses its long bill to take small creatures from water and mud.

On dry ground, the stilt bends its legs awkwardly to feed.

In flight, the stilt's legs stick out 18 cm (7 in) beyond the tail to counterbalance the head and neck.

SLEEPING
On an estuary, waders such as this dunlin feed when they can, and sleep when the tide comes in and covers their feeding grounds. They flock to the safety of high-tide roosts, such as small islands.

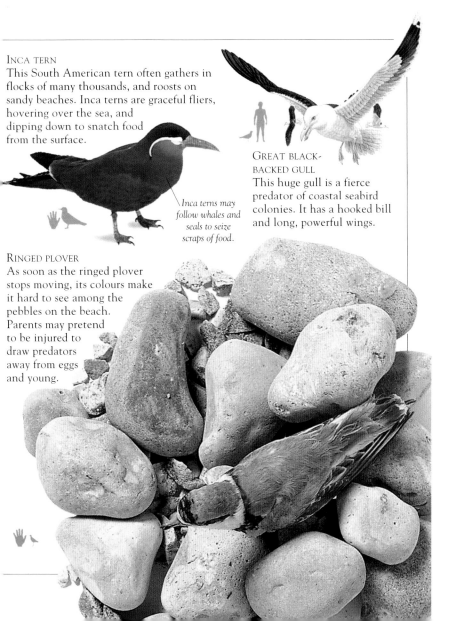

INCA TERN
This South American tern often gathers in flocks of many thousands, and roosts on sandy beaches. Inca terns are graceful fliers, hovering over the sea, and dipping down to snatch food from the surface.

Inca terns may follow whales and seals to seize scraps of food.

GREAT BLACK-BACKED GULL
This huge gull is a fierce predator of coastal seabird colonies. It has a hooked bill and long, powerful wings.

RINGED PLOVER
As soon as the ringed plover stops moving, its colours make it hard to see among the pebbles on the beach. Parents may pretend to be injured to draw predators away from eggs and young.

SEA AND CLIFFS

OVER THE OPEN OCEAN, seabirds search for food, also landing on the surface to rest and preen. Seabirds have waterproofed feathers, webbed feet for swimming, and sharp bills to catch slippery prey. Many nest on cliffs where eggs and young are safe from predators.

NESTING SPACE
To share the nesting sites on a cliff, the birds nest at different levels. Gannets and kittiwakes nest near the top, and razorbills and guillemots in the middle. Shags and cormorants nest lower down.

After fishing, the cormorant holds its wings open to dry.

GANNET SKULL
To catch fish, gannets plunge into the sea like torpedos from heights of up to 30 m (100 ft). They have a strong skull to withstand the impact when they hit the water with such a great force.

COMMON CORMORANT
The feathers of the common or great cormorant trap very little air, so the bird sinks in water more easily than other seabirds and can feed on bottom-living creatures.

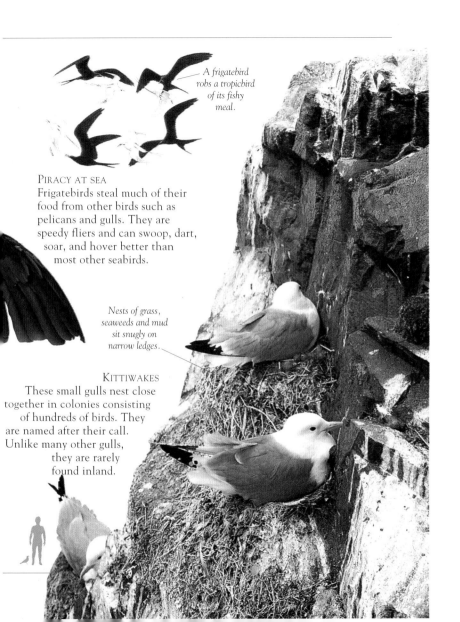

A frigatebird robs a tropicbird of its fishy meal.

PIRACY AT SEA
Frigatebirds steal much of their food from other birds such as pelicans and gulls. They are speedy fliers and can swoop, dart, soar, and hover better than most other seabirds.

Nests of grass, seaweeds and mud sit snugly on narrow ledges.

KITTIWAKES
These small gulls nest close together in colonies consisting of hundreds of birds. They are named after their call. Unlike many other gulls, they are rarely found inland.

DESERTS, SCRUB, AND GRASSLANDS

IN THESE MAINLY HOT, dry habitats, birds may have to travel long distances to find food and water, or migrate to avoid dry seasons. Seeds and insects are the main sources of food, but some larger birds also feed on reptiles, small mammals, and dead animals.

Bee-eaters often feed on flying insects, especially honey bees.

INSECT EATERS
Birds such as bee-eaters and warblers feed on the insects which are most abundant during a rainy season. In the dry season, insect eaters often have to migrate to find enough to eat.

ROADRUNNER

VARIED DIET
Food is often hard to find, so birds survive by eating any food they come across. Reptiles are a common source of food. This roadrunner has caught a lizard.

White-throated bee-eaters fly to wetter grasslands in the dry season.

WHITE-THROATED BEE-EATER

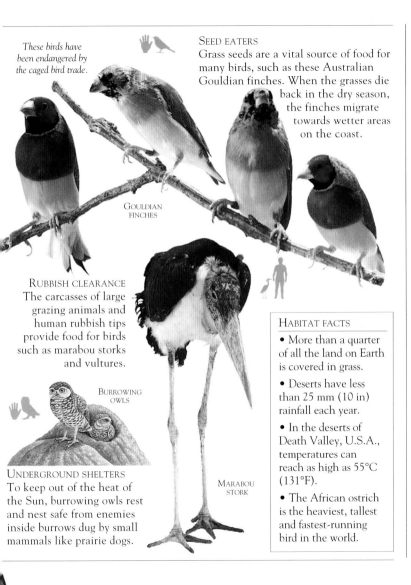

These birds have been endangered by the caged bird trade.

SEED EATERS
Grass seeds are a vital source of food for many birds, such as these Australian Gouldian finches. When the grasses die back in the dry season, the finches migrate towards wetter areas on the coast.

GOULDIAN FINCHES

RUBBISH CLEARANCE
The carcasses of large grazing animals and human rubbish tips provide food for birds such as marabou storks and vultures.

BURROWING OWLS

UNDERGROUND SHELTERS
To keep out of the heat of the Sun, burrowing owls rest and nest safe from enemies inside burrows dug by small mammals like prairie dogs.

MARABOU STORK

HABITAT FACTS
• More than a quarter of all the land on Earth is covered in grass.

• Deserts have less than 25 mm (10 in) rainfall each year.

• In the deserts of Death Valley, U.S.A., temperatures can reach as high as 55°C (131°F).

• The African ostrich is the heaviest, tallest and fastest-running bird in the world.

343

DESERTS

BIRDS THAT LIVE in deserts have to get most of their water either from their food or by flying long distances. By day, they may rest in the shade of rocks, or inside cacti or underground burrows. Some come out to feed at night, when it is cooler. Many birds of prey survive in deserts on a diet of reptiles and small mammals.

SANDGROUSE
These birds are strong fliers and travel many kilometres to find water. The male birds carry water back to their chicks in their belly feathers.

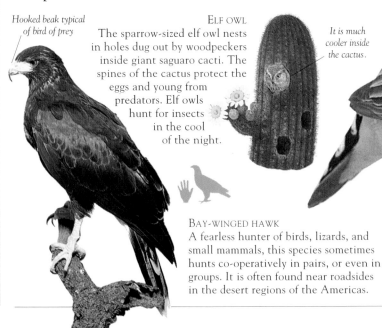

Hooked beak typical of bird of prey

ELF OWL
The sparrow-sized elf owl nests in holes dug out by woodpeckers inside giant saguaro cacti. The spines of the cactus protect the eggs and young from predators. Elf owls hunt for insects in the cool of the night.

It is much cooler inside the cactus.

BAY-WINGED HAWK
A fearless hunter of birds, lizards, and small mammals, this species sometimes hunts co-operatively in pairs, or even in groups. It is often found near roadsides in the desert regions of the Americas.

The female does not have orange cheek patches and her bill is a duller red.

The male has zebra-like stripes on the chest.

ZEBRA FINCHES
These lively little birds are common in the Australian outback. They nest after the rains when there are plenty of seeds and insects to feed to their young. They live in flocks of up to 100 birds, and several may nest together.

SCRUB AND BUSH

THE BIRDS OF these warm, dry, dusty habitats may roam widely in search of food, or follow the rains. The thorny bushes and shrubs often form dense thickets and these make safe nesting places. The berries that grow on the bushes and shrubs can be a useful source of food in colder weather.

Males have brighter markings on the face than the females.

COCKATIELS
These small cockatoos wander over the Australian bush country looking for fruits and grass seeds. They usually nest after rainfall at any time of year.

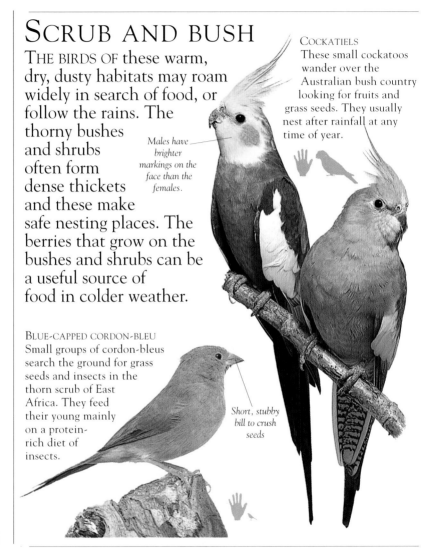

BLUE-CAPPED CORDON-BLEU
Small groups of cordon-bleus search the ground for grass seeds and insects in the thorn scrub of East Africa. They feed their young mainly on a protein-rich diet of insects.

Short, stubby bill to crush seeds

INDIAN GREY FRANCOLIN

These birds are common in southern Asia because they are able to survive in dry conditions. They usually live in small family groups, and feed on weed seeds and grain crops. In warm weather, they also eat insects.

Francolins try to escape danger by running.

EMU

Small flocks of flightless emus roam widely through the Australian bush in search of seeds, berries, and insects. The male looks after the chicks for up to 18 months.

WHITE HELMET SHRIKE

Tame and active white helmet shrikes live in small flocks of two to 20 birds. They hop through the African bush snapping up insects and spiders with their strong, hooked bills.

SCRUBLAND

The scrubland habitats of small trees and thorny shrubs are halfway between grassland and woodland. They include the Mediterranean scrublands, the Californian chaparral, and parts of the Australian bush or outback.

GRASSLANDS

A VARIETY OF seed- and insect-eating birds live in grasslands, especially those birds that can adapt to living near people. Some birds follow herds of grazing animals to snap up the insects disturbed by their feet. Other birds feed on the animals when they die. Long legs enable birds such as ostriches and rheas to see over tall grasses and watch for danger.

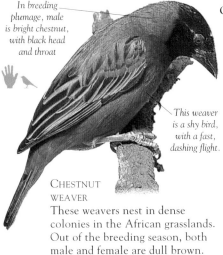

Oxpeckers and giraffe

OXPECKERS
These birds pick ticks and insects off the fur of large African mammals such as giraffes and zebra. They cling to the mammal's fur with their sharp claws.

In breeding plumage, male is bright chestnut, with black head and throat

This weaver is a shy bird, with a fast, dashing flight.

CHESTNUT WEAVER
These weavers nest in dense colonies in the African grasslands. Out of the breeding season, both male and female are dull brown.

OSTRICH
Able to survive in very dry conditions, ostriches stride over the African savannah grasslands on their long legs, searching for leaves, seeds, and insects. They are threatened by hunting and habitat destruction.

348

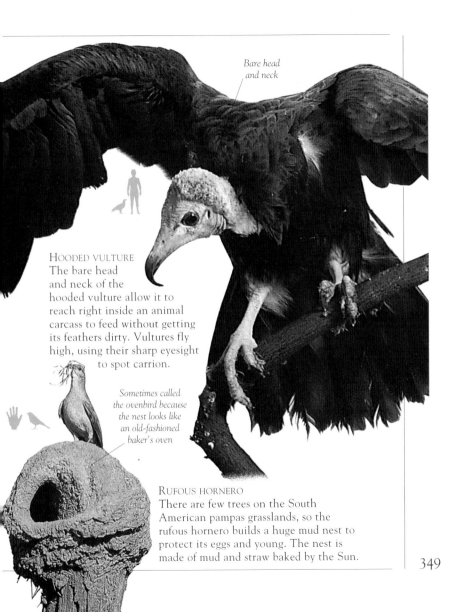

Bare head
and neck

HOODED VULTURE
The bare head
and neck of the
hooded vulture allow it to
reach right inside an animal
carcass to feed without getting
its feathers dirty. Vultures fly
high, using their sharp eyesight
to spot carrion.

*Sometimes called
the ovenbird because
the nest looks like
an old-fashioned
baker's oven*

RUFOUS HORNERO
There are few trees on the South
American pampas grasslands, so the
rufous hornero builds a huge mud nest to
protect its eggs and young. The nest is
made of mud and straw baked by the Sun.

349

MOUNTAINS AND MOORLAND

MOORLANDS TEND TO BE wet, boggy places while mountains can be very cold and windy. Only a few hardy birds live on mountains and moorland year-round because of the harsh climate and lack of food, especially in the cold seasons. However, these habitats are important breeding areas for some birds.

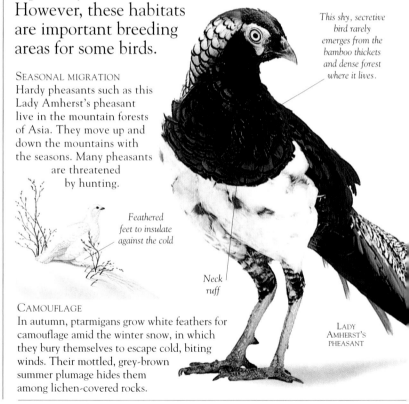

This shy, secretive bird rarely emerges from the bamboo thickets and dense forest where it lives.

SEASONAL MIGRATION
Hardy pheasants such as this Lady Amherst's pheasant live in the mountain forests of Asia. They move up and down the mountains with the seasons. Many pheasants are threatened by hunting.

Feathered feet to insulate against the cold

Neck ruff

CAMOUFLAGE
In autumn, ptarmigans grow white feathers for camouflage amid the winter snow, in which they bury themselves to escape cold, biting winds. Their mottled, grey-brown summer plumage hides them among lichen-covered rocks.

LADY AMHERST'S PHEASANT

NESTING CURLEW

MOUNTAIN FORESTS

The warmer forests on the lower slopes of mountains provide many birds with plenty of food and nesting places. In colder weather, birds may move down to these forests from the upper slopes.

RUFOUS-BELLIED NILTAVA

These Asian flycatchers live in mountain forest above 1,000 m (3,000 ft).

NESTING PLACES

Waders such as this curlew nest on windswept moorland in summer. They hide their nests among grasses and bushes. Their young feed on insects, worms, frogs, and snails. In winter, they move to the coast.

GROUSE EGG

MOORLAND EGGS

Heavy blotches of colour help to camouflage the eggs of moorland nesters such as grouse and waders among the heather and bracken. The eggs are laid in a shallow scrape on the ground.

CURLEW EGG

Male has long tail for display

HABITAT FACTS

• The Appalachians were formed over 250 million years ago; the Himalayas formed only 40 million years ago.

• The world's longest mountain chain is the Andes at 7,250 km (4,500 miles) long.

• Some moorland is created by a change to a wetter climate; others by people clearing trees for farmland.

MOUNTAINS

IN COLD WEATHER, food
is scarce on mountains, but
these areas are undisturbed
breeding areas for birds.
Birds' feathers keep them
warm when it is freezing
cold, and efficient lungs
enable them to get enough
oxygen from the thin air.
Many mountain birds are
powerful fliers.

RAVEN
The largest of
all perching birds, this
member of the crow family
patrols the mountain slopes,
searching for prey or carrion
with its sharp eyes.

WALLCREEPER
This nimble bird
clings on to rock faces
with its sharp claws,
probing for insects
with its slender bill.
In cold weather, it
moves to lower slopes
where there are more
insects for it to eat.

SWORD-BILLED HUMMINGBIRD
This hummingbird lives
high in the Andes. It has a
very long bill, which it uses
to sip nectar from flowers.

SNOW, ICE,
AND ROCK

GRASSY
MEADOWS

CONIFEROUS
FOREST

TEMPERATE
FOREST

HABITAT ZONES
Mountains have a variety of
habitats. There are warm,
deciduous forests on the lower
slopes, cooler coniferous
forests higher up, and, just
below the snow-covered peaks,
grasslands and scrub.

The lammergeier is also called the bearded vulture.

Lammergeiers fly to great heights and drop bones on to rocks to break them apart.

LAMMERGEIER
Soaring over the mountain slopes on rising warm air currents, the lammergeier searches the steep slopes for the carcasses of animals killed by the harsh climate. It drops the bones onto rocks to smash them open, then scoops out the marrow with its long tongue.

ANDEAN CONDOR
The Andean condor, the world's heaviest bird of prey, has sharp vision and long, broad wings. As it soars over the Andes, it scans the slopes below for dead animals to feed on. This bird has been heavily persecuted and also suffers from pesticide poisoning.

MOORLAND

THIS WATERLOGGED habitat of grasses and low-growing shrubs is found in cool, upland areas with lots of rain. It is an important breeding ground for waders and grouse. Predators such as hen harriers and golden eagles find many small birds and mammals to eat here, and there are plenty of insects breeding in the peaty bogs.

Golden plovers feed on insects, worms, and seeds.

Upper parts have golden colour all year round.

GOLDEN PLOVER
In late spring, golden plovers migrate to moorland to breed. They lay their well-camouflaged eggs in a shallow scrape in the ground.

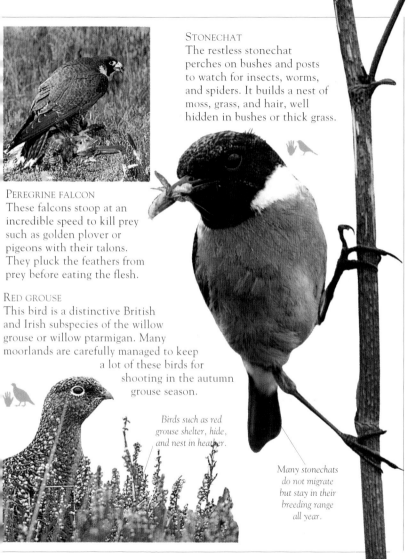

STONECHAT
The restless stonechat
perches on bushes and posts
to watch for insects, worms,
and spiders. It builds a nest of
moss, grass, and hair, well
hidden in bushes or thick grass.

PEREGRINE FALCON
These falcons stoop at an
incredible speed to kill prey
such as golden plover or
pigeons with their talons.
They pluck the feathers from
prey before eating the flesh.

RED GROUSE
This bird is a distinctive British
and Irish subspecies of the willow
grouse or willow ptarmigan. Many
moorlands are carefully managed to keep
a lot of these birds for
shooting in the autumn
grouse season.

Birds such as red
grouse shelter, hide,
and nest in heather.

Many stonechats
do not migrate
but stay in their
breeding range
all year.

355

EAGLES

WITH THEIR SHARP eyes, huge wings, and strong legs and feet, eagles are the most powerful of the birds of prey. Females are usually larger than males. Many species of eagle are threatened by people hunting them, poisoning them, and destroying their habitat.

Light-coloured crown and neck feathers

Strong talons to grip and crush prey

COURTSHIP
During courtship, many eagles show off their amazing flying skills. A pair of bald eagles may tumble and spin through the sky, while trying to touch or grip one another's talons.

Courtship display of bald eagles

IMPERIAL EAGLE
The imperial eagle belongs to a group called the booted eagles, which all have feathered legs. Imperial eagles are widespread in parts of Asia, but rare in Europe.

GOLDEN EAGLE
This booted eagle is a strong flier, soaring high on outstretched wings to search for prey. It gets its name from the golden feathers on the top of its head and the back of its neck.

Primary flight feathers for power and steering

BATELEUR EAGLE
This eagle's name comes from the French word for "juggler" because of its aerial courtship display. It has long wings and a short tail. When it is excited or angry, its crest is raised.

Raised crest

A bald eagle's eyrie

EYRIE
Eagle nests are called eyries and bald eagles have made some of the biggest eyries in the world. They use the same nest year after year, adding more and more twigs and sticks each time they nest.

EAGLE FACTS

• Family: *Accipitridae* – diverse family of about 70 species, including snake eagles, booted eagles, and others

• Diurnal

• Eat a variety of animals, alive and dead

• Habitat: wide range

• Nest: mass of sticks in tree or on cliff ledge

• Eggs: white or marked with brown

POLAR AND TUNDRA

THE FROZEN POLAR REGIONS are the coldest and windiest places on Earth. Few birds can survive there all year round. Most migrate there to breed in the short summer months, when the Sun shines 24 hours a day and there is plenty of food. These unique habitats are threatened by mining, tourism, and pollution.

TUNDRA LANDSCAPES

Around the edge of the Arctic Ocean lie the flat tundra lands, which have a frozen layer called permafrost under the ground. In summer, the soil above the permafrost thaws out, and lakes and marshes form on the surface.

Tundra means "barren land" in Finnish

Ice floating on water

Shoreline

Tundra with permafrost under the ground

Marshy tundra landscape in summer

MIGRATION

In summer, millions of ducks, swans, and geese, such as the barnacle goose, migrate to the tundra lands to feed and nest there. They eat new vegetation sprouting from the warm, moist ground.

ADAPTATIONS

The Arctic auks look like the Antarctic penguins. They have flipper-like wings for swimming, but unlike penguins, they can fly.

LITTLE AUK

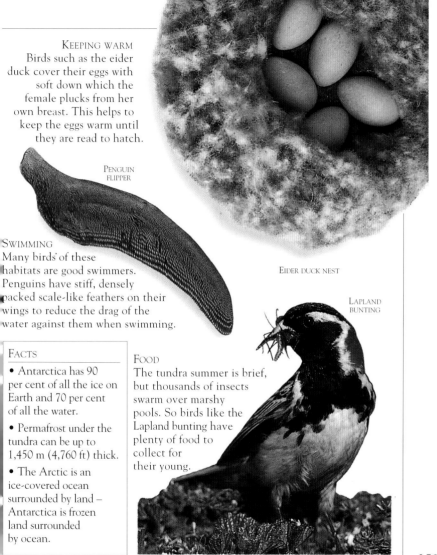

KEEPING WARM
Birds such as the eider duck cover their eggs with soft down which the female plucks from her own breast. This helps to keep the eggs warm until they are read to hatch.

PENGUIN
FLIPPER

SWIMMING
Many birds of these habitats are good swimmers. Penguins have stiff, densely packed scale-like feathers on their wings to reduce the drag of the water against them when swimming.

EIDER DUCK NEST

LAPLAND
BUNTING

FACTS
• Antarctica has 90 per cent of all the ice on Earth and 70 per cent of all the water.

• Permafrost under the tundra can be up to 1,450 m (4,760 ft) thick.

• The Arctic is an ice-covered ocean surrounded by land – Antarctica is frozen land surrounded by ocean.

FOOD
The tundra summer is brief, but thousands of insects swarm over marshy pools. So birds like the Lapland bunting have plenty of food to collect for their young.

ARCTIC AND TUNDRA

AROUND THE NORTH POLE is a huge ice-covered ocean surrounded by tundra landscape. This region is called the Arctic. In summer months, gulls, auks, and terns feed on the fish at sea, and nest on the coast. The insects and seeds on the tundra are food for waders, ducks, geese, and small songbirds. Before winter, the birds fly south to warmer regions.

Male giving his mate a fishy gift during courtship

ARCTIC TERNS
After courtship, terns raise their young in the Arctic summer, then fly all the way to Antarctica for the summer there. They do an incredible round trip of 35,000 km (22,000 miles).

SNOWY OWL FEET

SNOWY OWL
The plumage of the snowy owl camouflages it against the Arctic landscape, as it glides over the ground looking for prey. Feathers on its legs and feet help it to keep warm.

COMMON REDPOLL
This little bird can survive low temperatures. It eats a lot of seeds, and some small insects and their larvae in summer. Some redpolls nest in dwarf birches near the ground in tundra habitats.

Redpolls are named after their red forehead, or "poll".

EMPEROR GOOSE
This handsome goose breeds on the tundra in extreme eastern Russia and in Alaska, U.S.A. It winters farther south.

Adults have orange legs.

In winter, the male snow bunting turns browner and looks more like the female.

SNOW BUNTING
Hardy snow buntings breed in the Arctic – farther north than any other perching bird. They usually hide their nest from predators in crannies in the rocks.

Snow buntings may burrow in the snow to escape intense cold.

ANTARCTICA

THIS VAST AREA of frozen land surrounded by ocean has little rain or snow, so the birds have little fresh water to drink, apart from melted snow. The only land birds are two species of sheathbill. The rest are seabirds, including albatrosses, petrels, and penguins, millions of which nest around the Antarctic coast in summer. They have dense feathers or layers of fat to keep warm, and are strong swimmers or fliers.

BROWN SKUA
With their hooked bills and strong claws, skuas are fierce predators of penguin eggs and chicks. In summer, they regularly patrol penguin colonies in Antarctica.

ADELIE PENGUINS
Adelies are one of the two species of penguin that nest on the rocky coasts of Antarctica itself. In spring, they march inland from the sea to nest on the ground in huge rookeries.

BLACK-BROWED ALBATROSSES
Albatrosses mate for life and reinforce the pair bond each year when they return to the nest. This pair is bill-touching and preening each other.

SNOWY SHEATHBILL

The only bird found in Antarctica that does not have webbed feet

Relatives of plovers and other shorebirds, sheathbills scavenge around seal and penguin colonies for all sorts of food scraps, including penguin chicks, seal afterbirths, and even faeces.

IMPERIAL SHAGS

These impressive birds nest in large colonies on coastal ledges or among rocks. They have strong, hooked bills to grasp slippery fish. In the breeding season, they grow wispy crests.

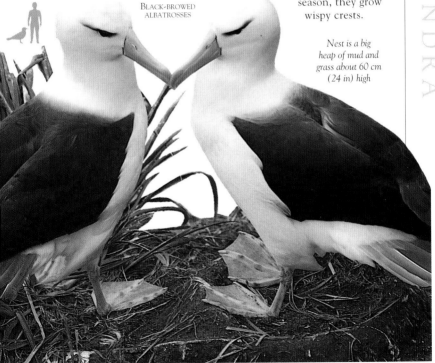

BLACK-BROWED ALBATROSSES

Nest is a big heap of mud and grass about 60 cm (24 in) high

PENGUINS

WITH THEIR SMOOTH, streamlined shape, and stiff, strong wings, penguins are expert swimmers. They dive to catch fish and squid with their spiky tongues. Dense, oily feathers, and thick fat under the skin keep them warm in the cold southern oceans. Penguins only come out of the water to moult and breed, some in colonies of thousands.

EMPEROR PENGUINS
These are the biggest penguins. They never come on land, but breed on the ice that floats around Antarctica in winter. Males incubate the single egg for about nine weeks.

KING PENGUINS
The striking golden-orange ear patches of these birds are used for display during courtship. The markings also help them to recognize other king penguins. These large penguins can dive as deep as 322 m (1,056 ft).

Powerful, narrow wings for swimming

Stiff tail feathers used to support body on land

Male king penguin incubates egg against bare patch of warm skin

Porpoising
Adelie penguins

In water,
penguins look dark
from above and
pale from below
– this helps to
camouflage them

SWIMMING AND DIVING
In order to breathe while swimming fast, penguins leap in and out of the water. This technique is called porpoising. By porpoising, penguins are thought to be able to swim at up to 27 km/h (17 mph), using their stiff wings to push themselves along.

MACARONI PENGUIN
During their courtship displays, these birds shake their bright yellow head crests. The crests also help them to recognize other macaronis.

Spread
flippers
cool bird
down

CHINSTRAP PENGUIN
These penguins are named because of the black line under their chin. They are noisy and quarrelsome birds.

Feet well
back on
body to act
as rudder

PENGUIN FACTS
• Family: *Spheniscidae*
• About 18 species
• Diurnal and nocturnal
• Flightless seabirds
• Eat fish, squid, and small sea creatures
• Habitat: southern oceans, cool temperate islands, tropical shores
• Nest: stones, grass, mud, caves, or burrows
• Eggs: whitish

365

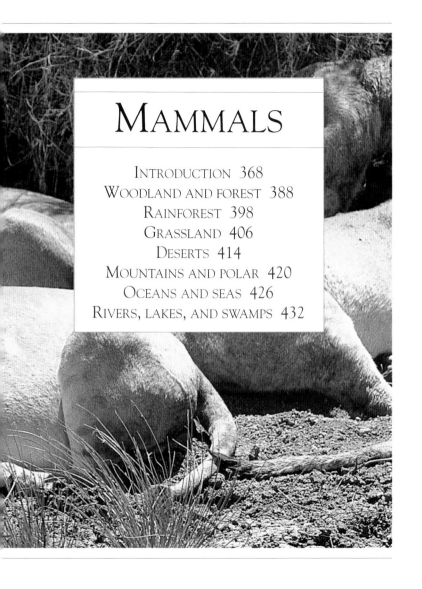

MAMMALS

MAMMALS

WHAT IS A MAMMAL?

ALL MAMMALS HAVE FUR or hair, a backbone for support, and are warm-blooded. Females give birth to live young and feed them with milk from their mammary glands – after which mammals are named. They are the most intelligent and adaptable of all animals and have come to dominate the animal world. There are over 4,600 different kinds of mammal, from enormous whales to tiny bats and shrews.

It takes just less than a year for a foal to grow inside its mother

Foal drinks milk from teats between mother's hind legs

YOUNG MAMMALS
Female mammals feed their young by producing milk in mammary glands. For a long time, as their young grow and develop, parents take care of them, passing on survival skills

HORSE AND FOAL

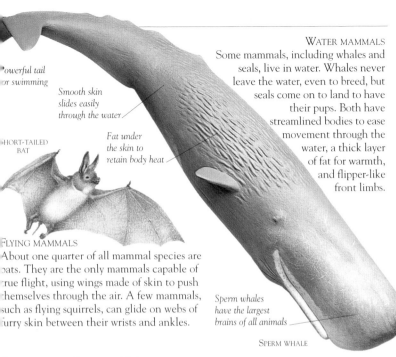

Powerful tail for swimming

Smooth skin slides easily through the water

Fat under the skin to retain body heat

SHORT-TAILED BAT

WATER MAMMALS

Some mammals, including whales and seals, live in water. Whales never leave the water, even to breed, but seals come on to land to have their pups. Both have streamlined bodies to ease movement through the water, a thick layer of fat for warmth, and flipper-like front limbs.

FLYING MAMMALS

About one quarter of all mammal species are bats. They are the only mammals capable of true flight, using wings made of skin to push themselves through the air. A few mammals, such as flying squirrels, can glide on webs of furry skin between their wrists and ankles.

Sperm whales have the largest brains of all animals

SPERM WHALE

HUMAN BABY

Humans need their parents for longer than any other mammal except the elephant

YOUNG CHIMPANZEE

Humans are closely related to chimps, gorillas, and orang-utans

CLOSE COUSINS

Humans are just one of the thousands of kinds of mammal. Chimpanzees are our closest living relatives, with a similar body structure and behaviour, and 98 per cent of the same DNA (genetic material).

369

REPRODUCTION

MAMMALS REPRODUCE in three ways. Most of them, including humans, are placental mammals that nourish their unborn young inside the mother's womb through an organ called a placenta. Marsupial mammals begin developing in the womb but, when still very tiny, crawl out to finish growing in their mother's pouch, called a marsupium. The third and rarest kind are monotremes, the only mammals to lay eggs. All three types of mammal feed their young on milk.

PREGNANT
WOMAN

Baby develops in mother's uterus

Baby, or foetus, facing head-down ready to be born

Placenta

Blood reaches placenta through umbilical cord

Muscles of uterus will contract to push baby out

PLACENTAL MAMMALS
The placenta is a disc-shaped organ that forms in the lining of the uterus after fertilization. The umbilical cord is attached to the placenta. This allows the baby to receive food, oxygen, and antibodies from its mother, and to pass waste products back into her blood.

Amniotic sac is filled with fluid to cushion the baby

Mucus plug blocks cervix during pregnancy

FOETUS AT 28 WEEKS

Platypus eggs have a soft shell

PLATYPUS

AMAZING FACTS

• At birth, a baby kangaroo would fit into a teaspoon.

• While a baby squirrel takes just 22–45 days to develop in its mother's womb, a young elephant takes as long as two years to be born!

• Female Norway lemmings can breed at just 15 days old.

MONOTREMES
The only egg-laying mammals are the platypus and two species of echidna. The platypus incubates its eggs in a nest for about three weeks. During incubation, the egg yolk nourishes the embryo. When they hatch from the eggs, young monotremes suck milk from their mother.

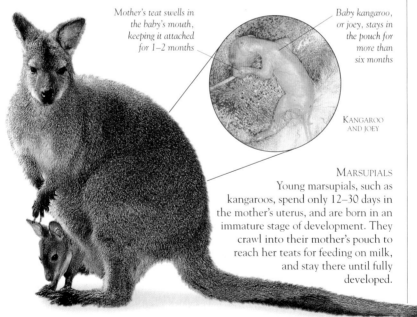

Mother's teat swells in the baby's mouth, keeping it attached for 1–2 months

Baby kangaroo, or joey, stays in the pouch for more than six months

KANGAROO AND JOEY

MARSUPIALS
Young marsupials, such as kangaroos, spend only 12–30 days in the mother's uterus, and are born in an immature stage of development. They crawl into their mother's pouch to reach her teats for feeding on milk, and stay there until fully developed.

BIRTH AND GROWTH

MOST FEMALE MAMMALS give birth to live young. Seals, whales, and monkeys and apes have only one or two young at a time. Other mammals bear up to 10 or 15 babies in a single pregnancy. Mice can have a litter of 18! Most tropical mammals are born at various times of the year; in temperate and cold climates, births usually take place in spring and summer. Mammals tend to spend a lot of time caring for and educating their young.

HAIRLESS BABIES

Baby mice are born without hair or fur. Unable to see or hear, they are totally dependent on their mother. Fur starts to appear when they are one week old, and after ten days, their eyes open. The young are ready to leave the nest after two or three weeks.

Nesting material helps keep mice warm

NEW-BORN MICE

HAIRY BABIES

Kittens are born with their fur. The mother licks the fur, making it dry and fluffy so it traps body heat and keeps the kitten warm. Though new-born kittens are active, their eyes and ears are sealed, leaving them temporarily blind and deaf. They will be ready to leave their mother in eight weeks.

Mother cuts through umbilical cord with her teeth

*Young hang upside
down while their
mothers go out
to feed*

*Each female
can recognize the
cry of her own young*

BAT ROOST

AMAZING FACTS

• Female rats may have
up to 100 babies a year.

• A mother chimpanzee
spends six years looking
after her young chimp.

• Baby giraffes can run
a day after they are born.

• Whales and dolphins
give birth in the water.

BAT NURSERY

Young bats are blind and
hairless when they are born.
They cling together in a
nursery roost, clustered
together for warmth,
while their mothers
go off to feed. Small
species fly within
about 20 days, but
larger species, such
as flying foxes, take
three months to fly.

PARENTAL CARE

Some mammals, including
primates such as gorillas,
spend many years raising
their young and teaching
them how to hunt and
feed. Mothers usually
provide most of the
care, but as in other
social species, like
bats, elephants, and
lions, the care of infants
may be shared among
members of the group.

*Gorillas teach
their young
life skills*

GORILLA
AND BABY

373

SKIN AND HAIR

A MAMMAL'S SKIN is a protective outer layer that, aided by hair, regulates body temperature. Hair, which is unique to mammals, grows as fur, whiskers, wool, prickles, and spines. It traps warm air and keeps out cold, heat, wind, and rain. Some mammals, like chinchillas, have thick, dense fur coats. Others, such as whales, have smooth skin with very little hair.

Movement of hairs can be detected by nerves

Hair

Hairs are toughened with keratin

As dead skin is rubbed off new skin grows underneath

Sebaceous gland coats hair with oily substance called sebum

HUMAN SKIN
Skin protects a mammal's insides and prevents its body from drying out. It keeps out dirt and germs and is sensitive to heat, pressure, and pain. The skin is also important in regulating the temperature of a mammal's body through sweat glands and hairs that grow out of little pits in the skin.

Sweat glands produce sweat to cool body down

Blood vessels expand when body is hot

Insulating layer of fat beneath the skin

CROSS-SECTION THROUGH HUMAN SKIN

BOTTLENOSE DOLPHIN

Fatty blubber under the hairless skin smooths out body contours

WATERPROOF SKIN

Members of the whale group, which includes dolphins, have smooth, tough, rubbery skin with few hairs. This makes them more streamlined in the water. Many seals have heavy, oily fur, which traps bubbles of air and keeps them warm and dry. Whales rely on their fat, called blubber, for warmth.

Camels don't need insulating layers of fat as they live in hot deserts

MOULTING

Many mammals moult, or shed, their fur coats with the changing seasons. This process is triggered by changes in temperature or light and enables mammals to grow thin summer coats and thicker winter ones. Some mammals, such as Arctic foxes, also change the colour of their coat with the seasons.

Fur looks ragged when camel moults its thick winter coat

MOULTING CAMEL

Teeth and limbs are used to comb and brush the fur

KEEPING CLEAN

To keep their skin and fur clean and free from parasites, mammals groom by licking, combing, and nibbling at their coats. Some, like elephants, bathe every day. Social mammals groom each other, which reinforces the bonds between individuals.

RAT GROOMING

INTRODUCTION

SENSES

MAMMALS PICK UP information about their surroundings, and communicate with each other through their senses of sight, hearing, smell, taste, and touch. They are the only animals that have external ear flaps. Most mammals see the world in black and white.

Some dogs are trained to sniff out drugs and explosives

SMELL

Vital for identifying individuals, food, and possible predators or mates, a sense of smell is highly developed in some insectivores, carnivores, (such as dogs) and rodents. In whales and higher primates, such as humans, it is much less developed.

BLACK LEOPARD, OR PANTHER

BEAGLE

A dog's sense of smell is a million times more sensitive than our own

Wet nose helps pick up scents

CATS WHISKERS

Whiskers are long hairs that grow out of the skin, usually on the face. Some mammals have whiskers on their legs, feet, or back. Whiskers respond when they are touched, helping mammals to feel objects in the dark and gauge the width of narrow spaces.

Long, sensitive whiskers

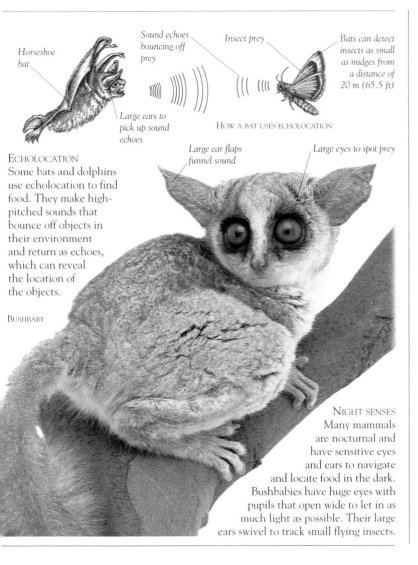

Horseshoe bat

Sound echoes bouncing off prey

Insect prey

Bats can detect insects as small as midges from a distance of 20 m (65.5 ft)

Large ears to pick up sound echoes

HOW A BAT USES ECHOLOCATION

ECHOLOCATION
Some bats and dolphins use echolocation to find food. They make high-pitched sounds that bounce off objects in their environment and return as echoes, which can reveal the location of the objects.

BUSHBABY

Large ear flaps funnel sound

Large eyes to spot prey

NIGHT SENSES
Many mammals are nocturnal and have sensitive eyes and ears to navigate and locate food in the dark. Bushbabies have huge eyes with pupils that open wide to let in as much light as possible. Their large ears swivel to track small flying insects.

377

FEEDING AND DIET

MAMMALS MUST EAT regularly to maintain a constant body temperature, and small mammals need to eat more often than large ones. Most are plant eaters, but some eat meat and others have a more varied diet. Most mammals have three kinds of teeth: incisors and canines for biting and tearing, and molars for grinding. These develop from two sets of teeth – milk teeth when they are young, and adult teeth, which grow as the jaws become larger.

PLANT EATERS

Herbivores, such as cows, horses, camels, sheep, goats, and deer only eat plants. They have long jaws that hold rows of molar teeth which grind and crush tough plant material. Many have a hard pad instead of top front teeth.

Deep lower jaw to anchor large chewing muscles

Horny pad

Jaws move sideways as well as up and down

GOAT SKULL

Gap for tongue to curl around bulky plant food

Carnassial teeth work together like shears

MEAT EATERS

Carnivores, like lions, tigers, and wolves eat meat. Their jaws are shorter and more powerful than those of herbivores. Carnivores have special cheek teeth called carnassials, which have pointed edges that can slice meat or crack bones.

JACKAL SKULL

Powerful canine teeth

378

BEAVER

Back part of tooth wears away more easily than the front, forming a sloping, chisel-like edge

AMAZING FACTS

• Shrews eat their own weight in food each day and can starve to death in just three hours.

• An adult elephant tooth weighs 4.5 kg (10 lb) – heavier than a brick!

• Vampire bats lap up two teaspoons of blood a day.

EVERGROWING TEETH

Rodents, such as beavers, have four strong front teeth called incisors that keep growing. They are continually worn down and kept sharp by constant use. The teeth of pet rodents can grow too long if they lack hard materials to gnaw on.

Curved upper jaw to hold long lengths of baleen

Section cut away to show baleen plates with fringes facing inside the mouth

FOOD STRAINER

Some whales, such as the humpback, grey, and blue whale, have no teeth. Instead, they have long, fringed plates hanging from their jaws. They draw sea water into their mouths and spit it back out through the baleen fringes, which trap food like a sieve.

BALEEN WHALE

BONES AND MUSCLES

ALL MAMMALS HAVE a skeleton, which is an internal framework of bones that supports the body and protects its delicate internal organs. As bones cannot move on their own, they are pulled into different positions by firmly attached groups of powerful muscles, enabling mammals to move. Some mammals have especially strong bones and muscles and can run and swim faster than other animals.

INSIDE A GORILLA
This model of a female gorilla's insides shows the position of the bones and muscles. The gorilla is pregnant and the baby inside its muscular womb is almost ready to be born.

Bony ridge over eyes

Flat shoulder blade or scapula for muscle attachment

Spine, or backbone

Rib cage protects heart and lungs

Long upper arm, or humerus

Long upper leg bone, or femur

Main shin bone, or tibia

Foetus in womb at eight months

FEMALE GORILLA

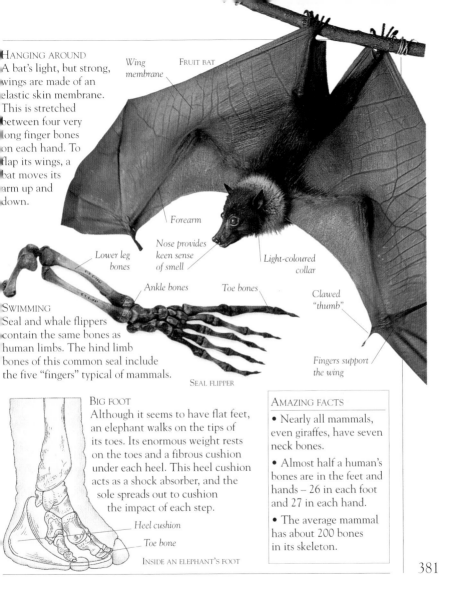

HANGING AROUND
A bat's light, but strong, wings are made of an elastic skin membrane. This is stretched between four very long finger bones on each hand. To flap its wings, a bat moves its arm up and down.

Wing membrane

FRUIT BAT

Forearm

Nose provides keen sense of smell

Light-coloured collar

Lower leg bones

Ankle bones

Toe bones

Clawed "thumb"

SWIMMING
Seal and whale flippers contain the same bones as human limbs. The hind limb bones of this common seal include the five "fingers" typical of mammals.

Fingers support the wing

SEAL FLIPPER

BIG FOOT
Although it seems to have flat feet, an elephant walks on the tips of its toes. Its enormous weight rests on the toes and a fibrous cushion under each heel. This heel cushion acts as a shock absorber, and the sole spreads out to cushion the impact of each step.

Heel cushion

Toe bone

INSIDE AN ELEPHANT'S FOOT

AMAZING FACTS

• Nearly all mammals, even giraffes, have seven neck bones.

• Almost half a human's bones are in the feet and hands – 26 in each foot and 27 in each hand.

• The average mammal has about 200 bones in its skeleton.

DEFENCE

PLANT-EATING MAMMALS, especially small ones, have
many enemies. These include meat-eating mammals,
humans, snakes, and birds of prey. To avoid detection,
herbivores might be
camouflaged. Others
bear weapons, from
sharp claws and
spiky coats to horns,
armour, and terrible
smells. Some find
safety in numbers.

Horns are not
shed each year,
like a deer's
antlers

Pointed tips of
horns could
injure a
predator

Curved
(annulated)
horn

ANTELOPE
SKULL

Joints
between
bones

Unlike antlers,
horns are never
branched, but
are curved and
twisted

PORCUPINE

HORNS, ANTLERS,
AND TUSKS
Used mainly to
fight other males
in competition for
a mate or defend
a territory, horns,
antlers, and tusks are
also useful weapons
of defence. The
horns of antelope,
cattle, and sheep are
hollow structures made
of bone that has a
slightly softer covering.

SPIKE ATTACK
If threatened, a porcupine will turn its
back, rattle its quills, grunt, and stamp
its feet. If the enemy does not retreat,
the porcupine runs backwards into its
attacker, sticking quills into its skin.

382

ODOUR POWER

The skunk's striking black-and-white colour warns enemies to stay away. If this fails, a skunk will turn its back, stamp, and raise its tail. It squirts foul-smelling liquid, which burns the skin and takes a long time to wear off.

Skunk sprays smelly liquid from 3.6 m (12 ft) away

Body armour is impossible to penetrate

ARMADILLO

ARMOUR-PLATING

The body of an armadillo is encased in bony plates, or scutes, covered by horn. Some of the 20 armadillo species roll up into a ball when attacked, to protect their soft underparts.

Handstand warns enemy to watch out!

SPOTTED SKUNK

OKAPI

CAMOUFLAGE

Stripes break up a mammal's shape, making it hard to spot. The okapi, a close relative of the giraffe, lives in rainforests.

AMAZING FACTS

• Opossums play dead if attacked – predators prefer live animals.

• Zebra stallions kick lions, sometimes smashing their teeth.

• Only two mammals are poisonous: the male platypus has poison spurs on its back legs and the water shrew has poisonous saliva.

MAMMAL HOMES

BUILT IN TREES, under the soil, in riverbanks and lakes, or even in people's houses, mammal homes provide a safe, warm shelter that protects them and their young from the weather and from enemies. Mammals build their homes from natural materials, such as grass, leaves, sticks, and fur and use their teeth and limbs to shape them. Many of these homes, such as badger setts, are permanent, while others are built daily or seasonally.

Outer layer of twigs and leaves

Cosy lining of grass, moss, leaves, bark, feathers, and sheep's wool

GREY SQUIRREL IN DREY

TREE HOUSES

As trees are exposed, they make windy homes. Squirrels build round, soccer-ball sized tree nests, called dreys, in which they rest, sleep, and raise their young. Most dreys are built in a new site each year. Winter nests are stronger than summer ones, and special nursery dreys are built for the young.

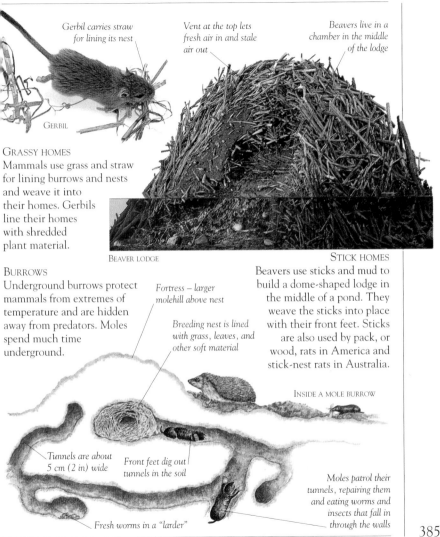

Gerbil carries straw for lining its nest

Vent at the top lets fresh air in and stale air out

Beavers live in a chamber in the middle of the lodge

GERBIL

GRASSY HOMES
Mammals use grass and straw for lining burrows and nests and weave it into their homes. Gerbils line their homes with shredded plant material.

BEAVER LODGE

BURROWS
Underground burrows protect mammals from extremes of temperature and are hidden away from predators. Moles spend much time underground.

STICK HOMES

Beavers use sticks and mud to build a dome-shaped lodge in the middle of a pond. They weave the sticks into place with their front feet. Sticks are also used by pack, or wood, rats in America and stick-nest rats in Australia.

Fortress – larger molehill above nest

Breeding nest is lined with grass, leaves, and other soft material

INSIDE A MOLE BURROW

Tunnels are about 5 cm (2 in) wide

Front feet dig out tunnels in the soil

Fresh worms in a "larder"

Moles patrol their tunnels, repairing them and eating worms and insects that fall in through the walls

385

WHERE MAMMALS LIVE

MAMMALS LIVE all over the world, from mountain tops and the icy poles to baking hot deserts. They can do this because they are warm-blooded, which enables them to keep a constant body temperature – even when their surroundings are extremely hot or very cold.

WOODLAND AND FOREST
There is plenty of food and shelter in these habitats, but mammals have to cope with seasonal changes that bring cold weather and less food.

- ■ Woodland and forest
- ■ Rainforest
- ■ Grassland
- ■ Deserts
- ■ Mountains and polar
- □ Oceans and seas
- ■ Rivers, lakes, and swamps

NORTH AMERICA

ATLANTIC OCEAN

PACIFIC OCEAN

SOUTH AMERICA

AFRICA

RAINFOREST
The year-round warm, wet climate encourages a variety of mammals that live in the trees and on the forest floor.

RIVERS, LAKES, AND SWAMPS
Mammals in these habitats are often strong swimmers with waterproof fur and webbed feet.

OCEANS AND SEAS
These habitats form 70 per cent of the earth's surface. Some mammals breed on land; others never leave the water.

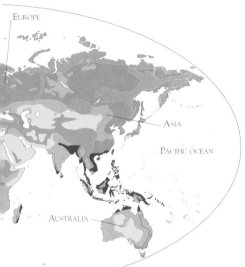

EUROPE

ASIA

PACIFIC OCEAN

AUSTRALIA

MOUNTAINS AND POLAR
With cold temperatures, strong winds, and little moisture, these habitats are home to some of the hardiest mammals.

GRASSLAND
Small burrowers and herds of grazers live in both hot and cool grasslands, which occur where it is too dry for trees.

DESERTS
Desert mammals are specially adapted to survive dry conditions and extreme temperatures. Many store food and rarely drink.

WOODLANDS AND FORESTS

PLENTY OF FOOD, shelter, and nesting places are to be found in woodland and forests. The main large herbivores are deer. Many small herbivores, such as mice and voles, live in the undergrowth, away from predators such as stoats and wolverines. Much of this habitat is protected, but some is still threatened by logging and pollution.

Powerful legs help pine martens climb

Long, bushy tail helps balance

FOOD AND FEEDING

From nuts and berries to leaves and bark, food for plant eaters such as chipmunks is abundant here and varies with the seasons. Small mammals scurrying through fallen leaves are a major source of food for predators

Chipmunks crack nuts with their strong front teeth

NIGHT HUNTERS

Many woodland mammals rest during the day, and become active at night, especially at dusk or dawn. The swift and agile pine marten is a hunter of birds and rodents, both in the trees and on the ground.

CHIPMUNK

MOVING THROUGH THE FOREST

Some woodland mammals climb trees, or glide or fly between them, to find food or places to shelter and nest. Climbers, such as squirrels and koalas, have sharp claws for gripping, while gliding mammals can parachute from tree to tree. Only bats fly freely though the branches.

WINTER SURVIVAL

Mammals survive the winter in many ways. Some, such as the sable, have a fur coat to keep warm, while others build up food stores ready for the hard times ahead. Certain mammals hibernate, or rest, during cold periods.

SUGAR GLIDER

Flaps of skin are spread along sides of body to glide between trees

Sable is up to 45 cm (18 in) long

Thick fur coat

Even the soles of the feet are furry

Hedgehogs have up to 5,000 sharp, stiff spines

HEDGEHOG

HIBERNATING HEDGEHOGS

When a mammal such as a hedgehog or a dormouse hibernates, its body processes slow right down so it is only just alive. In this deep sleep, there is no need to waste energy finding food or keeping warm. A hibernating mammal relies on stores of food or body fat and a protected den to help it survive.

No spines underneath body

DECIDUOUS WOODLANDS

IN TEMPERATE WOODLANDS, mammal lifestyles change with the seasons. Young are born in spring, so they can grow strong by the time winter comes. In summer and autumn, mammals feed as much as possible to gain stores of fat for winter's lean months. While larger mammals spend the winter resting in their burrows, many small ones stay active to keep warm.

Meadow vole is hard to see among dead leaves

UNDER COVER
Hidden in vegetation and leaf litter, small mammals, such as voles, depend on camouflage for survival. As they must feed frequently, many climb trees to collect nuts and other food for storage in underground chambers.

SKILLED CLIMBERS
Leaping nimbly from branch to branch, grey squirrels are masters of life in the trees. They can balance on the thinnest twigs and run up and down tree trunks by climbing with their sharp claws. Food is kept in their twiggy tree nests, called dreys, or buried in the ground.

Squirrels eat nuts and seeds

Bushy tail used for balance and signalling

Badgers have keen senses of smell and hearing but poor eyesight

Black-and-white face markings break up the outline of the badger so it is hard to see in twilight

Long, strong claws for digging underground homes

BURROWING BADGERS
A family of badgers lives in a system of underground burrows, called a sett, which may be hundreds of years old. Signs of an occupied sett include well-marked paths, piles of old bedding material, and dung pits.

Whiskers brush against surroundings to navigate in the dark

AMAZING FACTS

• The largest badger sett had 50 underground chambers and 178 separate entrances!

• Grey squirrels carry acorns up to 30 m (100 ft) from an oak tree before burying them.

• Dormice in some countries hibernate for as long as nine months.

WOODLAND PREDATOR
Ferocious hunters of small animals, weasels are slim enough to chase mice or voles right into their burrows. During the winter months in cold, snowy climates, weasels may grow a white coat, making it hard for both prey and predators to see them.

Sharp claws

Weasels often stand up on their hind legs to look for signs of food and danger

391

CONIFEROUS FOREST

STRETCHING ACROSS northern Europe, Asia, and North
America, coniferous forests provide year-round shelter
for mammals. In the bitter winters, some mammals
hibernate and others turn white for camouflage. To
conserve heat, mammals that live here have thick
fur coats and are larger than their southern relatives.

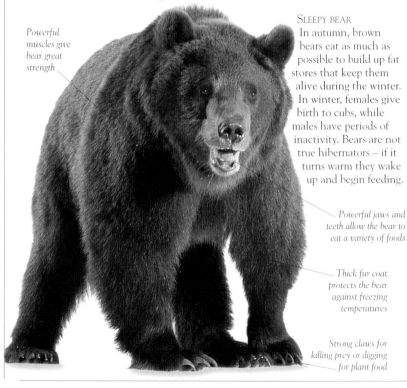

*Powerful
muscles give
bear great
strength*

SLEEPY BEAR
In autumn, brown
bears eat as much as
possible to build up fat
stores that keep them
alive during the winter.
In winter, females give
birth to cubs, while
males have periods of
inactivity. Bears are not
true hibernators – if it
turns warm they wake
up and begin feeding.

*Powerful jaws and
teeth allow the bear to
eat a variety of foods*

*Thick fur coat
protects the bear
against freezing
temperatures*

*Strong claws for
killing prey or digging
for plant food*

AMAZING FACTS

• A hibernating bat may breathe only once every 45 minutes.

• Red squirrels can smell and find pine cones buried 30 cm (12 in) underground.

• A wolverine can drag prey carcasses several times its own weight for many kilometres.

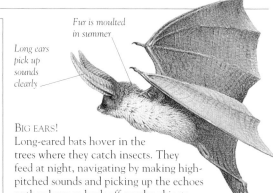

Fur is moulted in summer

Long ears pick up sounds clearly

BIG EARS!

Long-eared bats hover in the trees where they catch insects. They feed at night, navigating by making high-pitched sounds and picking up the echoes as they bounce back off nearby objects.

Thick fur keeps in heat

Powerful jaws give a crushing bite

Widespread toes help the wolverine to run over snow without sinking

Young have more distinct stripes than adults

PERSISTENT PREDATOR

As the largest member of the weasel family, the fierce wolverine can catch animals as large as caribou (reindeer) after pursuing them for 65 km (40 miles). Inuit peoples once prized wolverine fur for making parka coats because it can shed ice crystals.

WILD THING

The striped coat of the wildcat provides good camouflage as it stalks the forest. Wildcats live a solitary life, hunting at night. They are closely related to domestic cats.

EUCALYPTUS WOODLAND

AUSTRALIA'S HOT, DRY woodland provides food and shelter all year round. Most mammals here are marsupials (pouched mammals) that come out at night, using their sharp senses of smell and hearing to find their way around. Some, such as koalas and sugar gliders, live in the trees; others, including bandicoots, live on the forest floor.

POUCHED JUMPER
During the day, groups, or mobs, of grey kangaroos rest under the trees, but at night they search for plants to eat. Young kangaroos stay in the pouch for up to 11 months, longer than any other marsupial, suckling until they are 18 months old.

Large ears and eyes and keen sense of smell to detect signs of danger

AMAZING FACTS

• A baby kangaroo, or joey, is the fastest-growing animal. When born, it is thimble-sized, but it grows by 30,000 times in its lifetime.

• The common wombat is the largest burrowing marsupial. It burrows at 3 m (10 ft) an hour.

Front limbs have five clawed digits

Kangaroos graze with all four feet on the ground

Powerful back legs for bounding away from enemies

Tail helps keep balance

FUSSY EATERS

The tree-dwelling koala seldom comes to the ground, clinging to branches with its strong limbs and sharp claws. Koalas spend about 18 hours a day snoozing in the trees. When awake, they feed only on the leaves of 12 out of the 100 species of eucalyptus tree, eating about 1.5 kg (3 lb) of leaves each day.

A baby koala lives in its mother's pouch for six months, then spends another six months carried on her back

Koalas have a long intestine to help digest tough leaves

Tail can reach 20 cm (8 in) long

Numbats have about 50 teeth

TERMITE HUNGRY

One of the few mammals in these woodlands to be active during the day, numbats eat thousands of termites which they collect with their long, narrow tongue.

Striped coat camouflages numbat from predators such as eagles

NUMBAT

The name "devil" comes from its black colour and eerie call

LETHAL PREDATOR

The huge head and strong jaws of the Tasmanian devil allow it to crush and eat its prey, bones and all. Tasmanian devils live in dens under rocks or tree stumps and are mainly nocturnal. Their young stay in the pouch for 15 weeks and are left in the nest or carried around on the mother's back until 20 weeks of age, when they are weaned.

Sensitive nose to sniff out prey

395

DEER

WOODS and forests, which provide plant food and shelter, are home to many kinds of deer. Their shy nature and camouflaged coats make them hard to spot. Sharp senses help to detect danger, and long legs allow a speedy retreat.

Upper canines form tusks

MALE MUNTJAC SKULL

GRINDING TEETH
The narrow snout of the deer allows it to reach into small spaces to find food. Grinding molar teeth mash up tough plant material.

Long legs and broad hooves to move through deep snow, bogs, or lakes

Male moose have broad, flat antlers used to fight for females in the autumn

Overhanging top lip tears off leaves and branches

Flap of skin is known as the bell

Strong neck and shoulder muscles support heavy head and antlers

LARGEST DEER
Moose, or elk, are the largest deer, weighing up to 450 kg (1,000 lb) and standing 2 m (6.5 ft) tall at the shoulder. Unlike other deer, moose do not live in groups, and outside the breeding season are usually alone or with their young. In winter, moose eat woody plants but in summer, they wade into water for more tender vegetation.

ANTLER GROWTH

1. Antlers start to grow

2. Antlers are covered in soft skin, called velvet

3. Velvet dries up and peels off

4. Fallow deer have flat (palmate) antlers

RED DEER AND FAWN

DEER ANTLERS

All male deer, apart from Chinese water deer, have a set of bony antlers on their head as a sign of strength and dominance. They shed and grow a new set of antlers each year. In the autumn rutting (mating) season, male deer use their antlers in pushing contests to win females.

ROE DEER

The reddish brown coat of the roe deer blends in well with the summer colours of woods and forests. In winter it grows a thick, dense, grey-brown coat for camouflage and warmth.

Antlers no more than 30 cm (12 in) long

MALE ROE DEER

AMAZING DEER FACTS

• Deer are the only animals in the world to have antlers.

• The American wapiti and the caribou have the longest antlers, at over 1.5 m (59 in) in length!

• The South American pudu is the smallest deer, only 38 cm (15 in) tall!

• Red deer are likely to live for over 30 years.

RAINFORESTS

THE WORLD'S RICHEST habitat, rainforests provide
a year-round warm, wet climate and a variety
of food and resting places. Most
mammals here are agile climbers
that live in the trees, but large
predators stalk the forest
floor. Rainforests are
being destroyed at an
alarming rate.

*Thin
"wings"
of skin
run along
the sides
of the body*

COLUGO,
ALSO CALLED
FLYING LEMUR

GLIDING IN THE TREES
Gripping with long toes,
claws, or tails, gliding on
skin flaps, or flying with
wings, mammals move easily
from branch to branch in search
of food, mates, or to escape danger.

*Canopy:
monkeys, fruit bats,
sloths, gliders*

*Understorey:
jungle cats,
tree kangaroos,
lorises*

*Forest floor:
peccaries,
tapirs, okapis,
elephants*

LAYERS OF THE RAINFOREST
Mammals share the rich
resources of the rainforest
by living at various levels.
In the trees, there are leaves
flowers, insects, fruits, and
nuts on which to feed, while
the forest floor provides
a feast of millions more
insects, spiders, worms, and
other invertebrates as well a
plant roots, shoots, and fung

FOREST ECHOES
Visual communication is difficult among thick tangles of vegetation, so many mammals, especially monkeys and apes, rely on sound or scent signals instead. They mark territorial boundaries by scent or shrill cries, and give out alarms and remain in contact with one another by calling.

Tail can be 90 cm (3 ft) long

HOWLER MONKEY

A tiger's stripes help it stalk its unsuspecting prey without being seen

Every tiger has a different pattern of black stripes on its face

Calls of the howler monkey can be heard up to 3 km (2 miles) away

Tigers live in the forests of Southeast Asia and mark their territories with scent and droppings.

TIGER

WELL CAMOUFLAGED
Spots, stripes, and other markings on rainforest mammals help to camouflage them in the dappled forest light. They break up the animal's outline and blend it in with the background. Both predators, such as tigers, and their prey, such as deer, use camouflage. Young mammals are often better camouflaged than their parents.

399

IN THE TREES

HIGH UP IN the rainforest, tangled
tree branches form precarious
walkways. Mammals living here
may be either good climbers or flyers
that are able to move swiftly, or slow
movers that can grasp branches well.
Many tree-dwelling mammals come
out at night to avoid predators such
as cats, hawks, eagles, and snakes.

SPIDER
MONKEY

*Gripping
tail*

*Long fingers
to catch onto
branches*

JUNGLE ACROBAT
The strong tail of the spider monkey
supports its weight, allowing it to reach
fruits and leaves that would otherwise
be out of reach. Spider monkeys can
make acrobatic leaps of 10 m
(33 ft) through
the branches.

LAZING IN THE TREES
Hanging upside down from branches in
the rainforests of Central and South
America, sloths spend 20 hours a
day snoozing in the canopy. Their
fur grows towards the spine so that
rain runs straight off their backs.
Green algae grow in the hair,
camouflaging the sloth.

*Claws hook around branches
and only one limb is moved at a time*

SLOTH

*Nine
neck
vertebrae
allow sloth to
turn around more
than other mammals*

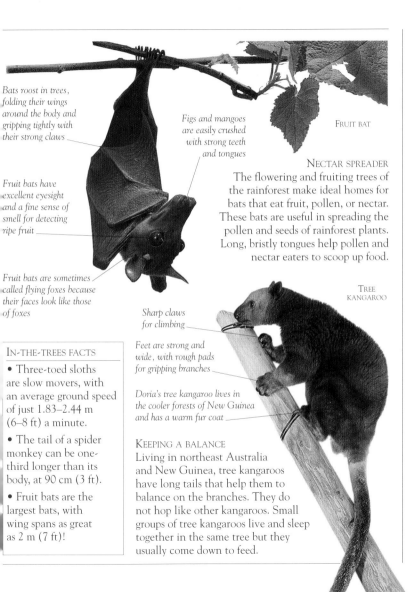

Bats roost in trees, folding their wings around the body and gripping tightly with their strong claws

Figs and mangoes are easily crushed with strong teeth and tongues

FRUIT BAT

Fruit bats have excellent eyesight and a fine sense of smell for detecting ripe fruit

NECTAR SPREADER
The flowering and fruiting trees of the rainforest make ideal homes for bats that eat fruit, pollen, or nectar. These bats are useful in spreading the pollen and seeds of rainforest plants. Long, bristly tongues help pollen and nectar eaters to scoop up food.

Fruit bats are sometimes called flying foxes because their faces look like those of foxes

TREE KANGAROO

Sharp claws for climbing

IN-THE-TREES FACTS
• Three-toed sloths are slow movers, with an average ground speed of just 1.83–2.44 m (6–8 ft) a minute.
• The tail of a spider monkey can be one-third longer than its body, at 90 cm (3 ft).
• Fruit bats are the largest bats, with wing spans as great as 2 m (7 ft)!

Feet are strong and wide, with rough pads for gripping branches

Doria's tree kangaroo lives in the cooler forests of New Guinea and has a warm fur coat

KEEPING A BALANCE
Living in northeast Australia and New Guinea, tree kangaroos have long tails that help them to balance on the branches. They do not hop like other kangaroos. Small groups of tree kangaroos live and sleep together in the same tree but they usually come down to feed.

ON THE FOREST FLOOR

THE RAINFOREST FLOOR is home to many large mammals. Herbivores, such as elephants, and gorillas feed on leaves, while anteaters, pangolins, and armadillos eat termites and other invertebrates. Groups of peccaries dig out roots, keeping a lookout for predators, such as jaguars and ocelots.

STURDY HERBIVORE
Consuming around 170 kg (375 lb) of fibrous plant matter a day, elephants need to have tough stomachs. Their trunks are also vital for reaching understorey plants while standing on the forest floor.

FOREST FLOOR FACTS

• The armadillo's front claws, used for digging up prey, are larger than any other animal's.

• You can tell an Asian elephant from an African one by its smaller ears and shorter tusks. Its dome-shaped forehead also contrasts with the African elephant's rounded one.

Long trunk reaches up to pick fruit or tear down branches

Trunk is a long nose and top lip joined together

Teeth have sharp ridges for grinding up tough plants

Adult bull elephant stands 3 m (10 ft) tall

Flat sole spreads out to carry the massive weight

AFRICAN ELEPHANT

SHY ANTELOPE
Rabbit-sized royal antelope, which live in African rainforests, are one of the smallest hoofed mammals. They are timid, coming out at night to feed on leaves. Royal antelope can slip away silently or leap as high as 3 m (10 ft) into the air to escape predators such as birds and snakes.

Females do not have horns

ROYAL ANTELOPE

Protective horny plates

CHAMPION DIGGER
Massive claws on its front feet enable the giant armadillo to smash its way inside rock-hard termite mounds. It also digs for other insects, worms, and spiders, and eats snakes.

GIANT ARMADILLO

Each ocelot has different fur markings

RARE PAINTED LEOPARD
The ocelot or painted leopard lives in the rainforests of Central and South America. Hunting at night, the ocelot has large eyes to navigate through the dark forest, and its spotted coat gives camouflage as it creeps up on prey. Ocelots are rare because of forest destruction and hunting for their fur.

JUNGLE APES

TROPICAL RAINFORESTS are home to all the world's apes, including gibbons, chimpanzees, gorillas, and orang-utans. Unlike monkeys, apes do not have tails. Gorillas and chimpanzees spend much of their time on the ground, while gibbons and orang-utans swing through the trees. Apes usually live in families, and feed by day.

HANGING AROUND
Lar gibbons are mainly vegetarian and live in small groups in Asian rainforests. Gibbons are confident, skilled climbers, that can run upright along branches and swing effortlessly through the trees.

Lower spine is short and inflexible and rib cage is solid to avoid distorting the trunk while swinging

Arms are longer than legs

OUR CLOSEST RELATIVES?
This chimp is investigating a toy brick. Chimps are intelligent, communicating by sound and gesture.

AMAZING APE FACTS
• The heaviest ape was a zoo gorilla weighing 310 kg (683½ lb).

• Some apes can live to be over 50 years old.

• Chimps have learned over 20 different ways of using everyday objects – such as stones, leaves, and twigs – as tools.

GIBBON SWINGING
THROUGH TREES

Arms are twice as
long as legs, with
an armspan of
about 2 m (6 ft)

Flexible hook-like
hands quickly grasp
branches or prey

Hand-over-
hand swinging
movement is
called brachiation

"Rowing" movements
with its legs help
gibbon propel itself
through the air

GENTLE GIANT

This male gorilla is the head of
a family group that wanders
through the forest eating fruit and
ferns. Females and young climb trees,
but males rarely
do as they are
so big and
heavy.

Mature male
gorillas have
silvery grey hair
on their backs
and are called
"silver-backs"

Fatty
throat
pouch

Long,
powerful
arms

FIVE-YEAR-
OLD MALE

MALE GORILLA

KING OF THE SWINGERS

In the forests of Borneo
and Sumatra, shy orang-
utans live a solitary life,
except in the breeding
season. Males are much
heavier and larger than
females, and mature males have
wide cheek flaps on their faces.

405

GRASSLANDS

LYING BETWEEN wet forests and dry deserts, grasslands fall into two categories– tropical, such as African savanna, and temperate, such as prairie or steppe. Grassland mammals include plant-eating herds, small burrowers, and the predators that feed on both these groups.

Prairie dogs live in colonies of thousands in underground tunnels

PRAIRIE DOG

Horns measure up to 40 cm (16 in)

Strong, grinding teeth for eating tough grasses and leaves

Long legs and sharp hooves to run swiftly away from danger

THOMSON'S GAZELLE

BURROWERS
To avoid the heat and cold, and to escape predators and fires, many small mammals burrow underground. Their burrowing mixes the soil and encourages plant growth. Most live off grass.

GRAZERS
The most common large grassland herbivores are grazers – grass-eating mammals like antelope, bison, and horses. Grasses, which sprout again when the tops are bitten off, produce a continuous supply of food. Grazers, such as Thomson's gazelle, live in herds of up to 100 for protection against predators.

HUNTERS

Most large hunters – like lions, cheetahs, leopards, and hyenas– are found on the African savanna. Since they hunt in groups, lions and hyenas can prey on animals much bigger than themselves. Cheetahs hunt alone but can run fast enough to catch swift antelopes.

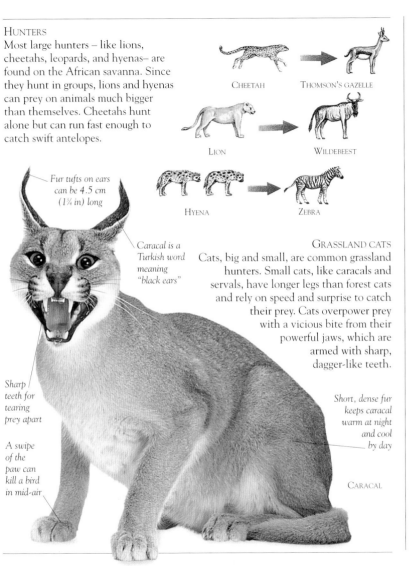

CHEETAH → THOMSON'S GAZELLE

LION → WILDEBEEST

HYENA → ZEBRA

Fur tufts on ears can be 4.5 cm (1¾ in) long

Caracal is a Turkish word meaning "black ears"

GRASSLAND CATS

Cats, big and small, are common grassland hunters. Small cats, like caracals and servals, have longer legs than forest cats and rely on speed and surprise to catch their prey. Cats overpower prey with a vicious bite from their powerful jaws, which are armed with sharp, dagger-like teeth.

Sharp teeth for tearing prey apart

A swipe of the paw can kill a bird in mid-air

Short, dense fur keeps caracal warm at night and cool by day

CARACAL

407

PAMPAS AND STEPPES

THE PLAINS called pampas in
South America and steppes
in Europe and central Asia
have hot summers and
cold winters. Many small
mammals, such as cavies
on the pampas and hamsters
on the steppes, shelter
underground. Herds of wild
grazers have mostly been
replaced by domesticated
cattle and horses.

*Coat turns white
and thickens in
winter*

*Nostrils can
be closed
during sand
storms*

SAIGA
ANTELOPE

STEPPE GRAZERS
The saiga antelope's long nose helps to
warm the air it inhales during cold
winters on the steppes. Huge herds of
saigas once roamed the steppes; they
are now a protected species.

*As anteaters have no teeth, food
is mashed up by hard ridges in
the mouth and a muscular
stomach.*

*Tongue pushes
out 150 times
a minute*

GIANT PREDATOR
Insects are the main grazers of the pampas,
and make a tasty meal for the giant anteater.
Anteaters feed mostly on ants and termites,
ripping open nests with their big claws and
licking the insects with their sticky tongues.

MANED WOLF

To escape danger, maras or Patagonian hares can use their back legs to cover 2 m (6½ ft) in one leap.

Viscachas dig with their strong front legs and can close their nostrils to stop soil from getting in

Cavies are wild relatives of the pet guinea pig

BUSY BURROWERS
Underground burrows provide safe shelter for small mammals of the pampas, such as the mara, cavy, and viscacha. Maras and cavies may live in old viscacha burrows in groups of up to 40.

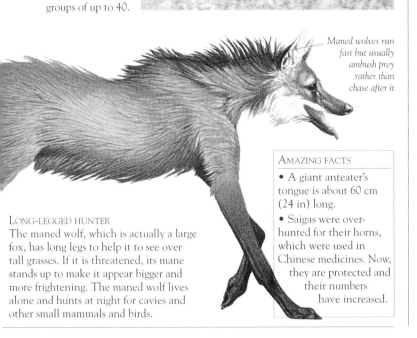

Maned wolves run fast but usually ambush prey rather than chase after it

LONG-LEGGED HUNTER
The maned wolf, which is actually a large fox, has long legs to help it to see over tall grasses. If it is threatened, its mane stands up to make it appear bigger and more frightening. The maned wolf lives alone and hunts at night for cavies and other small mammals and birds.

AMAZING FACTS

• A giant anteater's tongue is about 60 cm (24 in) long.

• Saigas were over-hunted for their horns, which were used in Chinese medicines. Now, they are protected and their numbers have increased.

AFRICAN SAVANNA

THE HUGE GRASSLANDS of Africa are
called savannas. They are home to
the last great herds of mammals, such
as elephants and antelope, and their
predators, including hyenas and large
cats. There are two main seasons – wet
and dry – and many grazers migrate
regularly in search of fresh grass to eat.

*Meercats
sit up on
their hind
legs to
watch for
danger.*

*Annual rainfall
is greater in the
north*

Dry season

*Serengeti National
Park, Kenya*

*Direction
of wildebeests' journey*

*Wet
season*

SAVANNA JOURNEY
Wildebeest trek 1,600 km
(1,000 miles) across the
savanna, following the
seasonal rains that bring
the dry grass back to life.
Living in large herds gives
them some defence
against predators.

SUN LOVERS
Meercats live in family
groups, sharing lookout
duty and diving for
cover if alarmed. Active
during the day, meercats
are often found basking in
the sun near the entrances
to their burrows.

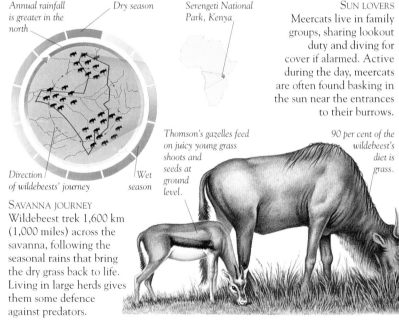

*Thomson's gazelles feed
on juicy young grass
shoots and
seeds at
ground
level.*

*90 per cent of the
wildebeest's
diet is
grass.*

Large, rounded ears

Giraffes can reach leaves up to 6 m (20 ft) above the ground.

Only four toes on front foot

EFFICIENT PREDATORS
Living in packs of 6 to 30, African hunting dogs are nomadic animals, roaming a wide area in search of prey. By hunting together, the dogs can bring down prey larger than themselves, even wildebeest. The pack shares a kill.

Many savanna animals have patterned skin for camouflage

SHARING FOOD
Various mammals live together on the savanna, sharing resources. Giraffes feed on the highest leaves; zebras crop the top of the grasses; wildebeest eat the medium-length grasses; and Thomson's gazelles nibble grass close to the ground.

Zebras feed on tough, grass tops and also dig for roots.

AMAZING FACTS

• Hyenas have jaws so strong that they can crunch through bones.

• Young wildebeest can run very soon after they are born.

• African hunting dogs may start to feed on their prey while it is still alive.

411

GRASSLAND CATS

INTELLIGENT, POWERFUL hunters with sharp senses, grassland cats, both big and small, have strong claws and teeth and a rasping tongue to scrape meat off bones. The spotted coats of leopards, cheetahs, and servals, and the tawny-coloured fur of caracals and lions, provide camouflage in the golden grasses. Lions are the only big cats to live in social groups.

Skull BIG CAT

Voice box

Cartilage provides looser connection

Skull

SMALL CAT

Bony link makes tighter connection

Voice box

TO ROAR OR PURR?
In most big cats, such as lions or tigers, the skull and voice box are loosely connected, allowing the cat to roar but not purr. In pumas and wildcats, the link between the skull and voice box is tighter and less flexible. They can purr, but they cannot roar.

Male lion's mane makes him look fierce and protects his neck during fights

MALE

Streamlined body

Flexible spine

At top speed, all four feet are lifted between strides

Tail helps balance when sprinting

FAST CAT
Cheetahs hunt by day, stalking and attacking prey with a short burst of speed. They can reach 96 km/h (60 mph) in just three seconds!

Long legs for fast running

Exposed claws grip the ground

Claws are made of keratin, like human nails

RELAXED

EXTENDED

KING OF THE CATS
Lions live in groups called prides, made up of 5 to 15 related adult females and their young and 1 to 6 adult males. Males defend the pride while females hunt and care for the young. Lions are the only cats to hunt together, share prey, and help rear each other's cubs.

CAT CLAWS
All cats, except cheetahs, can draw in their claws. This allows the cat to creep up on prey. A cat has four claws on its back paws and five on its front.

Male and female lions look more different than the two sexes of any other cat.

FEMALE

AMAZING CAT FACTS

• Lions sleep or doze for up to 20 hours every day.

• A lion's roar can be heard up to 5 km (3 miles) away.

• A cheetah can only run at top speed for 60 seconds, or it overheats.

• Adult lions eat as much as 18 kg (40 lb) of meat in one meal.

DESERTS

VERY LITTLE RAIN falls on the world's deserts. Most of them, such as the Sahara, are scorching hot all year round, although they get very cold at night. Some, such as the Gobi, have freezing winters. Many small desert mammals are nocturnal, burrowing by day to protect themselves from the extreme heat. Most desert mammals can survive with very little water. Their fur keeps out heat as well as cold.

LARGE MAMMALS
There are few large desert mammals because there is not enough food and water to keep them alive. Only a few kinds of specialized mammals, such as addax, camels, gazelle, antelopes, and kangaroos, manage to survive. They often have to travel long distances in search of water.

Both sexes have thin spiral horns, but the female's are thinner

The addax gets as much moisture as it can from food.

Addax travel around the African deserts in herds searching for food and water

Wide-spreading feet stop addax from sinking into the sand

ADDAX

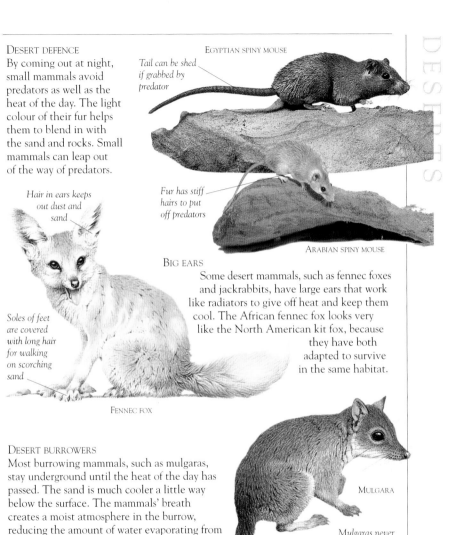

DESERT DEFENCE

By coming out at night, small mammals avoid predators as well as the heat of the day. The light colour of their fur helps them to blend in with the sand and rocks. Small mammals can leap out of the way of predators.

EGYPTIAN SPINY MOUSE

Tail can be shed if grabbed by predator

Fur has stiff hairs to put off predators

ARABIAN SPINY MOUSE

Hair in ears keeps out dust and sand

Soles of feet are covered with long hair for walking on scorching sand

FENNEC FOX

BIG EARS

Some desert mammals, such as fennec foxes and jackrabbits, have large ears that work like radiators to give off heat and keep them cool. The African fennec fox looks very like the North American kit fox, because they have both adapted to survive in the same habitat.

MULGARA

Mulgaras never drink and excrete concentrated urine to preserve water.

DESERT BURROWERS

Most burrowing mammals, such as mulgaras, stay underground until the heat of the day has passed. The sand is much cooler a little way below the surface. The mammals' breath creates a moist atmosphere in the burrow, reducing the amount of water evaporating from their bodies. Many small mammals store food in their burrows to last them through lean times.

415

HOT DESERTS

TEMPERATURES IN THE deserts of western North America, Australia, and the African Sahara are scorching during the day, but because there are no clouds to retain the heat, they drop to freezing at night. There are few plants to provide shelter from the extreme temperatures. Most mammals avoid the daytime sun. Others have large ears or light coats to lose heat, and some pant to cool down. The dew that forms at night may provide much needed moisture.

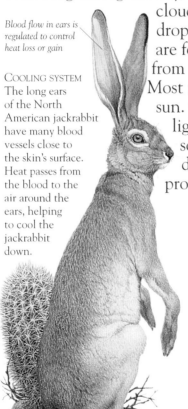

Blood flow in ears is regulated to control heat loss or gain

COOLING SYSTEM
The long ears of the North American jackrabbit have many blood vessels close to the skin's surface. Heat passes from the blood to the air around the ears, helping to cool the jackrabbit down.

Streamlined shape and smooth, silky fur help the mole slide easily through the sand

MARSUPIAL MOLE

Marsupial moles are blind

BLIND TUNNELLER
The Australian marsupial mole uses its long claws to tunnel through sand. Its nose is protected by a horny shield. The burrows are not permanent – the sand is soft and tunnels collapse quickly.

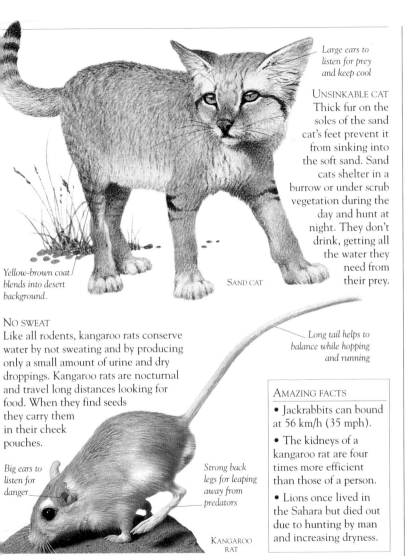

Large ears to listen for prey and keep cool

UNSINKABLE CAT
Thick fur on the soles of the sand cat's feet prevent it from sinking into the soft sand. Sand cats shelter in a burrow or under scrub vegetation during the day and hunt at night. They don't drink, getting all the water they need from their prey.

Yellow-brown coat blends into desert background.

SAND CAT

NO SWEAT
Like all rodents, kangaroo rats conserve water by not sweating and by producing only a small amount of urine and dry droppings. Kangaroo rats are nocturnal and travel long distances looking for food. When they find seeds they carry them in their cheek pouches.

Long tail helps to balance while hopping and running

Big ears to listen for danger

Strong back legs for leaping away from predators

KANGAROO RAT

AMAZING FACTS
• Jackrabbits can bound at 56 km/h (35 mph).

• The kidneys of a kangaroo rat are four times more efficient than those of a person.

• Lions once lived in the Sahara but died out due to hunting by man and increasing dryness.

COLD DESERTS

CENTRAL ASIA'S COLD DESERTS, such as the Gobi desert, are particularly difficult habitats for mammals. Besides great swings in temperature between day and night, there are freezing winters of -40°C (-32°F). Some mammals, such as Bactrian camels and dwarf hamsters, rely on their thick coats to keep warm. Small mammals survive desert conditions by spending a lot of time in burrows.

Coat is thicker in winter

MIGRATOR
Also called the Asiatic wild ass, the onager can run away from enemies at a speed of 65 km/h (40 mph). It migrates to find fresh grass and water.

Some turn white in winter for camouflage in the snow.

Camels can close their nostrils to prevent sand getting in.

Even the soles of the feet are hairy

HAIRY HAMSTER
As they forage for seeds and nuts, dwarf hamsters push food into their cheek pouches and then carry it underground for storage. Dwarf hamsters have very thick fur to help them survive the extreme climate. They stay in their burrows for much of the time.

DESERT JUMPER

In the darkness of the desert night, jerboas emerge from their burrows to feed on seeds, shoots, and insects. Jerboas are like tiny kangaroos, able to jump away from enemies on their strong back legs. Their long tail helps them to balance when they jump and supports their body when they rest.

Large ears and eyes to sense danger.

Back legs are four times as long as the front legs

WALKING WATER TANK

The thick fur of a two-humped Bactrian camel holds in body heat during the bitterly cold Asian winters. These camels moult their fur in spring when the weather gets warmer. Camels have long, thick eyelashes to protect their eyes from sharp grains of sand.

Humps store fat, which can be broken down to provide energy and water.

Fur is moulted in spring.

Webbed feet with thick pads prevent the camel from sinking into the sand.

AMAZING CAMEL FACTS

• A camel can drink up to 60 litres (13 gallons) of water in minutes.

• Camels do not sweat until their temperature reaches 40.5°C (105°F) – a high fever in a human.

• A 500-kg (1,100-lb) camel stores more than 50 kg (110 lb) of fat in each hump.

419

MOUNTAINS AND POLAR

LONG, COLD WINTERS, fierce winds, intense sunlight, and cold, dry air, with little moisture are the main features of mountain and polar regions. Mammals in these habitats rely on thick fur coats or layers of fat to keep warm. Some of these mammals' coats change colour seasonally, for camouflage. To escape the extreme winter cold, many polar mammals migrate to warmer habitats.

Vicuñas have thick fur and can run at up to 47 km/h (29 mph)

VICUÑA

MOUNTAIN CLIMBERS
Large plant-eating mammals living on mountains have to keep moving to find food and avoid predators and bad weather. These herbivores include wild mountain sheep and goats, as well as the vicuñas and alpacas of South America. Sure-footed and agile, these mammals have sharp, pointed hooves that grip on steep, slippery slopes.

About 600–700 sensitive whiskers to help find food

Fatty blubber more than 10 cm (4 in) thick

POLAR OCEANS
In polar regions, the sea is often warmer than the air. It is also very rich in food. Some mammals migrate to polar oceans for the summer months, while others live there all year round.

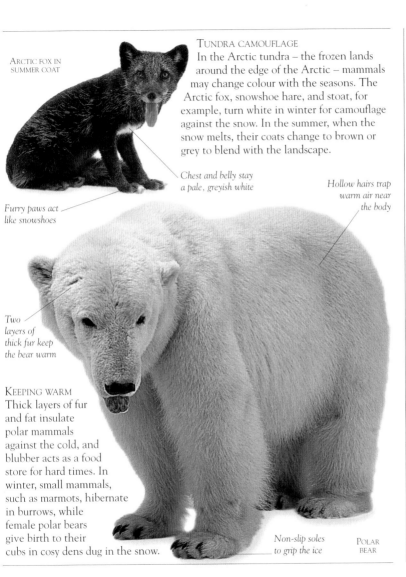

ARCTIC FOX IN
SUMMER COAT

TUNDRA CAMOUFLAGE
In the Arctic tundra – the frozen lands
around the edge of the Arctic – mammals
may change colour with the seasons. The
Arctic fox, snowshoe hare, and stoat, for
example, turn white in winter for camouflage
against the snow. In the summer, when the
snow melts, their coats change to brown or
grey to blend with the landscape.

*Chest and belly stay
a pale, greyish white*

*Hollow hairs trap
warm air near
the body*

*Furry paws act
like snowshoes*

*Two
layers of
thick fur keep
the bear warm*

KEEPING WARM
Thick layers of fur
and fat insulate
polar mammals
against the cold, and
blubber acts as a food
store for hard times. In
winter, small mammals,
such as marmots, hibernate
in burrows, while
female polar bears
give birth to their
cubs in cosy dens dug in the snow.

*Non-slip soles
to grip the ice*

POLAR
BEAR

ARCTIC TUNDRA

AROUND THE EDGE of the icy Arctic ocean is a flat, treeless region called the tundra, where the sub-soil is always frozen. Some mammals, such as musk oxen, are hardy enough to live here all year round. Others, including caribou, or reindeer, cannot stand the harsh climate and migrate here only for the summer months.

Long, curved horns for defence against wolves

Two-layered coat keeps out the cold

MUSK
OX

ARCTIC WOLF

SHAGGY COAT
Musk oxen have long, woolly coats lined with underfur that is eight times warmer than sheep's wool. Some hairs in the outer coat are more than 1 m (3 ft) long. Musk oxen have sharp hooves for digging through snow or ice to find food.

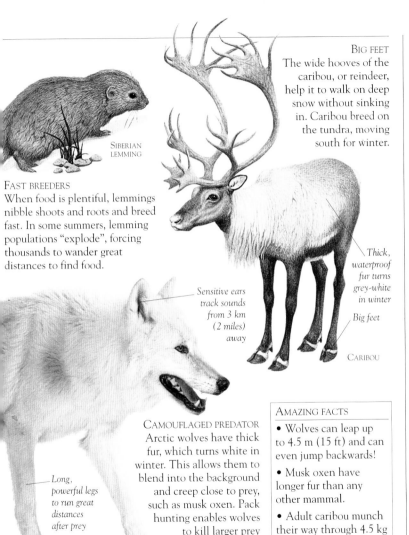

BIG FEET
The wide hooves of the caribou, or reindeer, help it to walk on deep snow without sinking in. Caribou breed on the tundra, moving south for winter.

SIBERIAN LEMMING

FAST BREEDERS
When food is plentiful, lemmings nibble shoots and roots and breed fast. In some summers, lemming populations "explode", forcing thousands to wander great distances to find food.

Thick, waterproof fur turns grey-white in winter

Sensitive ears track sounds from 3 km (2 miles) away

Big feet

CARIBOU

CAMOUFLAGED PREDATOR
Arctic wolves have thick fur, which turns white in winter. This allows them to blend into the background and creep close to prey, such as musk oxen. Pack hunting enables wolves to kill larger prey than if they hunted alone.

Long, powerful legs to run great distances after prey

AMAZING FACTS
• Wolves can leap up to 4.5 m (15 ft) and can even jump backwards!

• Musk oxen have longer fur than any other mammal.

• Adult caribou munch their way through 4.5 kg (10 lb) of food a day!

423

MOUNTAIN TOPS

MAMMALS ARE SCARCE on mountain tops. Many have adapted like Arctic mammals. To cope with the cold and wind, they have thick, shaggy fur coats to keep warm and may move up and down the mountain with the seasons. Some small mammals, such as marmots, hibernate in winter after building up layers of fat in the summer. The internal organs of mammals on high mountains may also differ from those in the lowlands. Many have developed large hearts and lungs to help them get enough oxygen from the thin air at high altitudes.

BATHING MACAQUE
To keep warm in winter, these monkeys from the mountains of northern Japan take hot baths in volcanic springs.

Thicker fur grows in winter

RARE HUNTER
The snow leopard, or ounce, hunts wild sheep and goats at up to 5,500 m (18,000 ft) high in the Himalayas. It roams its huge territory alone. The snow leopard is rare as it has been hunted for its thick fur.

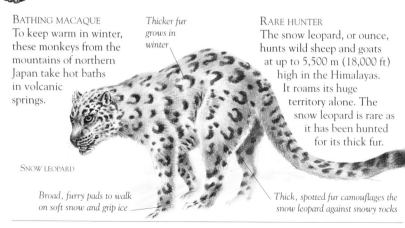

SNOW LEOPARD

Broad, furry pads to walk on soft snow and grip ice

Thick, spotted fur camouflages the snow leopard against snowy rocks

FURRY CHINCHILLA

High up in the Andes mountains, chinchillas huddle in rocky holes. Many have been hunted for their coats, so they are rare in the wild. Chinchillas eat plants, holding food in their paws.

Bushy tail is 15 cm (6 in) long

Soft, dense fur coat

CHINCHILLA
Summer coat is short and smooth; winter coat is long and dense with soft underfur

AMAZING FACTS

• The yak is the highest-living large mammal, grazing at 6,000 m (20,000 ft) in the Himalayas.

• Chamois can live for two weeks without food.

• According to legend, yetis, or abominable snowmen, live in the Himalayas, but no-one has proved they exist.

CHAMOIS

Both sexes have horns

SURE-FOOTED CHAMOIS

The chamois has a very good sense of balance and can jump about 4 m (13 ft) up sheer rock faces in the mountains of southern Europe and western Asia. Chamois browse on plants, moving down from the peaks in winter.

Hooves have a hard, thin edge for gripping rocks

Shock-absorbing legs and spongy hoof pads for extra grip on steep or slippery slopes

OCEANS AND SEAS

LIVING NEAR THE SURFACE of the world's oceans and seas are a variety of marine mammals that come to the surface regularly to breathe. Some, such as whales and dolphins, never leave the water, while others, such as seals, return to land to mate and have their pups. Sea mammals are streamlined, with modified limbs and tails for swimming and thick fat, or blubber, to keep them warm.

FURRY WARMTH

Unlike other marine mammals, the sea otter has no blubber for insulation. Instead it relies on thick, waterproof fur for warmth. An adult may have as many as 800 million hairs, which help provide buoyancy in the water.

SEAL GROUPS

Seals fall into three main groups. True seals, such as the one below, swim with their back flippers and have no visible ear flaps. Eared seals, like the sea lion on the right, swim with front flippers. Walruses are the third group.

TOP PREDATOR

Killer whales come top in polar food webs, feeding on fish, seals, penguins, and even other whales. Killing whales upsets the natural balance of life in the oceans.

Killer whale

Fish

Seabird

Seal

Minke whale

Squid

OCEAN FOOD WEB

Krill

Plankton

High nostrils to breathe almost underwater

Whiskers help to find food

DUGONG

No back legs, tail fluke for swimming

DUGONG

Slow-moving dugongs live in warm waters and are the only vegetarian marine mammals. Where they are still numerous, dugongs live in large herds.

SPEEDY SWIMMERS

Most sea mammals are fast swimmers. Seals propel themselves with flippers, while whales and dolphins rely on strong tail flukes. Dolphins and some seals "porpoise" or leap, out of the water when swimming.

Flat flippers to "fly" through the water

POLAR OCEANS

HARDY WHALES AND SEALS, such as beluga whales, and ringed seals, survive in polar oceans all year round. Many other sea mammals migrate to these cold waters in summer, when food is plentiful. This surge in sea life is fueled by the vast numbers of tiny creatures called plankton, which form the basis of food webs that include fish, whales, squid, seals, and seabirds.

Epidermis – outer layer of skin

Dermis – deeper layers of skin

Blubber – can be more than 25 cm (10 in) thick

Connective tissue

Fascia – band of connective tissue

Muscles

BLUBBER
Sea mammals have an insulating layer of fatty blubber between the skin and the muscles that prevents heat loss.

ELEPHANT SEAL
The gigantic male elephant seal does not eat during the breeding season, as he is busy defending a harem of females against rival males. He uses his nose like a loudspeaker to roar challenges to them. Male elephant seals are more than five times heavier than females.

Male's swollen nose looks like an elephant's trunk

ELEPHANT SEAL

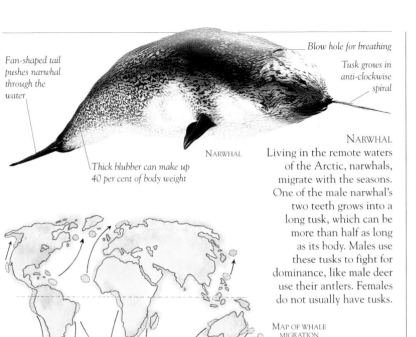

Fan-shaped tail pushes narwhal through the water

Blow hole for breathing

Tusk grows in anti-clockwise spiral

NARWHAL

Thick blubber can make up 40 per cent of body weight

SUMMER FEEDING PLACES
WINTER FEEDING PLACES
MIGRATION ROUTE

NARWHAL

Living in the remote waters of the Arctic, narwhals, migrate with the seasons. One of the male narwhal's two teeth grows into a long tusk, which can be more than half as long as its body. Males use these tusks to fight for dominance, like male deer use their antlers. Females do not usually have tusks.

MAP OF WHALE MIGRATION

WHALE MIGRATION

In summer, many whales travel to the cold polar waters of the Arctic and the Antarctic to feed. In winter, when the sea freezes over, the whales swim back to warmer waters in the tropics to mate and have their young. They eat little in the winter, using up the energy stored as body fat during the summer feast at the poles. Migrant whales include grey, blue, and humpback whales.

AMAZING FACTS

• Grey whales travel more than 20,000 km (12,000 miles) during migration.

• The elephant seal can survive without food for about 100 days.

• Male humpback whales sing the longest and most complex songs in the animal kingdom.

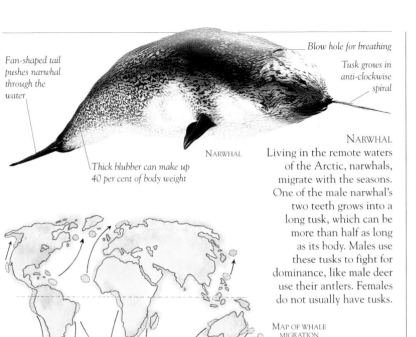

WHALES
AND DOLPHINS

GIANT WHALES and smaller dolphins travel
the oceans of the world, mating and giving birth
in the water. They dive deep into the ocean, surfacing
frequently to breathe air through a blow hole on the
top of their head. Whales and dolphins have large,
complex brains, live in groups, and communicate over
vast distances using sound, which travels well through
water. There are about 88 species of
whale, which fall into two main
groups: toothed whales
and baleen whales.

GREY WHALE

*Scratches
from other whales
or collisions with boats*

*The grey whale is
half the size of the
gigantic blue whale*

BALEEN WHALE
Blue, fin, grey,
and humpback whales are all
kinds of baleen whale, which are
larger than toothed whales. They
feed by straining fish and plankton
from the water, using fringed plates
of horny baleen which hang from
their great arched jaws like curtains.

BLUE WHALE

*An elephant could
stand on a blue
whale's tongue!*

*Grooves allow
throat to stretch so
whale can gulp huge
amounts of water*

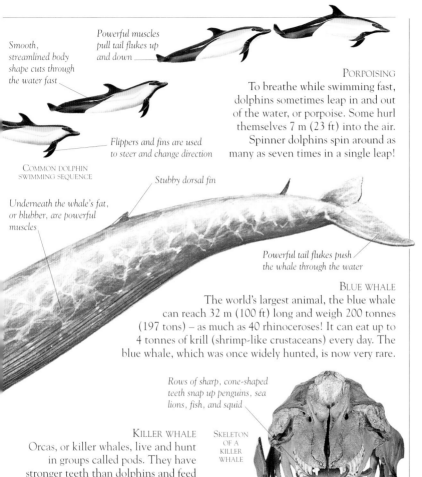

Smooth,
streamlined body
shape cuts through
the water fast

Powerful muscles
pull tail flukes up
and down

Flippers and fins are used
to steer and change direction

COMMON DOLPHIN
SWIMMING SEQUENCE

PORPOISING

To breathe while swimming fast,
dolphins sometimes leap in and out
of the water, or porpoise. Some hurl
themselves 7 m (23 ft) into the air.
Spinner dolphins spin around as
many as seven times in a single leap!

Stubby dorsal fin

Underneath the whale's fat,
or blubber, are powerful
muscles

Powerful tail flukes push
the whale through the water

BLUE WHALE

The world's largest animal, the blue whale
can reach 32 m (100 ft) long and weigh 200 tonnes
(197 tons) – as much as 40 rhinoceroses! It can eat up to
4 tonnes of krill (shrimp-like crustaceans) every day. The
blue whale, which was once widely hunted, is now very rare.

Rows of sharp, cone-shaped
teeth snap up penguins, sea
lions, fish, and squid

KILLER WHALE

Orcas, or killer whales, live and hunt
in groups called pods. They have
stronger teeth than dolphins and feed
on a great variety of prey – even
attacking other whales and dolphins.
Orcas, sperm whales, and dolphins are
categorized as toothed whales, which
are smaller than baleen whales.

SKELETON
OF A
KILLER
WHALE

Powerful
jaws

431

RIVERS, LAKES, AND SWAMPS

RIVERS, LAKES, AND SWAMPS provide inviting environments, rich in food and nesting places, that attract a wide range of mammals. These animals are often strong swimmers, gliding through the water to find food or escape danger. Some, like otters or river dolphins, spend most or all of their time in the water. Others, like raccoons, visit freshwater habitats to feed. These freshwater ecosystems are often threatened by drainage or pollution from industry, towns, or agriculture.

FRESHWATER SEAL
Living in and named after Siberia's largest lake, the Baikal seal is the only seal that lives in fresh water. About 70,000 seals live in the lake, feeding on fish and resting on lake shores and islands. Ancestors of Baikal seals may have migrated to the lake from the Arctic along a river during one of the ice ages.

BAIKAL SEAL

UNDERWATER LIFE
Otters are well adapted for swimming underwater. They have waterproof fur, webbed toes, and a long tail that acts as a rudder. Cubs are taught to enter the water but instinctively know how to swim.

Ears and nostrils can be closed under the water

Otters swim by undulating their body and tail and pushing with their back feet

Thick, fleshy, muscular tail

Front legs steer

OTTER

FISHING FOR FOOD

Fish are an important source of food for water mammals. The fishing cat of southern and Southeast Asian marshes and swamps can flip fish out of the water with its slightly webbed paws. It also dives into the water after fish and catches them in its sharp teeth.

FISHING CAT

Open mouth that shows off huge teeth is a display of threat.

Eyes, nose, and ears stay above the water's surface when hippo is underwater

HIPPOPOTAMUS

RARE MAMMALS

Large mammals are not common in watery habitats – the hippos and antelope of African lakes and swamps are an exception, as are the manatees of western Africa, the Amazon, and the Everglades. More common small mammals include muskrats, mink, beavers, and capybara.

RIVERS AND LAKES

MANY MAMMALS MAKE their homes in safe freshwater lakes, ponds, and rivers. Homes can be hidden away in riverbanks or lakesides, and beavers have even learned to build their homes in the middle of lakes where predators cannot reach them. Some freshwater mammals use sound or electric fields to find food in muddy water.

PLATYPUS

BOTTOM FEEDER
Feeding mainly along the bottom of lakes and rivers, the platypus probes the mud with its sensitive bill for small aquatic animals such as worms, insects, and crayfish. Platypuses, which have no teeth, crush food between horny, ridged plates inside their bill. They nest in burrows

Webbed feet with claws for burrowing

Underwater, the platypus can shut its eyes and ears to keep water out

EXCELLENT SWIMMERS
Muskrats have webbed hind feet and long, flattened tails, which they use as a rudder. They feed mainly on water plants, but also eat fish and frogs. Muskrats dig burrows or construct homes from plants.

Waterproof fur

MUSKRAT

AMAZING FACTS
• The platypus can detect electric fields given off by its prey.

• Strong enough to take the weight of a rider on horseback, the largest beaver dam measured 700 m (2,296 ft) long!

• Using its sharp front teeth, a beaver can fell a small tree in 10 minutes!

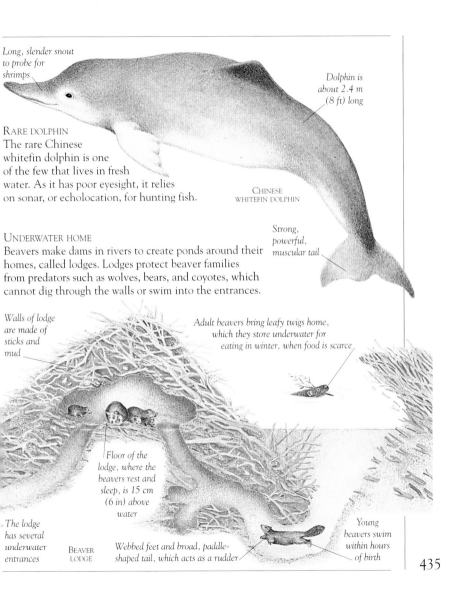

Long, slender snout to probe for shrimps

Dolphin is about 2.4 m (8 ft) long

RARE DOLPHIN
The rare Chinese whitefin dolphin is one of the few that lives in fresh water. As it has poor eyesight, it relies on sonar, or echolocation, for hunting fish.

CHINESE WHITEFIN DOLPHIN

Strong, powerful, muscular tail

UNDERWATER HOME
Beavers make dams in rivers to create ponds around their homes, called lodges. Lodges protect beaver families from predators such as wolves, bears, and coyotes, which cannot dig through the walls or swim into the entrances.

Walls of lodge are made of sticks and mud

Adult beavers bring leafy twigs home, which they store underwater for eating in winter, when food is scarce

Floor of the lodge, where the beavers rest and sleep, is 15 cm (6 in) above water

The lodge has several underwater entrances

BEAVER LODGE

Webbed feet and broad, paddle-shaped tail, which acts as a rudder

Young beavers swim within hours of birth

SWAMPS

WATERLOGGED, FORESTED AREAS, swamps can be fresh or saltwater and are more extensive in tropical than in temperate areas. At different times of year, the water level in swamps may rise and fall, affecting the lives of the mammals who live there. These mammal inhabitants may swim through the water, wade through the mud, or live high up in the trees. For the few that can survive the variable water level and muddy conditions, food and shelter are plentiful.

Nose goes red if monkey is angry or excited

BIG NOSE
The agile proboscis monkey leaps through the branches of mangrove trees in the swamps of Borneo. The male is much larger than the female and has a long nose, which makes his honking calls of danger louder.

Long 76-cm (30-in) tail for balance

PROBOSCIS
MONKEY

UNSINKABLE ANTELOPE
The long hooves and flexible ankles of the sitatunga antelope allow its feet to splay, preventing it from sinking into mud. The sitatunga swims well and often hides underwater.

WINGED HUNTER
The graceful fisherman bat detects its prey by echolocation, then uses its huge, powerful wings to swoop down into the water and catch it.

Sharp claws snatch fish and insects

AMAZING FACTS
• The nose of the male proboscis monkey can reach 17.5 cm (7 in).

• Fisherman bats are superb swimmers, using their wings as oars.

• Manatees munch through 75 kg (165 lb) of vegetation a day.

• Manatees can live for as long as 50–60 years.

Large, rounded tail pushes manatee through the water at speeds of 25 km/h (15 mph)

For breathing, only the tip of the snout is above the surface

SHY PLANT EATER
Manatees, often called sea cows, are shy, rare animals that feed at night mainly on sea grasses. Florida manatees of the Everglades swamps reach a maximum size of 3.9 m (12 ft 10 in) and weigh 1,660 kg (3,650 lb).

MANATEE

437

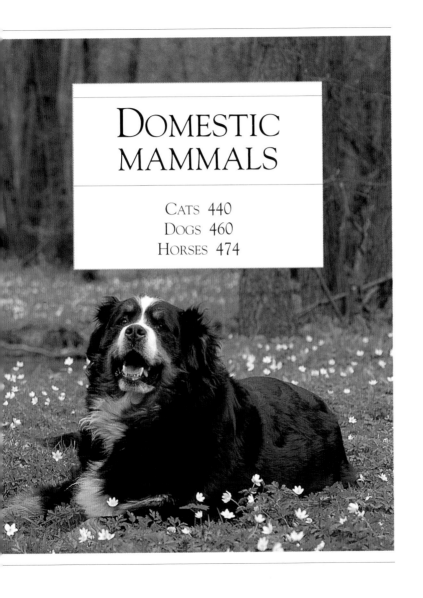

DOMESTIC MAMMALS

WHAT IS A CAT?

CATS ARE NATURE'S most efficiently designed hunting carnivores. They have powerful bodies, superb vision, and razor-sharp teeth and claws. Most cats are self-reliant, stalking their prey alone in dusk or darkness. One species has also succeeded in living with people, and is now kept as a pet around the world.

AFRICAN LION

ANCIENT EGYPTIAN CAT

Short, rounded head

Sandy-brown coat for camouflage

Cats lived near settlements, where they could easily find food.

Strong front legs and muscular neck for catching prey

Sharp claws are kept sheathed when not in use

HISTORY OF THE DOMESTIC CAT
Wall paintings show that cats were being tamed in ancient Egypt before 2500 B.C. Although the Egyptians forbade the export of their cats, they still spread to ancient Greece by 500 B.C. They were also recorded in India before 100 B.C.

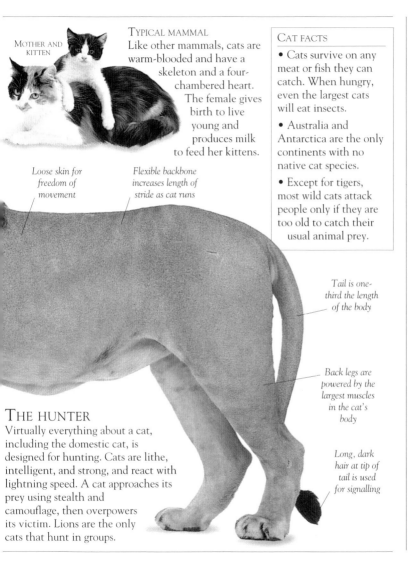

MOTHER AND
KITTEN

TYPICAL MAMMAL
Like other mammals, cats are warm-blooded and have a skeleton and a four-chambered heart. The female gives birth to live young and produces milk to feed her kittens.

CAT FACTS

• Cats survive on any meat or fish they can catch. When hungry, even the largest cats will eat insects.

• Australia and Antarctica are the only continents with no native cat species.

• Except for tigers, most wild cats attack people only if they are too old to catch their usual animal prey.

Loose skin for freedom of movement

Flexible backbone increases length of stride as cat runs

Tail is one-third the length of the body

Back legs are powered by the largest muscles in the cat's body

Long, dark hair at tip of tail is used for signalling

THE HUNTER
Virtually everything about a cat, including the domestic cat, is designed for hunting. Cats are lithe, intelligent, and strong, and react with lightning speed. A cat approaches its prey using stealth and camouflage, then overpowers its victim. Lions are the only cats that hunt in groups.

CAT ANATOMY

ALL CATS ARE AGILE and athletic predators. Their bodies are powerful and flexible, specially designed for running, jumping, and climbing. Some types of cat even excel at swimming. Superb hunters, cats first swiftly chase and then overpower prey with their strength. Sharp teeth are used to finish off the catch.

Tail provides balance

Muscular back legs propel cat forwards

Number of bones in tail varies in different species

POWER LEAP
Strong hind legs provide thrust so the cat can pounce on prey. Sure-footed, it lands safely even on slippery surfaces.

Neck vertebrae

Deep rib cage

Front legs are shorter than hind legs

Body elongates (becomes long and thin) as cat stretches out to leap

BARE BONES
A cat's skeleton has about 250 bones. The seven vertebrae in the neck are shorter than in most other mammals, and the spine is very flexible. This is a domestic cat skeleton, but the skeletons of the larger cats are similar.

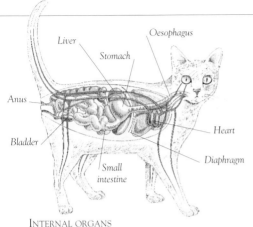

Oesophagus
Liver
Stomach
Anus
Bladder
Heart
Diaphragm
Small intestine

ANATOMY FACTS

• A cat breathes four times faster than a human, and its heart beats twice as fast.

• Cats do not chew their food, but swallow it in large chunks.

• The back muscles of a cat are very flexible.

• The record body length of a domestic cat is 105 cm (41.5 in).

INTERNAL ORGANS

The intestines of a cat are short and simple since they need to digest only meat and not plants. Most of the nutrients from the food are absorbed in the small intestine.

Powerful jaw muscles attach to side of skull

Incisor, or biting, teeth

Canine teeth to kill prey

Carnassial teeth to tear prey apart

Front legs take most of the impact of landing

Pads on the feet help cushion the cat as it lands

CAT SKULL

A cat's skull is large compared to the size of its body. The eye sockets are big to allow for good range of vision. The jaws are short and strong. All of a cat's teeth are sharp and scissor-like for tearing and cutting, rather than flat, like a human's, for crushing.

Eyes and ears

As predators, cats depend on their highly developed senses of sight and hearing to find prey. The majority of cats hunt at night, so they need to be able to see in near darkness. A cat can see about six times better than a person can at night. However, a cat's colour vision is not as developed as ours. Cats also rely on their acute hearing to pinpoint the exact location of prey. Sounds inaudible to humans, or even dogs, can be detected by cats.

SOUND DETECTORS
The serval, a cat from the African savannah, has large, mobile ears. It can pick up the high-pitched calls of rodents hidden in the grass.

THE OUTER EAR
A cat's outer ear acts like a funnel, channelling sounds to the eardrum. Each ear can rotate to locate sounds precisely.

Ossicles (ear bones) send sound into inner ear

Semi-circular canals filled with fluid

Cochlea changes vibrations into nerve impulses

Auditory nerve takes signals to brain

THE INNER EAR
Sound waves vibrate the eardrum, which then moves the ossicles. The vibrations change to electrical impulses and travel down the auditory nerve to the brain. Here they are deciphered into meaningful sounds.

Ear-drum picks up sound waves

Oval window takes sound waves to cochlea

Binocular vision occurs when two fields of vision overlap.

Peripheral vision

285°

130°

CAT VISION

210°

120°

HUMAN VISION

THROUGH A CAT'S EYES
Cats can see at a wider angle around their heads than people can. This means that cats can be alert to movements to the side or slightly behind them. Binocular vision allows them to see images as three-dimensional, as well as to judge distance and depth very accurately.

PUPILS IN DARKNESS

PUPILS IN DAYLIGHT

PUPIL DILATION
At night, the cat's pupils enlarge to let in more light. In bright light, some cats' pupils narrow to slits; others contract to small circles.

SEEING IN THE DARK
Cats see well in semi-darkness. This is because of a "mirror" of glittering cells (called the *tapetum lucidum*) behind the retina. These cells reflect light back, making objects clearer in the dark.

The mirror-like structures in cats' eyes shine when light reflects on them at night.

In the dark, the pupils dilate to become almost round.

Smell, taste, and touch

Cats have extremely acute senses. They rely on smell to identify the things around them, and on touch to feel their way around, particularly in the dark. Another sensory device cats possess is the Jacobsen's organ, located in the roof of the mouth. This structure seems to respond to both smell and taste, and helps the cat to detect scents that their nose cannot – for example, when a female is ready to mate.

The senses of smell and taste tell the cat if this toad is edible.

Cats never eat anything without carefully sniffing it first.

SENSE OF SMELL

A cat's nose contains some 19 million smelling nerves, compared to a human's 5 million. Cats are especially sensitive to rancid odours, such as meat that has gone off. They normally seek out fresh meat rather than scavenge dead animals.

ENTICING CATNIP

Many cats, especially tom (male) cats, find the smell of catnip irresistible. This garden herb contains a chemical that relaxes cats, or can make them roll around. About 50 per cent of cats do not react to catnip at all.

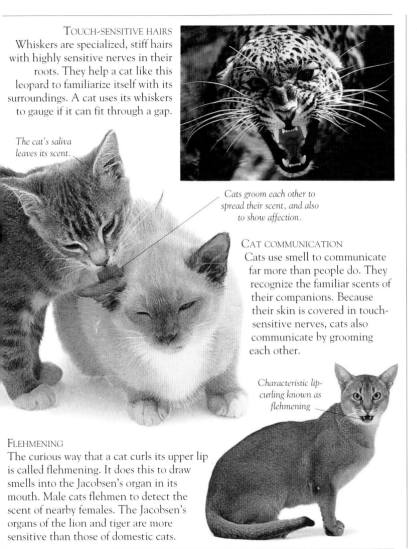

TOUCH-SENSITIVE HAIRS

Whiskers are specialized, stiff hairs with highly sensitive nerves in their roots. They help a cat like this leopard to familiarize itself with its surroundings. A cat uses its whiskers to gauge if it can fit through a gap.

The cat's saliva leaves its scent.

Cats groom each other to spread their scent, and also to show affection.

CAT COMMUNICATION

Cats use smell to communicate far more than people do. They recognize the familiar scents of their companions. Because their skin is covered in touch-sensitive nerves, cats also communicate by grooming each other.

Characteristic lip-curling known as flehmening

FLEHMENING

The curious way that a cat curls its upper lip is called flehmening. It does this to draw smells into the Jacobsen's organ in its mouth. Male cats flehmen to detect the scent of nearby females. The Jacobsen's organs of the lion and tiger are more sensitive than those of domestic cats.

447

Paws and claws

A cat uses its paws for everything from gentle grooming to fierce fighting. To aid a cat in one of its most important skills, running, the bones of the feet have evolved so that a cat permanently walks on its toes. In the wild, injuries to the paws can prove fatal, as these can prevent a cat from hunting successfully.

CLAWS FOR CLIMBING
Most cats are masterly climbers, and can make even a vertical ascent with ease. Coming back down is more problematic, since the claws curve the wrong way to grip when descending. Cats awkwardly make their way down a tree backwards.

Claws dig in to anchor the cat

Claws are made of keratin, like human nails.

Dew claw on front leg is placed like a thumb and helps to grip

Carpal pad on front paw prevents skidding when cat lands

SPECIALIZED FEET
A cat has furless pads of tough leather on the underside of its paws. These pads enable the animal to stalk silently, and they cushion the impact of landings. Pads also help the cat to "brake" suddenly in mid-run. The cheetah has unique grooved pads to improve its control when running.

SCRATCHING ITS MARK
This jaguar, like other cats, scratches trees to keep its claws clean and sharp. Scratching also marks a cat's territory. A cat leaves behind its scent from glands between its toes, while the scratches themselves show the cat has been in the area.

*Claws extended
to grasp toy*

HUNTING WEAPONS
Watching a cat play will reveal many of its hunting techniques. Cats use their front paws to swipe at, scoop up, rake, or grip their catch. Playing with toys is one way domestic cats practise these moves. Pets tend not to use their claws ferociously against their owners.

*This 3-week-old kitten is
already beginning to
develop its hunting skills.*

RETRACTABLE CLAWS
When a cat rests, ligaments keep its claws protected under extensions of the toe bones. The claws are only extended when needed. A cheetah, however, has its claws out permanently so it can grip the ground when it runs.

CLAWS
RETRACTED

CLAWS
EXTENDED

*Relaxed cat with claws
retracted out of sight*

*Ligaments slacken to unveil
claws when necessary*

CAT MOVEMENT

NORMALLY GRACEFUL and controlled, cats can also react with a sudden burst of energy. Balance, strength, speed, and quick judgement help cats to chase and seize elusive prey. The only physical quality cats lack is endurance. The cat is a particularly talented leaper, able to jump four and a half times its body length and land on a chosen spot with great accuracy.

JUMPING
Cats can leap vertically when necessary. The caracal and lynx are expert jumpers, leaping up into the air to swipe a bird as it takes off. With one paw, they can knock their catch to the ground.

A kitten extends its paws and claws to prepare for landing.

Head outstretched as cheetah accelerates to its full speed

CHEETAH

Claws help a cat climb and maintain its balance.

Looking before leaping, to judge its distance from the ground

TERRITORIAL MOVEMENTS
One of a cat's main daily movements is to patrol and mark its territory. It will roam around looking out for other cats or potential prey. Cats climb both to survey their area and because a higher position gives them an advantage over competitors.

LEAPING

A cat's most characteristic movement is its leap, demonstrated here by a lioness. The back muscles flex and relax as the cat leaps, with the tail extended for balance. The powerful back legs lift the cat and are the last part of the body to leave the ground.

The lioness stretches her body forwards as she takes off.

Tail is turned up for balance

Slender, light body and long legs enable the cheetah to reach high speeds

The tail is more than half the length of the body. It swings to counterbalance the body during sharp turns.

When running, the front paws never touch the ground at the same time as the back paws.

RUNNING

Most cats can leap better than they run, but the cheetah is built for speed. Its backbone is extremely flexible, so when the front legs touch the ground, the back end springs forwards. In mid-stride the body stretches full out and all four legs leave the ground. At full sprint the cheetah can reach 96 km/h (60 mph).

Balancing and falling

Some types of cat spend a significant part of their lives in trees, moving confidently along even the narrowest branches. However, if it does fall, the cat has evolved a unique method of protecting itself. Its eyes, brain, and sensitive balance organs in the inner ear ensure that the cat always lands on its feet.

The head rotates first to align with the ground.

1 INSTANT REACTION
The inner ear instantly reacts if the cat is off balance. This warns the brain that it needs to begin to respond to the fall.

2 ROTATING RAPIDLY
The front of the body receives signals from the brain and twists to follow the head. The backbone is so supple that it can rotate 180°.

Front legs pull around to upright position

GEOFFROY'S CAT

This cat lives in the mountainous forests of southern South America.

LIVING THE HIGH LIFE
Many of the small wild cats hunt and sleep in trees. The Geoffroy's cat from South America uses its sharp claws, keen eyesight, good reflexes, and superb sense of balance to stalk mammals and birds in the treetops.

PERFECT BALANCE
This leopard looks precariously balanced, but it will easily secure its kill off the ground and away from scavengers. The leopard is one of the biggest members of the cat family that spends a lot of time in the trees. It is strong enough to drag up a carcass heavier than its own body weight.

FALLING FACTS

• One cat is known to have survived a record fall of 61 m (200 ft).

• From heights of 18 m (60 ft), cats travel at 64 km/h (40 mph) before they hit the ground.

• If the front legs cannot absorb the force of impact, the cat's chin crashes into the ground. This is likely to cause a jaw fracture.

Back end still recovering

Eyes checking where it will be landing

The back legs will help to absorb the force of impact.

3 READY FOR IMPACT
As the cat's front legs begin to stretch out to make contact with the ground, the back of the body is still swivelling around. The collarbones at the top of the front legs will act as shock absorbers when the cat lands.

Legs prepared to run when cat touches ground

4 Landing on its feet
Only seconds after losing its balance, the cat is well positioned to land safely. The head and soft underparts are protected from injury. The cat instinctively relaxes its body before impact, which prevents it from tearing its muscles or jarring its joints.

Front legs take most of the shock of the landing

453

HUNTING

VIRTUALLY ALL CATS hunt on their own, so they must attack with surprise and speed. They stealthily approach their unsuspecting prey using any available cover. When they are close enough they suddenly pounce, seizing their quarry in a deadly grip.

HOUSEHOLD HUNTER
The domestic cat is famed for its prowess as a mouser. Some cats also excel at catching lizards, birds, or insects. However, hunting is a learned behaviour, so not all pet cats make efficient hunters.

GROUP CHASE
Unlike most cats, lions hunt in groups. This means they can kill animals larger than themselves. The lionesses of the pride do nearly all of the hunting. To improve their chances of a kill, they single out a weak-looking animal, surround it, and then chase it down.

Cat holds its body and tail close to the ground

FATAL BITE
This leopard pins down its victim to stop it from escaping. Then it bites through the neck of its catch to sever the spinal cord. If a cat cannot eat its kill all at once it will drag the carcass under cover to protect it from scavengers.

Spotted coat pattern keeps the animal camouflaged

FRUSTRATED KILLER
Domestic cats will play with a toy as if it were a prey animal. They creep up on the object, then bite and shake it. Wild cats sometimes toy with their quarry before killing it.

Mature cats play occasionally, but not as often as kittens.

ASIAN
LEOPARD CAT

SILENT STALKER
Except for the cheetah, cats can manage only short bursts of speed. They must steal quite close to an animal before they bound forwards. Approaching slowly and silently, the stalking cat is alert to every movement. When it is within striking distance it springs on its prey without warning.

The cat runs forwards in this position, then stops and crouches down.

455

FUR TYPES

SLEEK AND FINE, or long and luxurious, a cat's fur is its finest feature. The coat insulates a cat in hot or cold weather, carries its scent, and is sensitive to touch. Fur type is often suited to where a cat lives, although the wide variation of coats in domestic breeds is due to selective breeding by people.

Awn hairs

Down hairs   Guard hairs

A CAT'S COAT
There are three kinds of hair in a cat's coat, although not every breed has all three. The longest are the coarse outer guard hairs. In wild and domestic cats, these carry the fur pattern. Slightly shorter awn hairs lie beneath. Short, soft down provides insulation.

Persians have thick down and up to 10-cm (4-in) long guard hairs.

BRITISH SHORTHAIR
This breed is typical of short-coated cats. It has a short, dense, crisp coat. The thick, plush fur stands out from the body like a rug.

Coat is about 5 cm (2 in) thick

PERSIAN LONGHAIR
Persian cats have the longest and densest fur of any cat breed. The hairs are silky and fine, giving the cat a very fluffy appearance – even the paws are tufted. In warm summer months the cat moults, which makes its coat look shorter.

Fur is especially curly on back and tail

CORNISH REX
The unusual fur of the Rex breeds is wavy and crimped. All of the hairs in a Cornish Rex's coat are short and curly. The coat is made up solely of down and awn hairs, both of which are very soft to the touch. The fur is fine, so Rexes can be susceptible to the cold.

AMERICAN WIREHAIR
This cat's fur is distinctively wiry and springy. Every hair, including those in the ears and on the tail, is crimped, or even coiled. The Wirehair's fur is of medium length and very frizzy. It feels like lamb's wool to the touch.

Wiry coat makes pattern look raised

WILD CAT FUR
Wild cats have coats of two layers: warm down hair underneath and a resilient outer coat. In cold climates, cats have thicker fur. The Pallas's cat from Asia has the longest coat of any wild cat. It was once mistakenly believed to be the ancestor of domestic cats with long hair.

Longer fur on underside for warmth when lying on cold ground

PALLAS'S CAT

"HAIRLESS" SPHYNX
Although the Sphynx looks bald, it has traces of fur on its tail and a light covering of down on its body. It also has very short eyebrows and whiskers. This breed's lack of hair means that it is vulnerable to sunburn.

Coat is like suede

Colours and patterns

Cats come in a huge variety of colours and patterns. Many have distinctive markings that originally evolved to help cats in the wild stay hidden from their prey. Domestic cats often come in more conspicuous colours because they have little need for camouflage. Breeders have achieved some very striking colour and pattern combinations.

SEAL TORTIE
POINT SIAMESE

CORNISH REX
TORTOISESHELL

CHARACTERISTIC MARKINGS
Siamese cats have a characteristic pattern of darker areas on the tail, legs, ears, and face. These markings are described as points. Young kittens develop their points as they mature.

TORTOISESHELL
For genetic reasons, tortoiseshell patterns occur almost entirely in female cats. Tortoiseshell fur is a combination of black and red.

COLOUR RANGE
Some cats have unpatterned coats of one pure, solid colour. There are many varieties, some simply paler versions of the basic colours. Here the typical darker colours are shown above their lighter variants, with white shown on its own.

Black and red randomly but evenly distributed

WHITE

RED

BLACK

CHOCOLATE

CREAM

BLUE

LILAC

TABBY MARKINGS

This cat's spotted coat exemplifies the dark markings typical of tabbies. In different tabby cats, the patterning might be stripes, spots, or patches. These patterns are left over from the natural camouflage markings of wild cats. Tabby patterning is very common in feral cats (domestic cats that live in the wild).

SILVER SPOTTED BRITISH SHORTHAIR

Black spots are striking against a silver background

WILD CAT PATTERNS

The stripes or spots of a wild cat's coat are vital because they help the animal blend into its surroundings. Patterns camouflage a cat by breaking up the outline of its body shape. The markings of wild cats vary so considerably that the shape of the patterns is one way to distinguish the species. Individual cats of the same species also have slightly varying patterns.

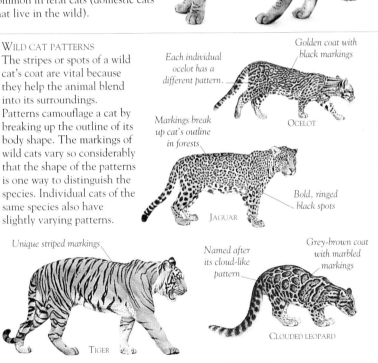

Each individual ocelot has a different pattern.

Golden coat with black markings

OCELOT

Markings break up cat's outline in forests

Bold, ringed black spots

JAGUAR

Unique striped markings

Named after its cloud-like pattern

Grey-brown coat with marbled markings

CLOUDED LEOPARD

TIGER

WHAT IS A DOG?

THE DOMESTIC DOG, scientific name *Canis familiaris* (from the Latin *canis*, meaning "dog"), is one of 34 living species of canids – meat-eating animals that evolved for the pursuit of prey across open grassland. The dog family ranges from the tiny Fennec Fox to the large Grey Wolf.

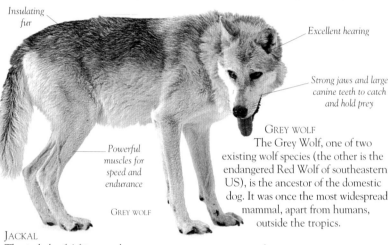

Insulating fur

Excellent hearing

Strong jaws and large canine teeth to catch and hold prey

Powerful muscles for speed and endurance

GREY WOLF

GREY WOLF
The Grey Wolf, one of two existing wolf species (the other is the endangered Red Wolf of southeastern US), is the ancestor of the domestic dog. It was once the most widespread mammal, apart from humans, outside the tropics.

JACKAL
The jackals of Africa, southeastern Europe, and Asia, have an undeserved bad name. Jackals are good parents to their young and do not scavenge as much as is supposed. Their diet ranges from fruit to small gazelle.

JACKAL

RED FOX

RED FOX
The Red Fox, like all foxes, is a small canid with a slender skull, large ears, and a long, bushy tail. Its coat comes in three colours – a flame red, a blackish silver, and the intermediate, "Cross" fox.

Dogs are social animals that adapt to their surroundings easily

PACK INSTINCT

Unlike more specialized carnivores, such as cats, which tend to hunt alone, most canids hunt in packs. Pack members also have a strong instinct to guard pack territory. Such instincts helped domestication, as canids readily adopted a human family as their "pack".

EVOLUTION

About 50 million years ago, in the Eocene epoch, *Miacis*, a small, weasel-like mammal with a well-developed brain, was the forefather of all canids, as well as more distantly related carnivores.

ANCESTORS OF THE DOG

RACOONS BEARS WOLVES WEASELS CIVETS HYENAS CATS

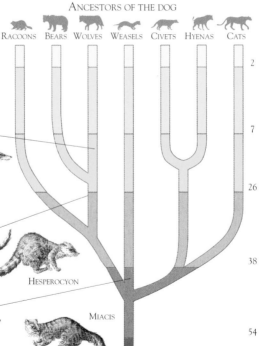

By the Miocene epoch, more than 40 ancestors of modern canids had emerged. Tomarctus *had the beginnings of modern canine tooth anatomy.*

TOMARCTUS

Hesperocyon was a long-bodied, short-limbed canid living in the later Eocene epoch. Fossils have been found in North America.

HESPEROCYON

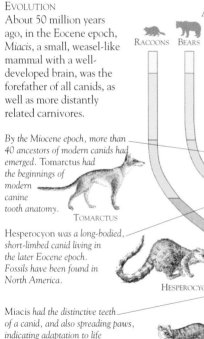

Miacis had the distinctive teeth of a canid, and also spreading paws, indicating adaptation to life in the trees.

MIACIS

2

7

26

38

54

MILLIONS OF YEARS AGO

DOMESTICATION

DOGS WERE FIRST DOMESTICATED from wolves more than 10,000 years ago. Human–dog contact may have evolved as wolves scavenged around human settlements and when wolf cubs were raised as pets. The dog's potential as a reliable guard and excellent hunting companion was soon realized.

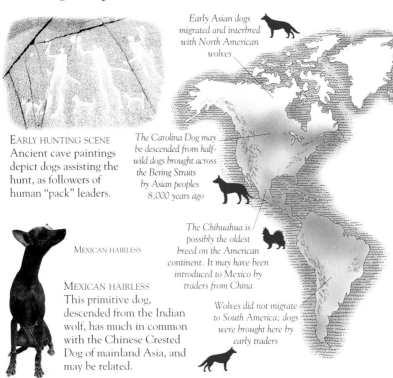

Early Asian dogs migrated and interbred with North American wolves

EARLY HUNTING SCENE
Ancient cave paintings depict dogs assisting the hunt, as followers of human "pack" leaders.

The Carolina Dog may be descended from half-wild dogs brought across the Bering Straits by Asian peoples 8,000 years ago

The Chihuahua is possibly the oldest breed on the American continent. It may have been introduced to Mexico by traders from China

MEXICAN HAIRLESS

MEXICAN HAIRLESS
This primitive dog, descended from the Indian wolf, has much in common with the Chinese Crested Dog of mainland Asia, and may be related.

Wolves did not migrate to South America; dogs were brought here by early traders

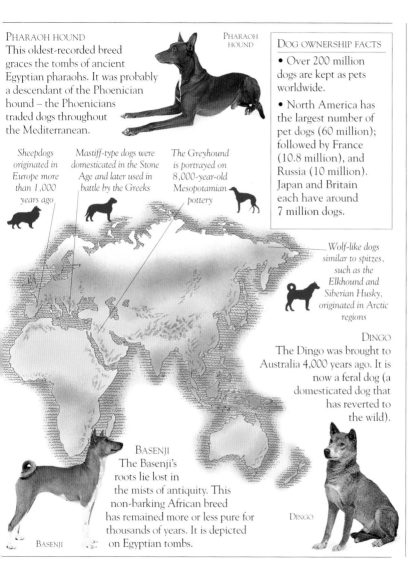

PHARAOH HOUND

This oldest-recorded breed graces the tombs of ancient Egyptian pharaohs. It was probably a descendant of the Phoenician hound – the Phoenicians traded dogs throughout the Mediterranean.

PHARAOH HOUND

Sheepdogs originated in Europe more than 1,000 years ago

Mastiff-type dogs were domesticated in the Stone Age and later used in battle by the Greeks

The Greyhound is portrayed on 8,000-year-old Mesopotamian pottery

DOG OWNERSHIP FACTS

• Over 200 million dogs are kept as pets worldwide.

• North America has the largest number of pet dogs (60 million); followed by France (10.8 million), and Russia (10 million). Japan and Britain each have around 7 million dogs.

Wolf-like dogs similar to spitzes, such as the Elkhound and Siberian Husky, originated in Arctic regions

DINGO

The Dingo was brought to Australia 4,000 years ago. It is now a feral dog (a domesticated dog that has reverted to the wild).

BASENJI

The Basenji's roots lie lost in the mists of antiquity. This non-barking African breed has remained more or less pure for thousands of years. It is depicted on Egyptian tombs.

BASENJI

DINGO

DOG ANATOMY

THE BASIC DESIGN of the dog is that of a highly developed carnivorous mammal of the chase. Over the centuries, humans have modified dog anatomy to exploit particular talents, and for aesthetic appeal.

Insulating coat

Loin

Brush, or tail

Croup

Flank

Stifle

Lower thigh

Knee

Hock

Pastern

INTERNAL ANATOMY

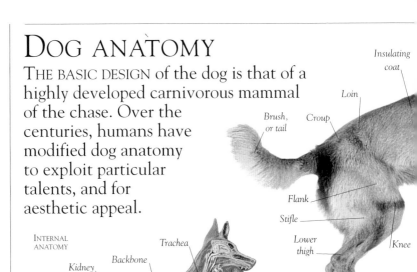

Trachea

Backbone

Kidney

Bladder

Tongue

Heart

Stomach

Duodenum

INTERNAL ORGANS

The organs of the dog are essentially the same as those of humans, and function in the same way. Although its attitude to food is that of a hunter-scavenger, the dog is not a pure carnivore, tending toward an omnivorous diet. Its digestive system can cope with anything from fruit and nuts to shellfish and raw meat.

PAWS

A dog's paws carry pads that act as shock absorbers, provide a good grip when running, and contain sweat glands. The claws, unlike those of most cats, cannot be retracted.

Small pads not sensitive to hot and cold

Stopper pad prevents slipping after a jump

Large pad bears most weight

Dewclaw

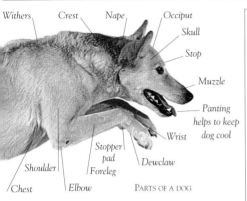

Withers, Crest, Nape, Occiput, Skull, Stop, Muzzle

Panting helps to keep dog cool

Wrist, Dewclaw, Stopper pad, Foreleg, Elbow, Chest, Shoulder

PARTS OF A DOG

CLASSIC DESIGN

The classic canine design is seen in most wild or feral dogs and many domesticated mongrels: a lithe body, long legs, a long tail for balance and communication, efficient prick ears, and excellent vision – all ideal features for a resourceful hunting animal with plenty of stamina.

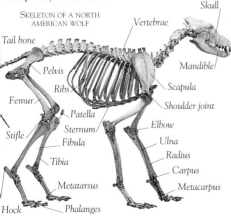

SKELETON OF A NORTH AMERICAN WOLF

Tail bone, Pelvis, Ribs, Femur, Patella, Stifle, Sternum, Fibula, Tibia, Metatarsus, Hock, Phalanges, Vertebrae, Skull, Mandible, Scapula, Shoulder joint, Elbow, Ulna, Radius, Carpus, Metacarpus

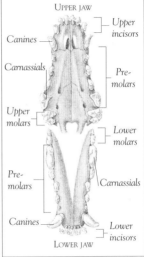

TEETH

An adult dog has 42 teeth, including four stabbing, canine teeth and four molar teeth called carnassials that are designed to shear through tough flesh.

UPPER JAW

Canines, Carnassials, Upper molars, Upper incisors, Pre-molars

Pre-molars, Canines, Lower molars, Carnassials, Lower incisors

LOWER JAW

THE SKELETON

The basic dog framework provides strength, flexibility, and speed. However, selective breeding has resulted in some breeds possessing weak areas. Extra-long spines can lead to "slipped-discs"; compressed skulls to breathing troubles; and short legs to knee problems.

DOGS

465

More on anatomy

All predatory animals depend on their sight, hearing, and sense of smell to catch prey. A dog's sense organs are some of the most sophisticated in the animal kingdom. Dogs' reproductive systems follow the basic mammalian pattern, but with some distinct features in the male.

Cerebral cortex

Frontal sinus

Nasal membranes

Vomeronasal organ

Tongue

Soft palate

Windpipe

CROSS-SECTION OF THE HEAD

SMELL AND TASTE

Dogs are marvellous smellers, in fact about one million times better than humans. Their long noses contain "smelling membranes" about 40 times larger than ours. Taste is not as important, as dogs "gobble" rather than "savour" food.

SIGHT

Dogs' eyes are more sensitive to light and movement than ours but they can often "miss" creatures that stand very still. Yet shepherds claim their working dogs will react to hand signals at a distance of 1 km (0.6 miles). Dogs are not totally colour-blind, but see mainly in black, white, and shades of grey. The anatomy of a dog's eye is very similar to ours.

Lacrimal gland

Sclera

Retina

Pupil

Optic nerve

Cornea

Iris covers anterior chamber

Lower eyelid

Third eyelid

Lens

CROSS-SECTION OF THE EYE

VISION

A dog has a wider field of vision than a human because its eyes are set towards the sides of its head. Its carnivorous, hunter ancestors needed lateral vision.

DOG'S EYE VIEW 250°–290°

HUMAN'S EYE VIEW 210°

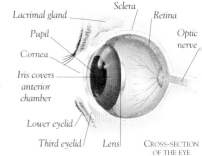

HEARING

Dogs have excellent hearing. Equipped with large external ears served by 17 muscles, they can prick and swivel these sound receivers to focus on the source of noise. They can register high-pitched sounds of 35,000 Hz (vibrations per second), compared to humans' 20,000 Hz. This greater hearing range assists in tracking down quarry.

Ear turns to detect sound

Pinna (Auricle)

Ear cartilage

Skull bone

Ear drum

Cochlea

Organs of balance

Ear canal

INSIDE THE EAR

HANGING EARS   POINTED EARS

EAR TYPES

Hanging ears protect the ear when hounds hunt through vegetation. Erect ears trap sound waves most effectively.

REPRODUCTIVE ORGANS

Testes   Bladder   Kidneys

Ureter

Spermatic duct

Bulbo-urethral gland

Urethra

Penis

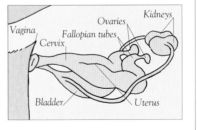

Vagina

Cervix

Ovaries   Kidneys

Fallopian tubes

Bladder   Uterus

MALE

The dog's penis contains a bone, through which the urethra passes, and a bulbo-urethral gland that swells up, thereby "tying" the dog and bitch together during sexual intercourse.

FEMALE

The female has a typical mammalian arrangement: vagina, cervix, uterus, Fallopian tubes, and ovaries. When a bitch is neutered, the ovaries, Fallopian tubes, and uterus are surgically removed.

467

LIFE CYCLE OF DOGS

ON AVERAGE, a dog's life span is about 12 years, though small breeds generally live longer than larger ones. In terms of ageing, the first year of a dog's life equals 15 human years, the second equals nine years, and thereafter each dog year counts for four human years.

GETTING ACQUAINTED

Exploratory sniffing before mating begins

THE "HEAT" PERIOD
The female is called the bitch. She becomes sexually mature at 8–12 months old. Twice a year, she goes into "heat", usually for 18–21 days. This is when ovulation occurs.

MATING

Female remains willing but passive

MATING
The male is sexually active all year and is attracted to the scent of a female in "heat". When a female is ready to mate, she draws her tail to one side. The transmission of sperm is completed within a minute but the couple remain "locked" together for half an hour.

DEVELOPMENT OF A PUPPY

7 DAYS
At this age the puppy only sleeps or suckles. Its eyes and ear canals are closed, but it responds to its mother's touch.

14 DAYS
The eyes are opening but they cannot focus properly for another 7 days. Between 13 and 17 days the puppy begins to hear.

3 WEEKS
At 3 weeks the puppy can focus its eyes and move around. Its nails should be trimmed to prevent it from scratching its mother.

1. The yolk sac provides nourishment to the embryo for the first few days

Yolk sac

Most puppies will emerge head first in diving position

2. By the third week of pregnancy, the embryo has a developing head, eyes, and limbs

Embryo

3. By mid-pregnancy, all the internal organs are developed

PREGNANCY

Pregnancy lasts an average of 63 days. Swelling of the mother's tummy is noticeable from the fifth week onwards. The breasts enlarge, the teats become bigger, and milk can often be produced 5–6 days before labour begins.

4. At six weeks, the skeleton has developed

BIRTH

When the puppies are ready to be born the mother may stop eating and find a nest site. She often gives birth to the first pups within two hours of the first contractions. After each puppy is born she may rest for minutes or for hours. Each pup's placenta is usually expelled within 15 minutes.

Mother sits contentedly while puppies suckle

Puppies huddle together for food and security

BONDING WITH MOTHER

30 DAYS
The puppy begins to play. Teething starts at 3–5 weeks. It should receive its first worming dosage.

6 WEEKS
Milk teeth are present, but the puppy is still weaning, and it should not be separated from its mother.

8 WEEKS
Mother and pup can be separated now, and the puppy should receive vaccinations against major diseases.

DOMESTIC MAMMALS

DOG BEHAVIOUR

DOGS EXHIBIT A BROAD RANGE of behaviour patterns that spring from their origins as social, hunting animals. Ear and tail movements are obviously expressive, but all patterns are vital rituals that express a dog's relationship with its environment.

SCENT MARKING

A dog marks out territory via deposits of urine or faeces, or by scratching the ground with its hind legs.

SCENT GLANDS

Distinctive scents are produced by sebaceous glands in the dog's anal sacs (anal glands) that are passed on to faeces, and by sweat glands in the hind paws. These scents lay down sniffable information that only dogs can interpret.

Dog shows interest in a scent

HOWLING

Howling is an ancient form of dog communication. Wild dogs and wolves howl to let other pack members know where they are and, in some cases, to inform strangers that they are in possession of territory. It can also be a sign of distress or loneliness.

DIGGING

Dogs inherit their love of digging from their ancestors who stored food in the ground in order to survive when hunting was poor. It leads well-fed dogs to bury bones and dig them up later.

AGGRESSION

Aggression can indicate possessiveness of prized objects, territory, or animals. It can be directed at outsiders who are not members of the home pack. Fear and pain also cause aggression.

SUBMISSION

Submissive individuals in the canine hierarchy reveal their position by their crouched postures, and by rolling onto their backs, looking away and appearing meek and defenceless.

DOMINANCE

Dogs asserting their dominance make eye contact, with tail raised and ears erect, and often place their neck on the other dog's shoulder. Size, though helpful, does not necessarily affect dominance.

Tail carried high indicates boldness

PLAY BOW

The play bow, often exhibited by puppies, is a clear request to human or fellow dog to meet on friendly terms. Indicating total lack of aggressive intent, it is usually an invitation to play.

Body is lowered to ground

Human pack leader offers food

Dog pack leader shows authority by rising above other dogs

HIERARCHY

Packs of wild canines have leaders to exercise authority and coordinate activity. This is usually, but not always, a male. Gatherings of domestic dogs behave in the same way.

471

INTRODUCTION TO BREEDS

AMONG DOMESTICATED ANIMALS only the dog has been selectively bred to produce such a wide variety of types. Worldwide, there are over 500 different breeds. National kennel clubs differ in the way they group breeds so, for the purposes of this book, general categories have been used.

GUNDOGS

Gundogs were developed to pick up the air scents of game and also be good sporting companions. They are highly responsive and amenable workers. Field trials are held regularly to test working skills.

IRISH RED AND WHITE SETTER

BORDER COLLIES HERDING SHEEP

CHOW CHOW

SPECIAL DOGS

This is a miscellaneous collection of breeds. Many, such as the Chow Chow, are highly distinctive, and some have specialized in particular types of work. Most make good companions; many popular pets fall into this category.

HERDING DOGS AND GUARD DOGS

These dogs were bred to protect and herd livestock, work as guards, pull and carry loads, or assist police and armed forces. Most of these dogs are happiest when they have access to open spaces and a job to do.

HOUNDS

These athletes with sensitive noses and sharp eyes were the first dogs used by humans. They helped their (much slower) masters by hunting down animals, such as deer, for food.

FOXHOUNDS

BREED FACTS

• Archaeological finds show that that there were four types of Bronze Age dog: wolf-like dogs, sheepdogs, hounds, and small house dogs.

• Breeds least likely to bite: Labrador, Golden Retriever, Shetland Sheepdog, Old English Sheepdog, Spinone.

TERRIERS

Developed from hounds to tackle small, burrowing animals, terriers are generally small, short-legged, stocky animals with alert and spirited temperaments. No group of dogs is more expert at tunnelling than terriers.

NORFOLK TERRIERS

TOY DOGS

These breeds' main function is to be loyal, decorative, and friendly companions. Many are useful for raising the alarm and nipping intruders' ankles. Small and dainty, they play a vital role in people's lives.

PEKINGESE

MONGRELS

Most dogs in the world are mongrels or "cross-breed" dogs that have interbred at random. Apart from their individual endearing qualities, they are often better-tempered, less disease-prone, and more adaptable than pure-breds.

WHAT IS A HORSE?

SOME 60 MILLION YEARS AGO the first horses ran on the plains of North America. The modern horse has single-hooved feet and a greater length of leg than its earlier ancestors. Like all mammals, horses suckle their young, and as herbivores, their natural food is grass. They are social creatures, and prefer to live in groups.

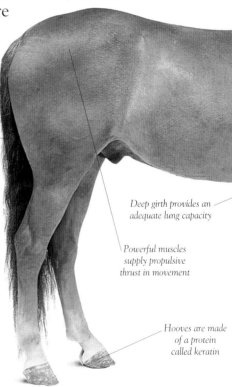

Long tail helps to keep flies off the body

Deep girth provides an adequate lung capacity

Powerful muscles supply propulsive thrust in movement

Hooves are made of a protein called keratin

HORSE FACTS

• Horses are measured from the ground up to the withers, which is the highest point of the shoulders.

• In 1910, North America had about 20 million domestic horses.

• There are over 150 officially recognized horse and pony breeds.

• Most modern horse breeds have been deliberately created to do a specific task.

Long hair on the back of the neck is called a mane

Horses have an excellent sense of hearing

Withers

Long head and neck allow horse to graze while standing

HORSES AND HUMANS
As this cave painting shows, early humans hunted horses for their meat and skin. By keeping horses in herds, these essential items became more readily available. Eventually, horses were used for riding and pulling carts, and later they were bred to perform all kinds of work.

It takes over two years for a horse foal to take on adult proportions

Long legs developed to run from danger

BORN TO RUN
Both wild and domestic horses give birth to fully developed offspring. This is because in the wild the young foal must keep up with its mother and the herd, while escaping from predators.

Main horse types

MOST MODERN HORSES are thought to be descended
from four types which inhabited Europe and Asia over
6,000 years ago. Their features can still be seen in
some breeds today. Domestication led to the variety of
modern breeds and their spread across the world.

Broad
forehead with
straight profile

Lean with
narrow body

PONY TYPE 1
This hardy pony looked similar to today's
Exmoor breed of Great Britain. It lived
in northwestern Europe.

HORSE TYPE 1
Originating from central Asia, this horse
lived in dry, arid conditions and
resembled the modern Akhal-Teke.

Small
head

PONY TYPE 2
Similar to Przewalski's horse, the Type 2
was powerfully built with a heavy head.
The breed roamed over northern Eurasia.

HORSE TYPE 2
Living in the hot deserts of western
Asia, this slim horse was possibly the
ancestor of the Arab and Caspian.

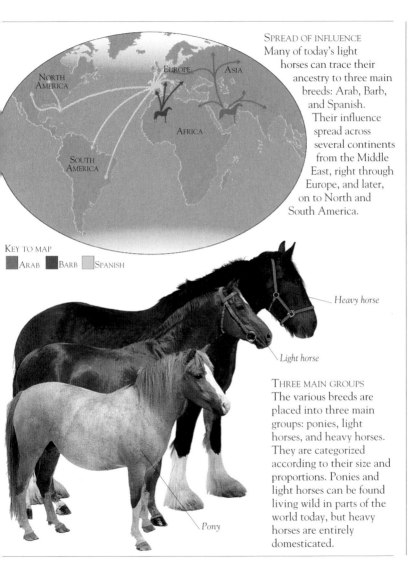

SPREAD OF INFLUENCE
Many of today's light horses can trace their ancestry to three main breeds: Arab, Barb, and Spanish. Their influence spread across several continents from the Middle East, right through Europe, and later, on to North and South America.

EUROPE
ASIA
NORTH AMERICA
AFRICA
SOUTH AMERICA

KEY TO MAP
ARAB   BARB   SPANISH

Heavy horse

Light horse

Pony

THREE MAIN GROUPS
The various breeds are placed into three main groups: ponies, light horses, and heavy horses. They are categorized according to their size and proportions. Ponies and light horses can be found living wild in parts of the world today, but heavy horses are entirely domesticated.

477

BODY AND CONFORMATION

A HORSE'S BODY IS perfectly designed for its way of
life. The neck is long so it can stoop to graze, and
long, muscular legs allow it to run away from danger.
The proportions of a horse's body, or conformation,
may vary according to the
group or breed.

Points

The external features of a
horse are called the points.
Each point has a different
name and together they
make up the horse's
conformation.

Mane

Crest

Withers

Throat

Jugular groove

Poll

Ear

Neck

Eye

Forehead

Shoulder

Facial crest

Breast

Nasal bone

Knee joint

Nostril

Cheek

Cannon bone

Lower jaw

Muzzle

Fetlock joint

Lower lip

Upper lip

PROPORTION

In a perfectly proportioned horse, certain measurements of the body should all be equal. Those shown in blue should correspond to each other, as should the lines drawn in both red and grey.

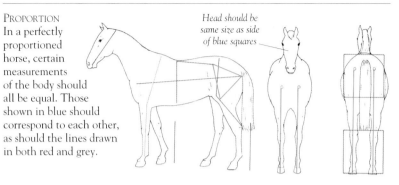

Head should be same size as side of blue squares

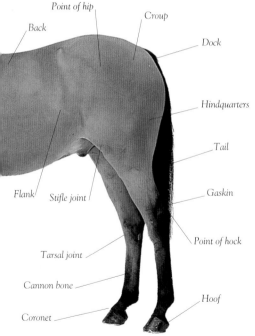

Point of hip
Croup
Back
Dock
Hindquarters
Tail
Gaskin
Flank
Stifle joint
Point of hock
Tarsal joint
Cannon bone
Hoof
Coronet

FRONT AND REAR LIMBS

When viewed from the front, a line from the shoulder should pass through the centre of the knees, fetlock, and foot. A straight line should also pass through the rear legs.

ANATOMICAL FACTS

• The body and head of a horse are streamlined and this helps to reduce wind resistance.

• A long neck and well-sloped shoulders may indicate that the horse is fast and good for riding.

• Large eyes usually show not only that the horse has good vision, but also a calm nature and intelligence.

Skeleton and muscles

The framework of the horse consists of a skeleton, made up of a number of connected bones that are moved by muscles. Along the spinal, or vertebral, column, which runs from the head to the tail, is the spinal cord – the connection between the horse's brain and body. When a horse wants to move, it sends a message from its brain down the cord via nerves to signal the appropriate muscle.

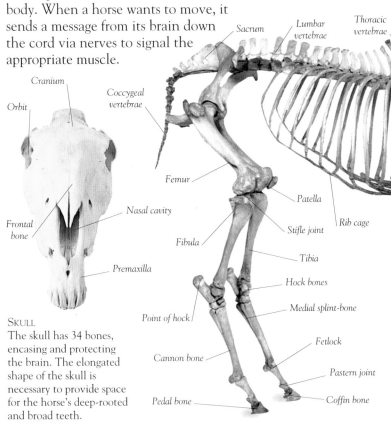

Sacrum

Lumbar vertebrae

Thoracic vertebrae

Cranium

Coccygeal vertebrae

Orbit

Femur

Patella

Nasal cavity

Frontal bone

Stifle joint

Rib cage

Fibula

Tibia

Premaxilla

Hock bones

Medial splint-bone

Point of hock

Fetlock

Cannon bone

Pastern joint

Pedal bone

Coffin bone

SKULL
The skull has 34 bones, encasing and protecting the brain. The elongated shape of the skull is necessary to provide space for the horse's deep-rooted and broad teeth.

SKELETON

The skeleton is a strong, jointed framework, made up of about 250 bones that support and protect the soft tissues of the body. The vertebrae of the spine keep the body rigid and strong.

Cranium

Orbit

Nasal bone

Atlas

Axis

Cervical vertebrae

Mandible

Scapula

Scapular spine

Shoulder joint

Sternum

Humerus

Ulna

Biceps femoris

Radius

Carpals

Suspensory ligament

Cannon bone

Fetlock joint

Pastern

Coffin joint

MUSCLE FACTS

• Forelegs ligaments and tendons govern movement and prevent muscle damage.

• Muscle development helps to create the horse's overall outline.

• Horses are sometimes made to swim in large water baths to help strengthen tired or injured muscles.

MUSCLES

Gluteal fascia

External intercostal

Trapezius

Splenius

Triceps

Pectoral

Abdominal

Carpal

Ligament binds bones together

Tendon attaches muscle to bone

MUSCLES

A horse has muscles in every part of its body. These are made up of fibrous bands of tissue that relax and contract to produce movement. There are two types of muscles: voluntary muscles which are near to the surface and controlled by the horse, and involuntary muscles which control the internal organs.

Patterns and markings

Individual horses can be identified by body markings, which can be either natural or acquired. Natural markings are often areas of white hair on the head, legs, and hooves. Acquired markings are the result of branding or injury. Branding has been carried out for more than 2,000 years and can help to identify the horse if it is stolen.

FACE MARKINGS
While some breeds are defined by their coat patterns, face markings help to identify individual horses. The most common face markings are named below.

BLAZE

WHITE MUZZLE

SNIP

LIP MARKS

WHITE FACE

STRIPE

STAR AND STRIPE

STAR

ERMINE   SOCK   STOCKING   ZEBRA

LEG MARKINGS

These markings are often white. They are called
ermine if they are just above the hoof, a sock if they
extend below the knee, and a stocking when extending
above the knee. Zebra markings are dark rings.

HOOF MARKINGS

The blue hoof is
made of hard blue
horn and is most
often associated
with ponies.
Hooves of black
and white
vertical stripes
are seen on the
Appaloosa and
other spotted
horse breeds.

BLUE HOOF

STRIPED HOOF

DORSAL STRIPE

This mark extends from the
tail to the withers. It is found
on primitive horses such as
the Tarpan, and is associated
with dun-coloured coats.

IDENTITY MARKINGS

Artificial markings help identify
ownership and sometimes breed.
Brand marks are applied by a hot
iron rod which stops the hair
growing back. Freeze marks are
frozen on in a similar way.

BRAND MARK   FREEZE MARK

FOOD AND DIET

LIKE ANY ANIMAL, horses get their energy from food. They are herbivores, which means they only eat plants. In the wild, horses survive well on grass and herbs as long as grazing is plentiful. In the winter, when it is cold and there is less food, wild horses get out of condition, while in the summer they put on weight.

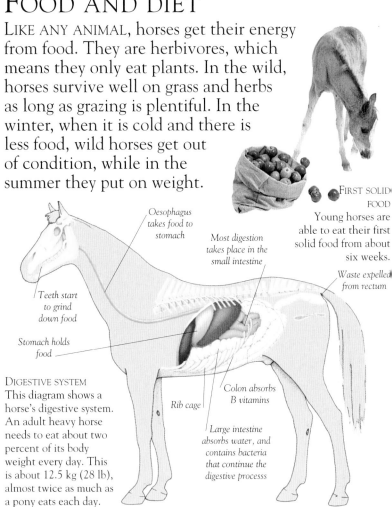

FIRST SOLID FOOD
Young horses are able to eat their first solid food from about six weeks.

Oesophagus takes food to stomach

Most digestion takes place in the small intestine

Waste expelled from rectum

Teeth start to grind down food

Stomach holds food

Colon absorbs B vitamins

Rib cage

Large intestine absorbs water, and contains bacteria that continue the digestive processs

DIGESTIVE SYSTEM
This diagram shows a horse's digestive system. An adult heavy horse needs to eat about two percent of its body weight every day. This is about 12.5 kg (28 lb), almost twice as much as a pony eats each day.

TEETH AND JAWS

Grazing wears down the foal's milk teeth and by the time the horse is five, these are replaced by a set of 36 adult teeth. The incisors cut the food into small pieces, and the molars grind it down, ready for digestion.

Hinge with top jaw

Mandible

Eye socket

Hard palate

Molars

Bottom incisors

Canines

Top incisors

BOTTOM JAW   TOP JAW

BALANCED DIET

Horses need a balanced diet, with enough vitamins and minerals to help them stay healthy and in condition. Horses should be fed little and often, and allowed constant access to fresh water.

Fruit and root vegetables must be chopped up lengthways so the horse does not choke

Feed bowl holds carrots, maize, linseed, nuts, chaff, and a slice of apple

Hay is grass that has been cut and dried

Bucket of clean, fresh water

FOOD DANGERS

• Plants like deadly nightshade, bracken, and ragwort may poison a horse if it eats them in any quantity. Pastures where horses are left to graze must be cleared of these plants.

• Horses should not graze in an area within 14 days of any spraying.

BEHAVIOUR

TODAY'S DOMESTIC HORSES show the same patterns of behaviour as their wild ancestors. The herd instinct still dominates, and horses prefer to be kept in groups rather than on their own. Much of their behaviour is linked to the way they communicate with other horses.

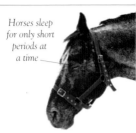

Horses sleep for only short periods at a time

SLEEPING
Horses are able to sleep standing up. In the wild, this increases their chances of escaping from predators.

EARS
The position of a horse's ears is an important indicator of its mood. If the ears point forwards, this shows curiosity. When the horse is uncertain, it keeps one ear forwards and the other backwards.

SHIRE HORSE

FLEHMEN
When a mare is close to a stallion, the stallion may fold back his lips and draw air into his mouth, over its Jacobson's organ, to detect the mare's scent to sense if she is ready to mate. This action is called flehmen.

MUTUAL GROOMING
Horses indulge in mutual grooming as a sign of a close relationship. They will gently nuzzle each other's backs, nibbling at the hair Such sessions may last for several minutes at a time.

REARING

A stallion rears up to intimidate a rival, often lashing out with his front feet at the same time.

Horse uses its front legs to balance

Horses often rear in play

ROLLING OVER

By rolling, a horse can exercise the muscles in its back, and also clean its coat. Horses often roll when turned out to graze in a field.

Stallions rear naturally in the wild

Horses nuzzle each other to establish their relationship

SHETLAND PONY

BEHAVIOURAL FACTS

• Horses will call out to warn others of approaching danger.

• The tail is used as a fly swish rather than for communication.

• Repeated pawing at the ground with the hooves is often a sign of nervousness.

• A horse's ears are very mobile and can rotate independently 180° forward and back.

487

USES OF THE HORSE

IN SPITE OF THE SPREAD of mechanization, the horse still has a place in society. Today, horses can be found hard at work in cities, forests, and farmland. While traditional horse sports like racing and steeple-chasing remain popular, they are now being joined by leisure activities like trekking.

Working horses

Horses work in forests because they cause less damage than tractors. Farmers in developing countries also find horses easy to keep as they can live off the land. Though no longer used in war, horses are retained in many countries for ceremonial duties and the police horse has so far proved to be irreplaceable.

MULE TRAINS
Even in the early 21st century, it has been hard to find anything to replace the mule to transport goods over uneven ground. Mules are still used in many parts of the world.

London police horses undergo about 40 weeks of training

ROYAL ARTILLERY HORSE AND RIDER

CEREMONIAL DUTIES
Many countries still use horses for ceremonial duties. This dates from wars where horses were used as cavalry and to haul artillery.

POLICE HORSES
Mounted police can be seen in many cities today. Horses offer the rider a good view and mobility, and can move through crowds more easily than either motorcycles or cars.

WORKING HORSE FACTS
• More horses are bred in the United States for leisure riding than for herding cattle.

• India employs more mounted police than any other country in the world.

• Heavy horses are used in Canadian forests to pull up trees and take them away, and to cultivate the soil afterwards.

Working cow ponies in the US tend to average 15 hands high (1hh=4in).

QUARTER HORSE

Average working life of a police horse is about 14 years

BRITISH POLICE HORSES AND RIDERS IN CEREMONIAL DRESS

HERDING CATTLE
Horses are still used to herd cattle and sheep in the Americas, the former USSR, Australia, and New Zealand.

Horses for sport and leisure

Since the end of World War II, there has been a tremendous increase in the use of the horse for pleasure. Sports such as horse racing remain as popular as ever, and interest in horse events like show jumping and dressage has been heightened by television. Riding holidays are now a popular and relaxing pastime for many people.

POLO
Probably originating in Persia, polo has been played for 2,500 years. Modern polo is played by two teams of four using long mallets to hit the ball into the opposition's goal.

VERSATILE MORGAN
The American Morgan Horse, once favoured by the US cavalry, is shown in ridden and harnessed classes. It is also used for Western and pleasure riding, and jumping.

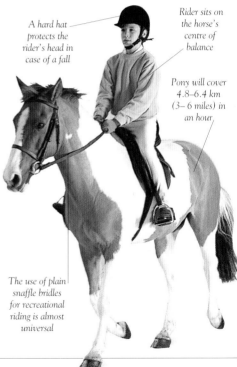

A hard hat protects the rider's head in case of a fall

Rider sits on the horse's centre of balance

Pony will cover 4.8–6.4 km (3– 6 miles) in an hour

The use of plain snaffle bridles for recreational riding is almost universal

RACEHORSES

Horse racing has become a huge international industry. This statue in the Kentucky Horse Park, US, is of the famous racehorse *Man O' War*, or *Big Red*, who was beaten only once in 21 races. When he died in 1947, more than 1,000 people attended the funeral.

HORSE SPORTS FACTS

• The longest-running horse race is the Palio in Siena, Italy, begun in the 1200s and still run today. The winning horse attends a special banquet afterwards.

• The word polo comes from the Tibetan *pulu*, meaning ball.

• The first steeplechase was held in 1830 at St. Albans, England.

Riders learn to use aids such as the reins

Each rider keeps a pony-length away from the next

A novice rider is given a quiet, reliable horse

Riding school ponies are frequently cross-bred animals

RIDING HOLIDAYS

Those who want to ride occasionally or just for pleasure, can take riding holidays. These involve treks that last from a single day to a whole week. The distances covered each day can vary from 16–40 km (10–25 miles). Trips are always supervised and provide an opportunity to reach beautiful and inaccessible areas of a country.

Index

Acknowledgements

Contributors to this title include:
Editors: Elise Bradbury, Laura Buller, Alan Burrows, Bernadette Crowley, Alastair Dougall, John Mapps, Susan McKeever, Miranda Smith, Leo Vita-Finzi, Selina Wood, Sarah Watson.

Designers: Alexandra Brown, Sarah Crouch, Janet Allis, Tanya Tween.

PAGEOne: Melanie McDowell, Chris Stewart, Suzanne Tuhrim, Sophie Williams.

Dorling Kindersley would like to thank: Hilary Bird and Mark Lambert for indexing, Robert Graham for research and editorial support, Caroline Potts for picture library services, Natural History Museum, University Museum of Zoology, Cambridge, Thurston Watson for model making.

Photographs by:
Julie Anderson, Dennis Avon, Akhil Bakhshi, Simon Battensby, Geoff Brightling, Jane Burton, Peter Chadwick, Gordon Clayton, Geoff Dann, Philip Dowell, Mike Dunning, Neil Fletcher, Steve Gorton, Frank Greenaway, Steve Gorton, Marc Henrie, Kit Houghton, Colin Keates, Dave King, Bob Langrish, Cyril Laubscher, Ranald Mackechnie, Andrew McRobb, Ray Moller, Tracy Morgan, Stephen Oliver, Oxford Scientific Films, Nick Parfit, Tim Ridley, Bill Sands, Karl Shone, Steve Shott, Harry Taylor, Kim Taylor, Michael Ward, Jerry Young

Illustrations by:
Graham Allen, Janet Allis, Stephen Biesty, Joanna Cameron, Rowan Clifford, Karen Cochrane, John Davis, Ted Dewan, Gill Ellsbury, Samantha Elmhurst, Angelica Elsebach, Giuliano Fornari, Chris Forsey, Will Giles, Craig Gosling (Indiana University Medical Illustration Department), Tony Graham, Nick Hall, Nick Hewetson, John Hutchinson, Mark Iley, Stanley Cephas Johnson, Aziz Khan, Richard Lewington, Kenneth Lilly, Ruth Lindsay, Mick Loates, Janos Marffy, Malcolm McGregor, Sean Milne, Richard Orr, Maurice Pledger, Sandra Pond, Bryan Poole, Sally Alane Reason, Colin Salmon, Tommy Swahn, John Temperton, Simon Thomas, Kevin Toy, David Webb, Amanda Williams, Ann Winterbotham, John Woodcock, Debra Woodward, Colin Woolf, Dan Wright.

Picture credits:

t=top b=bottom c=centre l=left
r=right

The publisher would like to thank the following for their kind permission to reproduce their photographs:
Dennis Avon 286b, 323bl;346bl;
Professor Edmund D. Brodie Jr. 165cr;
Lester Cheeseman 251c; Dr. Barry Clarke 23tr; John Holmes 175cl; Colin Keates 27cl; Dave King 25cr; Bob Langrish 487tl; Leszczynski 157cl
Ardea/M Krishnan 257bl; Eric Lingren 238tl
BBC Natural History Unit/Galleria Degli Uffizi, Florence 168tl
Bridgeman Art Library/210tl, 233br
Centaur Studios/175bl
Bruce Coleman/231bc; Jen and Des Bartlett 279tl; Erwin & Peggy Bauer 258-259, 216tl; Fred Bruemmer 203bl; John Cancalosi 236tl, 342bl; Eric Crichton 80cl; Gerald Cubitt 81br; Geoff Doré 81bc; M.P.L Fogden 154-155; P.A. Hinchcliffe 60tr; Dr. M. T. Kahl 344tr; Jan van de Kam 338br; Stephen J. Krasemann 379tl; Gordon Langsbury 354-355b; 355r; Cyril Laubscher 290br; Werner Layer 366-367; Luiz Claudio Mango 307tr; George Mcarthy 287b;351tl; Michael McCoy 237tl; Rinie van Meurs 338 tr; Charlie Off 330bl; Dr. Eckart Pott 30-31, 133tc; Dr Sandro Prato 139tr; Hans Reinhard 99tl, 352cl, 361b, 365bc, 438-439;

Hector Rivarola 349bl; Kevin Rushby 63tl; Dr Frieder Sauer 79br; Pacific Stock 142-143; Kim Taylor 51tr, 88cr, 94cr, 133tl, 272-273b, 302cl; 276c, 305b; 313cl; Norman Tomalin 106c
Corbis/Tony Arruza 50c; Joel W. Rogers 302cr
Mary Evans Picture Library/69ac, 151tr
FLPA/L Chance 237bl
Robert Harding/300cl; 301cr; 353b; 475tr
Chris Mattison Nature Photographics 185b
Musée Nationale d'Histoire Naturelle/158tr 159tc
Naturhistoriska Riksmuseet/158c
Natural History Museum/Frank Greenaway 98cr; 99br, 16cr, 170cl, 170bl, 170br, 171tl, 172t, 172b, 173t, 173c, 173br, 177c, 179tl, 212bl, 212cl, 215cl, 216bl, 217t, 218b, 219t, 221tl, 223cr, 223br, 224tl, 225b, 226t, 226bl, 227br, 228b, 229t, 230–231, 230cr, 230b, 231c, 231t, 233t, 237tl, 241cr, 243br, 248r, 252bl, 256b, 437br
Nature Photographers/289tr; E.Lemon 300br; H. Miles 358bl; Paul Sterry 337br; 341r; 337bu
Natural Science Photos/C Banks 221cr, 256tr, 256cl; M. Boulard 131bc; P. Bowman 92cl; M. Chinery 135cl; C Dani & I Jeske 209br; 221bl; Carol Farneti 106bl; Adrian Hoskins 95cr; G Kinns 246cl; JG Lilley 204c, 204b; Chris Mattison 227t, 246br; Jim Merli 176cr, 180bc, 188cl, 193tr, 255tl, 253t, 257tr; Pete Oxford 203tl, 205bl;

Queensland Museum 253c; Richard Revels 92tr, 132cr, 252tr; C & T Stuart 249bl. P.H. & S.L. Ward 61cr, 137c; David Yendall 101tr

N.H.P.A/Stephen Dalton 437tl; Melvin Grey 271cl; Peter Johnson 362 bl; R & D Keller 373tl; Peter Parks 153br, 282tr; Philippa Scott 301tl; John Shaw 301br; 348r

Frank Lane Picture Agency/ E&D Hosking 281t; 303tr; 355tl; 362-363; 365cr;/ T&P Gardner; F.Polking 304br; Silvestris 328tr;/Roger Tidma 353t;/ Roger Wimshurst 307tr;/ W.Wisniewski 359br

Mark O'Shea 199cr, 239t, 241bl
Oxford Scientific Films/Doug Allen 364l; Larus Argentatus 274-275, 301bl; Kathie Atkinson 57tr; G.I. Bernard 101cl; Raymond Blythe 130bl; Densey Clyne 127tr; C.M. Collins 68bl; J.A.L. Cooke 79c, 134tl; David B. Fleetham 387tr; Michael Fogden 125tl; Peter Gathercole 67tr; Howard Hall 153t; 387cr; Stan Osolinski 166-167; Papilio 296br; Alan Root/Okapia 371cr
Mantis Wildlife Films/32cl; Peter O'Toole 68cr; James Robinson 76cr, 99br; Harold Taylor 83c; Steve Turner 81cr, 125tr; P & W Ward 124cr
Museum der Bildenden Kuenste, Leipzig/24cl
Planet Earth/K & K Ammann 387br; Andre Barttschi 321 bc; John R. Bracegirdle 386cl; Richard Coomber 436bl; Carol Farneti-Foster 449tr, 459tr;

386br; Daniel Heuclin 245bl; Gerard Lacz 217cr; John Lythgou 308b, 347tr; Mark Mattock 336cl; E Hanumantha Rao 244cl; Brian Kenney 232t, 236bl, 238bl, 255bl; Jonathan Scott 387bl; 387tl; Anup and Manoj Shah 451tr; Yuri Shibbnev 311tl; Martin Wendler 239c
Premaphotos/K.G. Preston-Mafham 59tr, 67br, 71br, 73cl, 74br, 80br, 106br, 110bl, 123t, 123cr. Dr Bill Sands 70cr
Science Photo Library/Dr Jeremy Burgess 47tl; Mark Deeble & Victoria Stone 213cr; John Downer 214br; Michael Fogden 215tr, 249tr; J.C. Revy 114cr; Tui de Roy 186cr; David M. Schleser/Nature's Images 74br; Alastair Shay 247cr
Tony Stone Images/Mike Surowiak 101bc; 196cl; Maurice Tibbles 189c
Werner Forman Archive/14cl
Wild Images/Romulus Whitaker 193br; 214tr; Howard Hall 153 cl
Jerry Young/12c, bl, br
Zefa/J. Schupe 7tr; 447tr, 455t.

Every effort has been made to trace the copyright holders and we apologize in advance for any unintentional omissions. We should be pleased to insert the appropriate acknowledgment in any subsequent edition of this publication.

All other images © Dorling Kindersley
For further information see:
www.dkimages.com